STORMTROOP TACTICS

STORMTROOP TACTICS

INNOVATION IN THE GERMAN ARMY, 1914–1918

BRUCE I. GUDMUNDSSON

PRAEGER

New York
Westport, Connecticut
London

Library of Congress Cataloging-in-Publication Data

Gudmundsson, Bruce I.
    Stormtroop tactics : innovation in the German Army, 1914–1918 /
    Bruce I. Gudmundsson.
       p.   cm.
    Bibliography: p.
    Includes index.
    ISBN 0–275–93328–8 (alk. paper)
    1. Germany. Heer—History—World War, 1914–1918. 2. World War,
    1914–1918—Campaigns.   I. Title.
    D531.G85   1989
    940.4′13′43—dc19   89–3882

Library of Congress Catalog Card Number: 89–3882
ISBN: 0–275–93328–8

First published in 1989

Praeger Publishers, One Madison Avenue, New York, NY 10010
A division of Greenwood Press, Inc.

Printed in the United States of America

∞™

The paper used in this book complies with the Permanent
Paper Standard issued by the National Information Standards
Organization (Z39.48–1984).

10 9 8 7 6 5 4 3 2 1

Quality Printing and Binding by
MAPLE-VAIL BOOK MANUFACTURERS
P.O. Box 1005
Binghamton, NY 13902 U.S.A.

Contents

Illustrations

Acknowledgments

This book would not have been written were it not for the support of my parents and the patience, faith, and forbearance of my wife. Professor Stephen Ross, of the Naval War College and Yale University, sparked my interest in World War I and inadvertently sowed the seeds of this project when he allowed me to write first a term paper and then a senior thesis on the subject of this book. William S. Lind, of the Institute for Cultural Conservatism, provided both advice and encouragement, as did of Lieutenant Colonel Jack English of the Canadian Defense Forces. Dr. Bradley Meyer, in addition to offering lots of helpful comments on various drafts and providing lots of useful sources, helped me clarify the distinction between operational art and tactics. Professor Dennis Showalter made sure that I was up to date on the recent literature about the tactical debates of the prewar period and corrected a number of grievous errors of fact that managed to survive into late drafts. Most of all I would like to thank my older brother, First Lieutenant Brian Gudmundsson, USMC, who read and commented on every single draft of this work, and who was a great help in ensuring that what I wrote was of use to the serving officer. However, all errors of fact and interpretation in this work are, of course, my own.

Introduction

In the spring of 1940, the defenses of the Kingdom of Belgium, and with Belgium, the northern flank of France, depended almost entirely upon a belt of ultramodern concrete fortresses along the border that Belgium shared with Germany. The greatest of these, in both strength and importance, was Eban-Emael. Covering almost four square kilometers, the fort, with its artillery, antitank guns, and machine guns, dominated the terrain around it and made an infantry assault against it unthinkable. Artillery or air bombardment would be equally futile—the bulk of the fortress was located deep underground.

On May 11, however, the Germans took this fortress, not with a division or even a regiment, but with a battalion of combat engineers acting in concert with a glider-borne engineer platoon. The German heavy artillery fired, not in a vain attempt to destroy the fort, but to create craters in the flat terrain covered by the field guns in their armored cupolas. Other German guns fired at the cupolas themselves, again not to destroy, but to suppress the fire of the occupants.

When darkness fell, the German engineers crossed, in rubber boats, an artificial lake that separated them from Eban-Emael. Using the shell holes made by their own guns for cover, they crept forward. At dawn, flamethrowers sent streams of burning oil onto the embrasures from which the machine guns responsible for the close defense of the fort were expected to fire. Reeling from the heat and blinded by the smoke, the machine gunners failed to see the small team that had rushed forward with a huge shaped charge. A few seconds later, the charge went off, punching a hole in one of the main cupolas of the fort. Other explosions followed. One by one, the steel turrets that housed the teeth of Eban-Emael were destroyed. By the end of the morning, the fort was defenseless and surrendered.

German infantry poured across the bridges that Eban-Emael was supposed to cover. The infantry was followed by panzer and motorized divisions, which pushed deep into Belgium and Holland. Farther south, in France, other panzer divisions and motorized divisions pushed through the lightly defended Ardennes. In the course of the next month, in a campaign that combined the visions of General Schlieffen and H. G. Wells, these mobile troops succeeded in doing to France, Belgium, and Holland what the battalion of combat engineers had done to Eban-Emael. Using deception, swift movement, and fire to avert the eyes and destroy the concentration of the enemy, the panzer divisions pushed deep into his territory, isolating his armies in little pockets that could be reduced at leisure.[1]

Both the assault on Eban-Emael and the subsequent blitzkrieg came as a great surprise to the victims. Neither operation, however, should have surprised anyone. It was not, after all, any special security measures on the part of the Germans that kept the Allies from learning about their war plans. (These were sufficiently bad to allow a staff officer carrying a full set of plans for the invasion of France to fly over enemy territory in an unarmed liaison aircraft.) Neither can it be entirely blamed on the shortsightedness or sloth of Allied leadership, although these vices were very much in evidence during the first year of the war. Rather, it was their ignorance about how the Germans had fought World War I that prevented the overwhelming majority of French, British, Dutch, and Belgian leaders from adequately preparing for the German attack.

By the time that the German attack against the West was carried out in the spring, the fundamentals of the blitzkrieg at both the tactical and operational level had been present in the German army for almost a quarter century. By the end of 1915, German infantrymen and combat engineers fighting on the western front had developed the techniques that were the direct forbears of those used to reduce Eban-Emael. In that same year, German divisions and corps had begun to conduct campaigns of deep penetration that approached, though never equaled, the blitzkrieg campaigns of 1939 and 1940 in terms of their rapidity of movement and the degree of success achieved.

Despite the hundreds of volumes written about World War I between 1919 and 1939, the tradition of operational maneuver that manifested itself so often in the East was largely unknown outside of Germany. Historians writing in English or French largely ignored the great campaigns of maneuver in the East: Tannenberg, Gorlice-Tarnow, East Galicia, and Riga. Not only were the archives that contained the most information about these battles, those of Germany and Soviet Russia, largely closed to

Western researchers, but the reading public was more interested in the war that they, or their neighbors, had fought in, not a conflict between strangers half a continent away.

The lack of source material, however, was not what prevented adequate coverage of stormtroop tactics. These, after all, had been developed on the western front, and, as they had resulted in the deaths of many Englishmen, Frenchmen, Belgians, and Americans, should have been of intimate interest to the reading public. The handicap that prevented adequate coverage of stormtroop tactics was twofold. First, military writers were mostly products of the French approach to tactics. Seeing tactics as an exercise in engineering, these writers were looking for the formula for German tactics—how many guns per yard of front and how many waves of infantry per battalion. They thus missed the intangibles—the social relations between officers, noncommissioned officers (NCOs), and men, for example—that were the essence of stormtroop tactics. Second, like all members of their generation, military writers were effected by wartime propaganda, which depicted the Germans as heartless automatons who were as incapable of independent action on the battlefield as they were of human feeling. That such "Huns" were capable of the most fluid infantry tactics of the war would be a difficult proposition for such writers to swallow.

Those Western writers who accurately described stormtroop tactics usually referred to them as "infiltration tactics" and explained them away as the product of individual genius. A popular French magazine credited the invention of "infiltration tactics" to General Oskar von Hutier, a cousin of Erich Ludendorff who had been the commander of the German Eighteenth Army during the great offensive that began on March 21, 1918. Others ascribed their development to a Frenchman, André Laffargue, copies of whose pamphlet on tactics had been captured by the Germans in 1916 or 1917.

A partial exception to this general trend of Western ignorance of German tactics in World War I took place in Britain. Displaying that peculiarly Anglo-Saxon capacity to identify with one's enemies, a handful of Englishmen attempted to understand the German army on its own terms. The most successful of these was Capt. G. C. C. Wynne of the King's Own Yorkshire Light Infantry. In a series of articles published in the *Army Quarterly* between April 1937 and October 1939, Wynne described the evolution of German defensive tactics during World War I. While the chief characters in Wynne's articles are officers serving on the staff of the German High Command and the central theme of the book is the process by which the High Command was convinced to change defensive doctrine, Wynne provided a great deal of information about what was happening on the battlefield.

Wynne's series of articles was not completed until after World War II had broken out. Early in 1940 they were republished in the form of a book,[2] in which he predicted many of the tactical aspects of the blitzkrieg. (Not having studied Germany's campaigns on the eastern front, he lacked a clear conception of German operational art.) However, 1939 was too late a date to start educating the leaders who would soon face the blitzkrieg at both tactical and operational levels. Wynne's work would not provide any significant fruit until 40 years after its publication.

In the United States of the 1970s and 1980s both producers and consumers of military literature were in much better shape to undertake the study of the German army of World War I. The failure of the United States to subdue a state that might well be called the Prussia of Asia preserved serving soldier and military enthusiast alike from the kind of chauvinism that had infected the military literature of the interwar period. In fact, if there was any prejudice at all, it was in favor of the Germans. A generation of readers of military history had grown up with postwar accounts of the German Army in World War II that, while they decried the ends that army served, lauded the skill with which its members fought. In the minds of many observers of military affairs, both in and out of uniform, the German became a paragon of military virtue whose institutions and tactics were worthy of close study, if not outright imitation.

It was in this atmosphere of "Germanophilia" that the second major contribution to the English-speaking world's knowledge of World War I German tactics was written. Capt. (now Major) Timothy T. Lupfer, U.S. Army, then serving on the faculty of the United States Military Academy at West Point, wrote a short book entitled *The Dynamics of Doctrine: The Changes in German Tactical Doctrine During the First World War.* True to its name, *The Dynamics of Doctrine* dealt chiefly with the problem of changing military doctrine at the General Staff level. Building upon Wynne's work and drawing from the memoirs of officers who had taken part in the great doctrinal debates of 1915, 1916, and 1917, Lupfer's book also made a connection between the defensive doctrine and the new offensive tactics that were made official in 1918.

My goals in writing this book are both academic and practical. On the one hand, I want to contribute to the historical investigation begun by Wynne and Lupfer. On the other, I want to provide serving officers with a standard of excellence in infantry tactics that few units in the English-speaking world have attained in this century. This book therefore deals, in terms that I hope are accessible to both the historian and the professional soldier, with those areas left largely unexplored in the English language literature of World War I—the tactical heritage of the German infantry, the evolution of the squad as a tactical unit in its own right, the use of new weapons for close combat, the role of the elite assault units in developing and promulgating the new tactics, and the offensive battles, both large and small, that provided both the inspiration and the testing ground for a new way of fighting.

If there is a single thesis to this book, it is that there is no single explanation for the transformation of the German infantry that occurred during World War I. As I hope will become clear by the end of this book, the process by which the German infantry adapted itself to modern warfare was anything but straightforward. A large number of personalities, ideas, situations, and organizational forces interacted to push the German Army towards the "infiltration" tactics that won the spectacular tactical victories of late 1917 and early 1918. Sometimes the actions that pushed the German Army toward the new tactics were deliberate. Sometimes they were quite accidental and unintended. Most of the time, however, they were mere improvisations, ways of dealing with a pressing situation that were later sewn together in that patchwork quilt that Germany's enemies called "infiltration" tactics.

NOTE ON DEFINITIONS

One of the central ideas of this book is the distinction between *operational art* and *tactics*. For the most part, I have used both words in a way that is consistent with current U.S. Army doctrine as promulgated in the 1982 edition of FM 100-5 *Operations*. Thus, as the rule of thumb, operational level of war is of concern to corps commanders and higher while tactics is the province of echelons below corps. More strictly speaking, operational art is the art of winning military campaigns, while tactics is the art of winning engagements.

Out of consideration for the general reader, I have used as few German words as possible in the text. The only exceptions to this are the words *Jäger, Landwehr,* and *Landsturm,* which, I trust the reader will agree, are handier than their respective translations of "light infantry," "territorial army," and "second-line territorial army." German, however, is a language that is rather hard to translate and, as an aid to the reader who might wish to delve further into the subject of German military history, I have given the original German word in parentheses almost every time I introduce a German concept, title, rank, or organization.

The ranks of noncommissioned officers have been translated so as to make sense to Americans. *Gefreiter* I have translated as "corporal," *Unteroffizier* as "sergeant," *Sergeant* as "staff sergeant," *Vizefeldwebel* as "platoon sergeant," and *Feldwebel* as "first sergeant." Britons will have to deflate these ranks somewhat, as *Gefreiter* corresponds more to the British rank of "lance/corporal," *Unteroffizier* to "corporal," *Sergeant* and *Vizefeldwebel* to "sergeant," and *Feldwebel* to "company sergeant major" or "colour sergeant."

Officer ranks are easier to translate: There is a one-to-one correspondence with British and U.S. ranks from second lieutenant through colonel. U.S. readers should be aware, however, that German officers of World War I of a given rank tended both to be older and to command larger units than corresponding U.S. and British officers. A German captain, for example, had at least ten years of commissioned service under his belt and, soon after the outbreak of the war, often found himself in command of a battalion with an official strength of over a thousand men.

General officer ranks of the Imperial German Army, on the other hand, do not correspond well with either U.S. or British ranks. The holder of the title *General Major,* the most junior general officer rank, might command a brigade, a division, or even a corps. A *General Leutnant* might also command a brigade, a division, or a corps. A *General der Infanterie, Kavallerie, Artillerie,* and so on, might command a corps or an army, while a *General Oberst* (often translated as "colonel general") might command an army or an army group. To further complicate matters, most generals were promoted at least once during the course of the war. I have therefore decided to refer to all general officers simply as general. The description of their billet should give the reader a sufficiently accurate idea of their importance vis à vis one another.

Units are designated according to the following system. Most companies and all battalions, regiments, and divisions are designated by cardinal Arabic numerals. We thus have the "1st Company", the "7th Battery", and the "3rd Battalion", the "124th Regiment", and the "50th Reserve Division." (British and U.S. companies use letter designations, e.g. "A Battery".) Corps are designated by cardinal Roman numerals; "XXIV Corps" is thus pronounced "the Twenty-Fourth Corps". The numbers of armies are spelled out. We thus have the Fourth German Army and the First French Army.

The terms I use to describe artillery are translations of German terms from World War I. A 105mm howitzer, until recently considered to be medium artillery in the English-speaking world, is described as the 10.5 cm light field howitzer. Likewise, pieces that today would fit into the heavy category—those larger than 175mm—would fit into the German "super-heavy" category. The German classification of trench mortars, moreover, can be somewhat confusing. German light trench mortars of World War I, so heavy that they had to be mounted on wheeled carriages and drawn by teams of three or four men in harness, bear little resemblance to the light and handy 60mm and 2-inch mortars with which much of the world's English-speaking infantry is equipped.

Whenever one exists, the English spelling of a place name is used. When an English spelling does not exist, I have usually used the French (France and Belgium) or German (Eastern Europe, Italy, and Alsace) version.

NOTES

1.   The attack on Eban-Emael is often, in books the main purpose of which is to glorify parachutists, credited to the parachutists who were dropped on Eban-Emael on May 10 and 11. The first group of "paras," however, was captured by the Belgians and the second was trapped between the fortress and the Albert Canal until the assault engineer battalion linked up with them. Daniel Vilfroy's *War in the West, the Battle of France, May–June 1940* (Harrisburg, Pennsylvania: Military Service Publishing Company, 1942), p. 40. This book remains the best and most concise description of that campaign written in English.

2.   The book, published in 1940, was unfortunately entitled *If Germany Attacks: The Battle in Depth in the West.* The publisher apparently wanted to take advantage of the invasion scares of that year to boost sales. *If Germany Attacks* has subsequently been republished by Greenwood Press, Westport, CT, as part of the West Point Military Library.

STORMTROOP
TACTICS

Prologue: The Massacre of the Innocents

They evidently intend to handle their infantry in close lines in the next war. The average German private is not a person to be turned loose in a skirmish line and left to a certain degree to his own devices. . . . They prefer to lose men than lose control of the officers over them.

1st Lt. Carl Reichmann, U.S. Army, Infantry Division,
observing the German maneuvers of 1893

In keeping with the predictions of the experts, World War I began as a war of grand maneuvers in which each side sought victory at the operational level. In such a war, the art of tactics, concerned with winning battles, was far less important than operational art, concerned with winning campaigns. The loss of a battle, the destruction of a regiment, or even the destruction of a division was seen by the general staff virtuosos who directed the movement of million-man armies as inconsequential when compared to considerations that affected the campaign as a whole.

The goal of the German campaign in France in 1914 was the destruction of the French army in the field. The means by which this was to be accomplished, outlined in the Schlieffen Plan, was a march by the German First through the Fifth Armies through northern France and Belgium. This maneuver of five armies provided the hammer with which to smash as much of the French army as possible against the anvil of the Sixth and Seventh Armies that guarded the Franco-German border. If, in the course of this maneuver, certain French units succeeded in stopping the forward movement of certain German units, other German units would simply bypass the battlefield and be in a position either to attack the offending French units from the rear or push forward so far that the local French victory would have no significance for the outcome of the campaign. This was how the Germans had won the first Franco-Prussian War and this was how they planned to win the second.

The French unwittingly cooperated with the Schlieffen Plan, sending the bulk of their forces against the German Sixth and Seventh Armies.[1]

From the point of view of operational art, this move made no sense. It pitted strength against strength far from the center of gravity of the German armies in the West. From the point of view of tactics, attacking the Germans in the wooded and mountainous terrain along the Franco-German border that offered so much advantage to the defender, made even less sense. From the point of view of French strategy, however, much was to be gained from this attack. The German Sixth and Seventh Armies barred the way to the lost provinces of Alsace and Lorraine, the liberation of which was a major goal of French policy.

This pursuit of a strategic goal where neither the tactical nor the operational situation was favorable led to disaster for the French. The shrapnel shells fired by the already famous 75mm field pieces did little significant damage to the defending Germans.[2] The latter had been well schooled in the use of the spade and were invariably well dug-in whenever the French encountered them. Following this ineffective artillery preparation, the French infantry would move forward in thick skirmish lines. Advancing almost shoulder to shoulder with fixed bayonets, the red-trousered Frenchmen provided easy targets for German riflemen and machine gunners. The sacrifice of wave after wave of the flower of the French peacetime army failed to bring any results. By the middle of the month of August, the French had lost 300,000 men and were pulling back from Alsace and Lorraine. Every single French soldier would be needed to fend off the attack of the five German armies sweeping down from the north.[3]

The progress of the five German armies through Belgium and France was hindered more by logistical problems than by enemy action. The railroads that served the conquered territories were not up to the task of moving the massive amounts of supplies needed by the advancing armies, nor could they relieve the German soldier of the burden of marching 30 or 40 miles a day. Those supplies that did reach the railheads tended to stay there. The wagon trains set up to move supplies to the troops had to compete with other troops for the roads. Even if they had had open roads, however, there were far too few wagons to meet the needs of five hungry armies. While the German soldier did not starve as a result of these logistical problems—he was, after all, in the middle of a prosperous agricultural region at harvest time—much energy was diverted from the task of moving south as fast as possible by the need to forage. This, coupled with the sheer physical exhaustion of the average German soldier, slowed down the march of the five German armies.[4]

Far more dangerous from the operational point of view than supply problems, however, was the fact that each passing day brought the battlefield closer to Paris and its environs. This area was home to a dense railway system that radiated from the city center, a railway system that gave the French the ability to move units rapidly from one location to another. During the confused Battle of the Marne (6–9 September, 1914), the appearance of strong French and English forces at unexpected places caused Lieutenant Colonel Hensch, the general staff officer who had been authorized to give orders in the name of the High Command, to order a general retreat.

By September 13, the Germans had stopped retreating and the French had stopped pursuing. The belligerents faced each other across a line that stretched from the Swiss border to a point near the juncture of the Oise and the Aisne, between the French cities of Noyon and Compiègne. Along this frontier between two exhausted armies, trenches were being dug and barbed wire was being strung. Europe was about to get its first taste of trench warfare.

Generals on both sides knew the terrible cost of attacking entrenched troops. Those who had forgotten the lessons of the American Civil War and the Franco-Prussian War, not to mention the more recent Anglo-Boer and Russo-Japanese Wars, were quickly reminded of this fact by the casualties that resulted from hastily organized attacks against thoroughly prepared positions. This, combined with a widespread desire to seek decisive victory at the operational level, made the generals on both sides eager to resume the war of grand maneuvers. Maneuver to the south was inadvisable. The muscular neutrality of the Swiss forbade it. The only space available for maneuver was to the north.

Thus began the "race to the sea." First the French, and then the Germans, and then the French again tried to move around the open north flank with the ultimate goal of delivering a crushing blow to the enemy from the rear. Such a maneuver, had it succeeded for either belligerent party, would not have trapped enough of the enemy to result in a campaign-winning victory. It might, however, permit further large-scale maneuvers that would lead to the victory at the operational level that both sides desired.

While each attempted envelopment brought the fighting closer to the North Sea, German second line formations cleared the pockets of resistance that remained in those parts of Belgium overrun in August. On October 9, the fortress city of Antwerp fell to General von Beseler's Third Reserve Corps, a formation composed mostly of *Landwehr* and reserve units.[5] A few of the Belgian and British defenders were captured in the city, more were chased into neutral Holland. Five Belgian infantry divisions, however, escaped toward the west. To pursue the retreating Belgians along the coastline to the Channel Ports of Dixmude, Dunkirk, and Calais, and with the ultimate goal of some as yet unnamed operational maneuver, the Germans formed a new army on October 15.

Command of the new army was given to Albrecht, duke of Württemberg, who had been in charge of the Fourth Army since the end of July. Perhaps to confuse the French and the British, who did not realize its existence until October 18, the new army was also called the Fourth

Army. Albrecht's new Fourth Army was composed of five corps. One was von Beseler's Third Reserve Corps, the conquerors of Antwerp. The other four, the newly minted Twenty-second, Twenty-third, Twenty-sixth, and Twenty-seventh Reserve Corps, were untried formations composed almost entirely of hastily trained troops led by officers and NCOs that had been brought back from retirement.[6]

By October 14, the four new Reserve Corps had detrained in Belgium and were marching west. To the north, the Third Reserve Corps marched along the coast. To the south, a weary Sixth Army held a line south and southeast of the city of Ypres. In between was western Flanders, a strip of land noted for its flatness. It was through this territory that the four Reserve Corps would have to pass on their way to the Channel ports.

THE KEY TO THE COUNTRY

From the coast of the North Sea to the French border, the variation in elevation between any two points in Flanders is rarely more than 50 meters, and is often far less than that. Most of the higher ground is located south and east of the city of Ypres. These "highlands" contain Mount Kemmel, the only proper hill in western Flanders. From there, one can see the city of Dixmude 28 kilometers to the north and Menin 20 kilometers to the east.

In many parts of the world, Kemmel would not qualify as a mountain. Its peak is no higher than 156 meters above sea level.[7] For the armies that fought in Flanders during World War I, however, Kemmel and the surrounding heights were of immense importance. Before the war was to end, hundreds of thousands would die to take control of these little Flemish hills. The slaughter began in October and November of 1914 with the sacrifice of the four German Reserve Corps at the First Battle of Ypres.

The Germans were not the only ones to recognize the value of the west Flanders plain. To the Belgians retreating from Antwerp to a line just east of the Yser River, it was the last sliver of their homeland to remain free from the German occupation and its attendant outrages. To the French, it was the last open route to the Rhine. And to the British Expeditionary Force (B.E.F.), it was the gate to the Channel ports that had to be defended at all costs. Control of the towers of Ypres and the surrounding heights gave the British the ability to see and to call artillery fire upon any massing of German troops. The same heights masked British troop concentrations and provided the British artillery with good defilade positions. In short, Ypres was the key to the country.

The first German attempt to reach the Channel ports had not been aimed at Ypres but rather at the more direct route along the North Sea coast. After the Fall of Antwerp, the Third Reserve Corps had taken Ghent and Ostende in quick succession. Their forward march had been stopped, however, on the east bank of the Yser where the Belgians could occupy strong fortifications and count on support from the guns of British torpedo boats and cruisers in the North Sea. Some units of the Third Reserve Corps made limited progress against this line. A handful of German soldiers even succeeded in crossing the river. The bulk of the Third Reserve Corps, however, was unable to break through the Belgian position.

The baton now passed to the four new Reserve Corps. From October 14 to 18 they had marched through Belgium unmolested by enemy forces of any significant size. Belgian *franc tireurs* occasionally shot at them, but caused far fewer casualties than the combination of hard marches, new jackboots, and soft feet. The advancing battalions of the Reserve Corps were followed by caravans of civilian carts filled with those suffering from various foot ailments.[8]

Until October 18, the forward march of the four Reserve Corps had been undetected. The British General French had been convinced that there were no German troops between the Third Reserve Corps in the north and the Sixth Army in the south. On that day, however, a bicycle patrol sent out ahead of the German main body found itself surrounded by British cavalry.[9] The British got the best of the German cyclists and captured a few. The testimony of these prisoners told French that the gap that he had been hoping to exploit was about to be closed.

On October 19, General French made an attempt to place a division in the path of the four advancing Reserve Corps. The gesture was futile. In the face of odds of over eight to one, the division was pulled back. As the British, Belgians, and French tried desperately to form a solid line in Flanders, the four Reserve Corps linked up with Beseler's Third Reserve Corps to the north and the Sixth Army to the south. From Menin to the North Sea, a front a hundred kilometers long had been formed. Along its length, across dykes and canals, in little Flemish villages, and on the outskirts of the city of Dixmude, a hundred fire fights raged. The First Battle of Ypres had begun.

THE IRON YOUTH

In the center of the German line, the four new Reserve Corps, still unbloodied, pushed forward with an enthusiasm born of ignorance of the horrors of modern war. Where the enemy was weak, this enthusiasm served them well. In the first three days of the battle, they poured through the gaps in the Belgian, British, and French lines. Small bands of cavalrymen caused casualties, as did Belgian civilians firing from their houses. Neither these, nor the isolated garrisons of villages and towns, however, did much to retard the forward movement of the Fourth Army. The cavalry could not stand against the masses of infantry that appeared before them. The franc tireurs could do little more than fire a few shots and hide. When night fell, the villages and towns were cleared out at the point of a bayonet.

Where the enemy was strong, however, progress was slow. In the daylight, when the enemy could dig a shallow trench and put enough rifles in the line, each advance of a hundred yards cost the attacking Germans thousands of casualties. By October 22, there were no more gaps in the French, British, or Belgian lines to exploit. The thin screen of cavalry that had been thrown up to delay the advance of the Fourth Army had been relieved. In its place was a thin but solid line of infantry.

For two weeks, working in concert with the continuing attempt of the Third Reserve Corps to cross the Yser as well as the westward push of the Sixth Army south of Ypres, the four Reserve Corps tried to break through this line. Each day followed the same pattern. First the German artillery would bombard the defender's trenches. The light field howitzers (10.5cm) and heavy mortars were especially effective. A direct hit could kill an entire squad. In one case, an entire troop of dismounted British cavalry was buried alive.[10]

The artillery, however, could not kill all of the defenders. There were neither enough guns, enough shells, nor enough time. The divisions of the four Reserve Corps did not have their full complement of artillery, and what they had consisted mostly of light field guns (7.7cm).[11] The German logistical system had yet to sort itself out; low inventories of shells combined with transportation bottlenecks resulted in shell rationing in the gun pits. Finally, each day that passed, the British and French got stronger and the chances of being able to turn a tactical breakthrough into an operational victory became slimmer. The German High Command[12] was eager to achieve a breakthrough and thus resume the war of maneuver, cost what it might in the short term.

So, time after time the infantry was sent in, advancing shoulder to shoulder in thick skirmish lines reminiscent of those of the American Civil War. A young Austrian volunteer serving with the 16th Bavarian Reserve Infantry Regiment described one of these attacks in his memoirs.

And then came a dark cold night in Flanders, through which we marched in silence, and when the day began to emerge from the mists, suddenly an iron greeting came whizzing at us over our heads, and with a sharp report sent the little pellets flying between our ranks, ripping up the wet ground; but even before the little cloud had passed, from two hundred throats the first hurrah rose to meet the first messenger of death. Then a crackling and a roaring, a singing and a howling began, and with feverish eyes each one of us was drawn forward, faster and faster, until suddenly past turnip fields and hedges the fight began, the fight of man against man. And from the distance, the strains of a song reached our ears, coming closer and closer, leaping from company to company, and just as Death plunged a busy hand into our ranks, the song reached us too, and we passed it along: *Deutschland, Deutschland, Über Alles, Über Alles in der Welt!*[13]

At times the attacking Germans would reach their objectives and clear them with the bayonet. Once they were upon the enemy, the ferocity of the "Iron Youth" gave them a certain advantage. This advantage, however, did not bring any concrete benefit to the attacking Fourth Army. The effort of the attack tended to use up all of the energy of the attackers and there was no second echelon to exploit any breach that might have been made. The surviving defenders would pull back a few hundred meters and reform the line. Once again, the attackers would have to cross open fields swept by the fire of a thousand rifles and the occasional well-handled machine gun.

The lack of success of the Fourth Army could not be blamed on the troops, for their fighting qualities were excellent. Twenty-five percent of the private soldiers of the four new Reserve Corps were "extra" men from the three reserve contingents of the German Army—the Reserve, the *Landwehr,* and the *Landsturm.* Some of the older men had already lost sons in the war. The other 75 percent were war volunteers *(Kriegsfreiwilligen),* young men who by virtue of their youth or their studies had not yet served their term of national service. Many of these were the well educated sons of the middle classes, young men being trained for the universities and the professions. When the war broke out, hundreds of thousands of these young men made their way to the local barracks and reported for duty.[14]

The major deficiency of the units of the Fourth Army lay in the area of training. In the course of the months of August and September 1914, the volunteers had been trained by officers and NCOs largely ignorant of modern warfare. The officers and NCOs of the active army, as well as the younger reserve officers and NCOs, were already at the front when the regiments of volunteers had been formed. The spots that they vacated were filled by retired officers and NCOs, as well as civil servants with temporary commissions.[15] The overwhelming majority of these leaders were not familiar with machine guns. Many were new to the latest model (M1898) Mauser rifle and the tactics that had been developed to make the most of its virtues. As a result, the training that was imparted to the eager young men in surplus dark blue uniforms consisted mostly of close order drill and bayonet fighting.[16]

THE DRILL BOOK OF 1888

One of the chief tactical lessons of the Franco-Prussian War—that men packed together in skirmish lines and columns were no match for breach-loading rifles—had never been learned by the retirees that taught the young volunteers. During the 1880s the German Army had all but abandoned open order tactics.[17] Military authors such as Fritz Hönig and J. Meckel had painted terrifying pictures of attacks conducted in open order falling apart because large numbers of troops took advantage of the fact that they were far enough away from their officers to permit them to hide during the battle. The belief that the increased casualties that resulted from dense formations were a fair price to pay for the guarantee that troops would remain under the direct supervision of their officer became widespread.

The fear of losing control of troops in battle reinforced an entrenched belief in the moral value of the bayonet charge. The battles of the second half of the nineteenth century provided numerous examples of close formations attacking with the bayonet prevailing over rifle-firing skirmish lines. That the close formations had suffered horrific casualties was rarely considered cause to worry—European wars of the second half of the nineteenth century were so short and infrequent that a regiment might only fight one battle in a generation. So distributed, the loss of half of a regiment's effectives in less than half an hour tended to contribute to, rather than diminish, belief in the *Furor Teutonicus*.

This belief in the continuing value of close order tactics was incarnated in the *Drill Regulations of 1888 (Exerzier Reglement von 1888)*. While they made mention of the growing importance of the junior officer and NCO on the battlefield, as well as of the necessity for cultivating a spirit of initiative in every soldier, the *Drill Regulations of 1888* recommended that the best means of gaining fire superiority over the enemy was to move against him with infantry arrayed in close order. Although particular formations were not prescribed, the battalion and sometimes the company commander being free to use whatever formation he saw fit, the most popular formation for the attack at the company level was the column of platoons (see Illustration 1). This was the formation that the old Prussian Army, which had called it the company column, had used since the Napoleonic Wars. With a front of about 25 meters, it permitted the company commander to keep his entire company in sight and within the sound of his voice. At the same time, it could easily be transformed into a dense firing line in which every rifle in the company could be employed against the enemy.[18]

It was this and similar formations that the war volunteers learned in the last three weeks of September and the first two weeks of October when their time was devoted to unit training. When whole battalions took part in mock attacks, the companies were formed into broad and deep columns (*Breitkolonne* and *Tiefkolonne*) where they were formed four abreast and four deep, respectively.[19] Larger-scale attacks were also practiced, although there were no prescribed formations for regiments, brigades, or divisions.

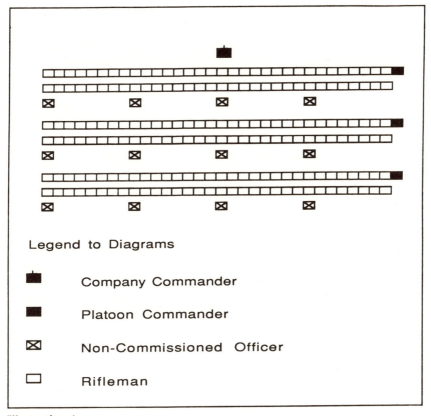

Illustration 1
Column of Platoons, 1914

The exercises of the volunteers were cut short during the second week of October by orders to move to the front. The old dark blue tunics and trousers were hastily exchanged for new field grey uniforms. The belts, cartridge pouches, and packs[20] that had not been available during training were issued, and the troops boarded the trains that were to take them to Belgium.[21]

The soldiers of the British Expeditionary Force (B.E.F.) who held the line against the German Fourth Army were volunteers of a different sort. Most were professionals serving out a seven-year enlistment. A few were reservists who had done their time "with the colors" and had been obliged to return to active duty at the outbreak of hostilities. Many of these latter men, as well as some of the senior NCOs and officers, were veterans of the Anglo-Boer War. Almost all were crack shots.

The training of the British regular soldier in the years before World War I had consisted of close order drill, gymnastics, and the use of the short magazine Lee-Enfield rifle. The Lee-Enfield was distinguished from the other bolt action, magazine-fed rifles of the day by the remarkable smoothness of its action. With it, the average professional soldier could fire 15 aimed shots a minute. Those who displayed a particular aptitude for the weapon could manage thirty.

Where skill at arms is concerned, the Belgian and French soldiers that guarded the flanks of the B.E.F. could not compete with the British soldier. Their rifles lacked the smooth action of the Lee-Enfield and, as short-term conscripts, they had not spent much time on the rifle range. The cavalrymen and sailors who were thrust into the line when it threatened to break were even less well trained in the use of their rifles and carbines. As slow and inaccurate as it was, the fire of the French and Belgian troops was deadly enough. In their dense formations, the volunteers provided an easy target for even the most hastily trained rifleman.

PINCER ATTACK

By November 4, it was clear to the German High Command that no more progress could be made across the Yser. The Belgians had opened their dykes and flooded the battlefield. The Third Reserve Corps was therefore sent south to reinforce the four Reserve Corps and the Fourth Army was ordered to change its direction of attack. Instead of pushing west, as it had since the beginning of the battle, the Fourth Army was now to push south. In fulfilling this new mission, the Fourth Army was to form the northern half of a pincer, the southern half of which was already present in the form of the Sixth Army. This pincer movement, the German High Command hoped, would cut off a major portion of the B.E.F. and capture the high ground south and east of Ypres.[22]

However it may have worried the staff officers in B.E.F. headquarters, the pincer was not strong enough to turn the tide of attack in favor of the Germans. In the course of a week of daily attacks, the defenders of Ypres were occasionally pushed back a few hundred meters. On the whole, however, the thin line of riflemen in shallow trenches was maintained. Small gaps that were torn in the line were quickly filled by counterattacks and the bringing up of still more German troops did little to alter the situation.

On November 11, almost a month after the battle had begun, the German High Command threw in its last trump. On the personal order of the Kaiser, who had traveled to Flanders to personally supervise the attack at Ypres, units of the Imperial Guard were sent into the battle. A week before, four of the eight infantry regiments of the Guard Corps had been pulled out of the fighting south of Arras, formed into a provisional division under the command of General Winckler, and marched north.[23] By November 10, all of "Division Winckler" was in position.

Tall, fit, and superbly disciplined, the men of the Imperial Guard were the inheritors of a tradition that dated back to the Thirty Years' War. Unlike the four Reserve Corps, the Guard had had plenty of opportunity to train. When the Guard Corps had marched west at the beginning of the war, there had been no need to requisition carts to carry those whose jackboots disagreed with their feet.

The officers of the Guard were likewise quite different from the middle-aged middle-class retirees who led the men of the four Reserve Corps. Arrogant and dashing throwbacks to the previous century, the officers of the Imperial Guard were the idols of German high society.[24] Ambitious hostesses took pains to ensure that their parties were well attended by officers of the Guard while hundreds of lovelorn Berlin ladies readily identified with the popular singers who sang "Forget me not, my darling Guard officer."[25] In their approach to infantry tactics, however, the officers of the four Reserve Corps and the Guard Corps were very much alike.

In the long peace that preceded the outbreak of war, officers of the Imperial Guard and other prestigious units displayed an unfortunate distaste for the serious study of the military profession. The officers leading the young volunteers had not had the opportunity to prepare for modern war. The officers leading the Guard seem not to have had the inclination. The cost of this neglect was demonstrated by the attack of Division Winckler on November 11, 1914.

The direction of Division Winckler's attack roughly coincided with the road that led from Ypres to Menin. The immediate objective was the British position in the "nose" of the Ypres salient (see Illustration 2). The artillery preparation against the woods where the British trenches had been dug, provided by the two fully equipped artillery regiments attached to Division Winckler, was heavier than those which had prepared the attacks of the war volunteers. Three-fourths of the field pieces in those regiments, however, were still field guns—weapons the shrapnell rounds of which, like those of the French 75mm guns, were of use primarily against troops in the open. Thus, the shelling of the British trench, which began at 7:30 A.M. with the registration of the guns, increased in intensity at 9:00 and stopped at 10:00,[26] was sufficient only to harass the British sharpshooters, cause a few casualties, and warn them that an attack was imminent.

Shortly before 10 A.M., the Guard regiments deployed in their old-fashioned skirmish lines with the sergeants behind the tightly packed rows of guardsmen "to encourage those who might otherwise stay back"[27] and began to move forward. British artillery, rifle fire, and, in a few places, machine gun fire, tore gaps in the advancing ranks. Seemingly indifferent to the killing around them, the Guardsmen reformed their lines and continued their advance up the gently sloping meadows that

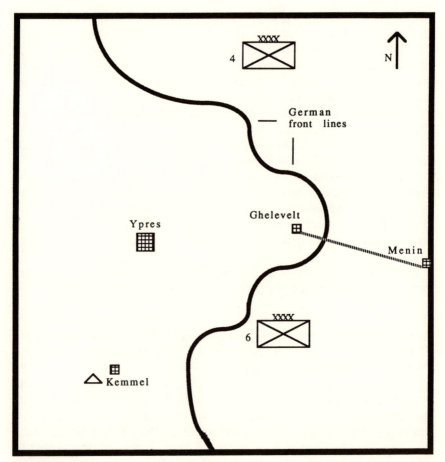

Illustration 2
The Ypres Salient, November 11, 1914

gave the British riflemen such excellent fields of fire. One hundred meters from the British trenches the attack started to fall apart. At 50 meters, the thick skirmish lines had been reduced to groups of 20 or 30 men
following whatever officer remained alive.

Most of these groups succeeded in reaching the British trenches and
even pushing beyond into the woods and tiny groups of houses that the
British were defending. Even in such close quarters, however, the bayonets of the Guard could not contend with the aimed fire of sharpshooters
trained to fight as individuals. The small groups of Germans were quickly
whittled down. While the experience of the young reserve lieutenant who
rushed alone into an English position shouting orders at a company that
no longer existed was a unique one,[28] the killing and wounding of so many

of the Germans through rifle fire made it possible for the British to speed-ily eject the survivors from the woods and villages and recover most of their original line.

The casualties—dead, wounded, and captured—among the Guard were comparable to those suffered by the four Reserve Corps a few days before. The 2nd Guard Grenadier Regiment, the 3rd *(Fusilier)* Battalion of which had succeeded in reaching the British line only to be surrounded and destroyed, lost 15 officers and 500 men.[29] The 1st Foot Guard Regiment, with an officer roster that read like a "Who's Who" of the Prussian aristocracy, lost eight officers, most of whom were company or battalion commanders, and 800 men.[30]

The attack of Division Winckler was the last major event of the First Battle of Ypres. The failure of the Germans to break through at Ypres meant that they would be unable to pursue victory at the operational level until the tactical problem of how to pierce a modern defensive position was solved. In the decades before the outbreak of war the German General Staff had, in concentrating its collective attention on operational problems, relegated tactics to the status of a subsidiary art. The whole aim of operational art, after all, was to avoid those situations where the success of a campaign depended on the outcome of a single engagement. With the onset of position warfare, however, tactics assumed a far greater importance. Good tactics had become the prerequisite for the resumption of the war of grand maneuvers upon which the Germans pinned their hopes for ultimate victory.

NOTES

1. The plan for this attack was referred to by the French as Plan XVII.

2. The entirety of the artillery of a French infantry division consisted of batteries equipped with the *soixante-quinze,* as was most of the artillery directly subordinate to each army corps. While its accuracy and rate of fire were quite satisfactory, this most famous of all French field pieces was limited to firing at relatively flat trajectories. This meant that the shells fired by these guns were only a danger to well dug in troops in the rare occurrence of a shell either landing in the trench or bursting directly above it.

3. Pascal Marie Henri Lucas, *L'Évolution des idées tactiques en France et Allemagne pendant la guerre de 1914–1918* (Paris: Berger Levrault, 1923), p. 38.

4. See Martin van Creveld, *Supplying War: Logistics from Wallenstein to Patton* (New York: Cambridge University Press, 1982), pp.109–21.

5. The *Landwehr* was the second line reserve force of the German Army. It was made up of older reservists who had served their time with the colors and the first line reserve. Landwehr units were used both as field units and as the garrisons of fortresses.

6. Otto Schwink, *Die Schlacht an der Yser und bei Ypern im Herbst 1914* (Oldenberg: Verlag von Gerhard Stalling, 1918), p. 16.

7.   Schwink, *Die Schlacht an der Yser,* pp. 22–26.

8.   Hans Willers, *Königlich Preussisches Reserve Infanterie Regiment Nr. 215* (Berlin: Verlag Gerhard Stalling, 1926), pp. 21–22.

9.   The divisions of the Twenty-second, Twenty-third, Twenty-sixth, and Twenty-seventh Reserve Corps did not have a full complement of cavalry. The deficiency was made up by forming volunteer bicycle detachments.

10.   John Buchan, *A History of the Great War* (Boston: Houghton Mifflin Company, 1922), p. 360. American readers should note that a British cavalry troop, roughly corresponding to an infantry platoon of the time, was much smaller than a U.S. cavalry troop, which corresponded to an infantry company.

11.   Wilhelm Balck, *The Development of Tactics—World War* (Fort Leavenworth, KS: The General Service Schools Press, 1922), p. 24. This is the English language translation of the first edition of Balck's *Entwickelung der Taktik im Weltkrieg,* and will be referred to hereafter as Balck, *Development of Tactics.* The second edition, greatly expanded from the first, which was published in Berlin by R. Eisenschmidt in 1922, will be referred to as Balck, *Entwickelung.*

12.   *Oberste Heersleitung* (OHL), now led by Chief of the General Staff General von Falkenhayn.

13.   Adolf Hitler, *Mein Kampf,* quoted in Joachim Fest, *Hitler* (New York: Harcourt, Brace, and Jovanovich, 1974), pp. 69–70.

14.   Schwink, *Die Schlacht an der Yser,* p. 10.

15.   The civil servants were former NCOs who had been given posts in the customs office, post office, and police at the ends of their terms of service.

16.   W. Rohkohl, *Reserve Infanterie Regiment Nr. 226* (Berlin: Verlåg Gerhard Stalling, 1923).

17.   Open order tactics are those in which soldiers advance as individuals or in small groups rather than as part of a closely packed formation.

18.   Carl Reichmann, *Observations on the German Imperial Manoevers in 1893* (Fort Leavenworth, KS: U.S. Infantry and Cavalry School, 1894), pp. 17–21; and A. Hillard Atteridge, *The German Army in War* (New York: McBride, Nast, and Company, 1915), p. 86.

19.   Wilhelm Balck (Walter Krueger, translator), *Tactics,* Vol. I (Fort Leavenworth, KS: U.S. Cavalry Association, 1915), pp. 56–59. This book, written by Balck before the outbreak of World War I, is cited hereafter as Balck, *Tactics.*

20.   Many of the packs issued to the volunteers had, only days before, been captured from the Belgians. Some of them were still stained with the blood of the former owners.

21.   Josef Schatz, *Geschichte des badischen (rheinischen) Reserve-Infanterie-Regiments 239* (Stuttgart: Chr. Belser A.G., 1927), p. 6.

22.   General von Kuhl, in his two-volume history of World War I, sees this decision as an admission of the impossibility of achieving any operational level decision in the West. Hermann von Kuhl, *Der Weltkrieg 1914–1918,* Vol.I (Berlin: Verlag Tradition Wilhelm Kolk, 1929), p. 75.

23.   General Oskar von Hutier, the commanding general of the 1st Guard Division who gave up half of his command to General von Winckler, will be a major character in Chapters 7 and 10.

24.   Grover Cleveland Platt, *The Place of the Army in German Life 1898–1914* (unpublished doctoral dissertation, State University of Iowa, 1941), p. 100.

25.   *Vergißt mir nicht, mein kleiner Gardeoffizier.*

26.   The details of the attack of the four infantry regiments of the Prussian Guard are taken from articles written by German officers who participated in that attack. F. von Unger, "Der Angriff des Regiments Augusta am 11. November 1914 bei Ypern"; Fritz Baehrecke, "Tage vor Ypern"; and von Rieben, "Ypern" in Ernst von Eisenhart Rothe and Dr. Martin Lezius, *Das Ehrenbuch der Garde, Die preußische Garde im Weltkriege 1914–1919* (Berlin: Wilhelm Kolk and Verlag Oskar Hinderer), pp. 133–43, hereafter referred to as von Unger, Baehrecke, and von Rieben, *Das Ehrenbuch der Garde.*

27.   Ibid., p. 139.

28.   Ibid., p. 140.

29.   von Winterfeldt, *Das Kaiser Franz Garde-Grenadier Regiment Nr. 2: 1914–1918* (Berlin: Verlag Gerhard Stalling, 1922), p. 21.

30.   Eitel Friedrich Prinz von Preußen, *Erstes Garde-Regiment zu Fuß* (Berlin: Verlag Gerhard Stalling, 1922), p. 52.

1

Open Order Tactics

> It is no less important to educate the soldier to think and act for himself. His self-reliance and sense of honor will then induce him to do his duty even when he is no longer under the eye of his commanding officer.
>
> *German Field Service Regulations, 1908*

During the long peace that preceded the outbreak of World War I, each autumn after the crops had been gathered it was the custom of the German Kaiser to invite one of his army corps to engage in a week-long mock battle. Observers at the Imperial Maneuvers, as these exercises were called, usually took note of the density of the German infantry formations and the apparent fondness on the part of German commanders for bayonet and cavalry charges.[1] When, after the First Battle of Ypres, military writers—whose image of the German soldier had been largely formed by the reports of these observers—heard reports of how the Guardsmen and volunteers had fought at Ypres, they made the false assumption that the entire German infantry fought that way.[2]

Aided by the stereotype of the mindless Prussian militarist that was becoming popular in the English-speaking world at the time, this phenomenon produced the myth of the German soldier as an unthinking automaton whose personality was so stunted by years of "cadaver discipline" that he was incapable of independent action on the battlefield. What most English-speaking military writers of the period did not know, however, was that during the 14 years that passed between the turn of the century and the outbreak of war, the dense formations that had served the Germans so poorly at Ypres had fallen into disrepute in many military circles. As a result, when war broke out in 1914, there was no consensus within the German Army about how the infantry should fight. This lack of consensus, combined with the decentralized nature of the

German Army, resulted in a variety of radically different approaches to infantry tactics in the first months of the war.

A DECENTRALIZED ARMY

The German Army of 1914 was the most decentralized in Europe. Only one official, the Kaiser himself, could be said to have complete authority over all military functions. Below this "Supreme War Lord" there were a number of autonomous organizations that answered only to him. The General Staff, which unlike the general staffs of other European armies of the time, concerned itself exclusively with the planning of campaigns, is perhaps the best known. Those few administrative matters that were dealt with at the national level were divided between the War Ministry (tables of organization, standardization of weapons, procurement, drill regulations) and the Military Cabinet (officer assignments). Although each was powerful within its own sphere, neither these agencies nor any of the many inspectorates and commissions that reported directly to the Kaiser controlled any troop units in peacetime. This was the prerogative of the commanding generals of the 22 corps districts[3] into which the German Empire was divided.

Each corps district was responsible for providing a certain number of formations and units—usually one active and one reserve corps plus additional cavalry, heavy artillery, engineer, and support troops—the enlisted men of which were recruited from within the boundaries of the district. Subject only to the annual visit of the inspectors of each branch of service and the official regulations promulgated by the War Ministry, the commander of each corps district was free to train his troops as he pleased. As a rule, most of this discretion was passed down the chain of command until it rested with company commanders.[4]

Free from all but the most general supervision and relieved by a promotion system based on strict seniority of the need to constantly please superiors, the German battalion or company commander was free to train his troops according to his own lights. "As regards the method of training," wrote a British officer observing the German Army in the late 1880s, "the Captain is practically unfettered by regulations, and no one has a right to interfere with what he thinks fit to do, unless such action is directly contrary to the spirit of existing regulations or manifestly would give but insufficient results."[5] This tradition was reiterated in German regulations in force at the outbreak of World War I.[6]

ORGANIZATION

The most significant restrictions on this freedom were the organization and social composition of his unit. A German infantry company, for example, had an authorized strength of 259 men, almost all of whom were riflemen; the only exceptions to this were officers, senior NCOs, and musicians. The lack of any other means of attaining fire superiority organic to the company made it impossible for a company commander to dispense with the idea of putting as many rifles as possible into the firing line.

The company was divided into three platoons *(Züge)* of 80 men, each commanded by a lieutenant. There was no tactical rationale behind the large platoons—even relatively conservative tacticians such as Wilhelm Balck realised that it was difficult for one man to control such a unit in combat. Companies and platoons were large, however, because there weren't enough captains and lieutenants to make smaller companies and platoons.[7]

In the early years of the twentieth century the German War Ministry repeatedly and explicitly decided to suffer shortages of junior officers rather than to commission those without the requisite social, moral, and intellectual qualifications. These decisions, made with the full blessing of the Kaiser, are often mentioned in connection with the War Ministry's reluctance to call a larger percentage of Germany's population to the colors. What is not often realised is that the unwillingness of the German Army as an institution to put anyone but members of the traditional officer caste in command of units on the battlefield had a profound effect on the tactics that the German infantry would use in the opening months of World War I.[8]

THE BACKBONE OF THE ARMY

Each platoon was divided into a number of eight-man squads *(Gruppen)*, the number depending on the size of the platoon rather than any predetermined idea of the ideal number of squads in a platoon. While a platoon entered the battlefield as a formed unit, separated by other platoons by a few meters of open space and led by an officer who would maneuver it so as to take advantage of the terrain and the peculiarities of the situation, the squad had no such independent function. It was an integral part of the column or firing line, joined with its neighboring squads into a seamless tactical garment.

The squad leader, a sergeant *(Unteroffizier)* or corporal *(Gefreiter)* was not a tactical decision maker. "The backbone of the Army," Rudyard Kipling had written late in the previous century, "is the non-commissioned man" and the German squad leader of the prewar period was expected to serve as "backbone" in more ways than one. The squad leaders responded to the commands of the platoon leaders to form or move the skirmish line by stepping out in front of the ranks and forming what the Germans called the "skeleton" of the skirmish line. They served as examples to the private soldiers, models of military deportment and martial prowess. Finally, they were disciplinarians, enforcing regulations in garrison and discouraging slackers in battle.

If there were more than three squads in a platoon, as was often the case even in peacetime companies with a strength of less than 200 men, the platoon was divided into two half-platoons *(Halbzüge)*. These, like the squads, did not have a separate role on the battlefield but rather were little more than subdivisions that facilitated drill. The leader of each half-platoon was a noncommissioned officer—a sergeant, senior sergeant *(Sergeant)* or the platoon sergeant *(Vizefeldwebel)*. Neither squads nor half-platoons, however, had any permanent standing within the company. Instead, each time the company assembled for parade the men lined up by height in two ranks, the tallest on the right and the shortest on the left. This accomplished, squads and half-platoons were counted off—the first four men in the first rank and the four men immediately behind them forming the first squad and so forth.

For administrative purposes, the platoon was divided into "corporalcies" *(Korporalschaften)* of two squads (16 men) under the supervision of a sergeant. These corporalcies allowed the first sergeant *(Feldwebel)* to take care of the day-to-day administration and training of the company (e.g. guard duty and fatigues) through an administrative chain of command run entirely by NCOs, leaving the officers free to concentrate on other matters. The "corporalcy" had no role to play on either the parade ground or on the battlefield.

BOER TACTICS

The first major blow against the column tactics that had been so popular in Germany in the late nineteenth century was delivered by reports coming out from South Africa. During the Anglo-Boer War of 1899–1902, Boer irregulars armed with Mauser rifles decimated, on a regular basis, British troops attacking in the column of platoons formation that they had copied from the Germans. This repeated humiliation of the British regular army by a frontier militia convinced many German officers, including some influential General Staff officers, that the close order tactics then practiced by the German Infantry were obsolete. By 1902, the German military journals and the files of the General Staff were full of articles warning of the impracticality of advancing in close order against an enemy armed with modern repeating rifles.

As a substitute for the charge of massed infantry inspired by the *Furor Teutonicus* the authors of these articles suggested that riflemen should imitate the Boers and patiently work their way forward in small groups and as individuals, using every fold in the ground for cover. These riflemen, trained to fire as individual marksmen, would destroy the enemy's will to resist by accurate fire rather than by the weight of their own bodies.

The year 1902 saw the high point of German enthusiasm for "Boer tactics." In that year, infantry units of the Guard Corps held demonstrations where the Guardsmen crept rather than charged into mock battle. At the Imperial Maneuvers of 1902, German infantry was observed working its way toward the "enemy" in widely dispersed skirmish lines, each rifleman moving from one covered position to another as an individual. After a few months, however, German interest in imitating the Boers waned. It had been discovered that it was difficult, if not impossible, for a platoon commander to control his 80-man platoon when it was stretched out over 300 or so meters. It was even more difficult for a battalion commander to control his 960-man unit when it was extended over 3000 or so meters. By the autumn of 1903, most German units had reverted to the column of platoons as the chief attack formation.[9]

Beginning in 1904 the debate over Boer tactics was revived by reports coming from German officers observing the battles of the Russo-Japanese War. Soon after the end of the Franco-Prussian War, the Japanese dismissed the French advisers who had been training their army since the 1860s and replaced them with German officers. Ever since then, the Japanese had slavishly followed German military methods. The success of the Japanese army in Manchuria, even though it had cost the lives of many Japanese infantrymen, was seen by many German officers and military writers as a vindication of column tactics.[10] Other German commentators, however, took the opposite view. The Japanese, they noted, had responded to their unacceptable losses in the early battles of the war by attacking in more open formations, with more space between individuals, and greater freedom for platoons and squads to move independently.

THE DRILL REGULATIONS OF 1906

The infantry training manual that appeared in May of 1906 reflected the lack of a consensus about tactics in the German Army of the prewar decade. With the exhortation "forward upon the enemy, cost what it may" the *Drill Regulations of 1906* expressed the still well entrenched belief that only a bayonet charge could seal the doom of the enemy infantry and bring victory in battle. This belief was balanced by a repetition of the admonition contained in the *Drill Regulations of 1888* that the obtaining of fire superiority was a precondition to a successful bayonet charge. The *Drill Regulations of 1906* further recognized that in order to gain this fire superiority the infantry might have to, on occasion, be released from the direct control of commissioned officers.[11]

In the ideal battle described in the *Drill Regulations of 1906* the German infantry would enter the battlefield in the traditional closed formation. As the German infantry approached within a thousand meters or so of the enemy force, the light field guns of the division's artillery brigade would start to shell the enemy. This would serve to encourage the enemy riflemen and machine gunners to seek shelter, thus reducing the amount of fire that could be brought to bear upon the advancing infantry columns. If the artillery preparation was wholly successful, the German infantry would maintain its closed formation until it began firing its rifles at the enemy. If the artillery hadn't been successful in suppressing enemy rifle and machine gun fire, the columns would deploy into smaller formations. Platoons, half-platoons, and, in extreme cases, individual squads would rush from cover to cover. The breaking up of the larger formation, however, was regarded as an evil to be avoided whenever possible.

At a covered position 400 or 500 meters away from the enemy, the forwardmost German infantry would halt, form a single line, and commence firing. Whenever possible, platoons, half-platoons, and squads would fire as units under the direction of an officer or NCO. The infantry that followed the forwardmost troops would also join this line, filling in gaps to ensure that as many rifles as possible were firing at the enemy. The object of the rifle fire was fire superiority—keeping down the heads of the enemy and thus their ability to return effective fire. Once this was achieved, the infantry would take advantage of the enemy's temporary paralysis and charge home with the bayonet.[12]

It was widely recognized, both by proponents and detractors of the modest tendency toward open order tactics in the *Drill Regulations of 1906* that the adoption of such an approach would require a change in the spirit in which the German infantry was trained. The *Drill Regulations of 1906,* as well as the *Field Service Regulations of 1908 (Felddienst Ordnung)* contained a number of passages reminding the German officer that close order drill alone would no longer guarantee the type of discipline that was needed on active service. To prepare him to be alone on the modern battlefield, the officer was advised to cultivate the initiative, self-reliance, and sense of honor of the individual soldier.

Initiative, self-reliance, and honor would not be enough, however, to guarantee that small groups of men working forward from covered position to covered position would do so skillfully. More leaders were needed within the platoon and the German NCO was called upon to fill that role. Recognizing this, the *Field Service Regulations of 1908* mandated "special tactical exercises" for NCOs, where the "same principles laid down for the training of officers apply in a modified sense."[13]

UNEXPLOITED ASSETS

The German Army was fortunate in that its NCOs were, by and large, capable of receiving such instruction. The German NCO of the early twentieth century had either risen from the ranks or had been directly appointed following graduation from one of the NCO academies where indigent children of former soldiers received a free education. As a result of these academies and the excellent German primary schools, the German NCO could be counted on to be literate. He was also, as a rule, quite ambitious. A major inducement to service as an NCO was a substantial gratuity and a position in the police force, customs service, or post office at the end of 12 years service with the colors. In a society with relatively few opportunities for social mobility, such a retirement plan, combined with the relatively high social status that NCOs enjoyed, attracted high quality applicants.

Reserve NCOs, as a rule, were even better qualified for leadership than their active duty counterparts. Educated young men of the middle classes usually performed their military service as "one year volunteers" *(Einjärige Freiwilligen)*. Serving without pay while paying for their own uniforms and food, these volunteers served in the ranks for one year, during which time they were exempted from many of the menial tasks performed by ordinary soldiers while being given additional instruction in military subjects. At the end of their year of service, the volunteers took an examination. Those who received high scores and were considered suitable from a social point of view were eventually given reserve commissions. Those with lower scores, and those (such as members of nonconformist religious sects and men whose fathers were artisans or shopkeepers) who were not considered to be of sufficient standing in the community to be granted a commission, were made reserve NCOs.

Despite this advantage in the quality of its NCOs, the German Army was slow to give them formal command of even the smallest tactical unit. This reluctance went hand in hand with the fear of letting soldiers loose on the battlefield. At a time when a greater and greater percentage of recruits came from the urban working classes, among which the still-Marxist and anti-patriotic Social Democrats were gaining in popularity, the German officer could easily succumb to a certain uneasiness about the reliability of his troops in battle. This seems to have been especially true in those units, such as those raised in Alsace, Lorraine, and in regions inhabited primarily by Poles or Danes, where the gap between officers and men was geographic as well as social.[14]

As a result of the compromises inherent in the *Drill Regulations of 1906,* the German infantrymen who marched to war in August of 1914 fought in ways that reached across the spectrum of small unit tactics. Those German units fortunate enough to have officers who understood the effect of modern firepower went into battle in dispersed skirmish lines, with as many six meters between each man and with each man granted the freedom to make use of whatever cover was available during his forward movement. In some regiments, squads had even been taught to act as units on the battlefield. The 124th *(Württemberg)* Infantry Regiment, the unit with which Lieutenant Erwin Rommel went to war in 1914, had squads well practiced in the technique of fire and movement, one squad moving from one covered position to another while a second squad provided covering fire.[15] Other units, those commanded by officers who had rejected Boer tactics, went into battle in dense columns or thick skirmish lines.

BOER TACTICS IN ACTION

The contrast between the Boer tactics and close order tactics is perhaps best illustrated by the successful attack of the 43rd Infantry Brigade on September 8, 1914, against Russian troops conducting a hasty defense near Gerdauen in East Prussia. The brigade, consisting of two regiments of three battalions each, attacked with four battalions in the front line and two battalions in the second line. Fifteen of the 16 companies in the first line advanced in open order, with half-platoons (30 to 40 men) formed in open skirmish lines moving as units. Of the 2250 men of those 15 companies, 2225 survived the attack. The sixteenth company, commanded by a reserve officer who disobeyed the order of the brigade commander to advance in open order, moved forward in a dense formation. Only half of his 150 men lived to see the end of the attack.[16]

After the first engagements of the war, news of the unsuitability of dense formations travelled quickly, through official and unofficial channels, through the German Army. The tactical debate of the last decade or so was over; Boer tactics had been vindicated. The dense column had given way to the open skirmish line. Even the four Reserve Corps of Duke Albrecht of Württemberg's Fourth Army, whose training had left them firmly in the nineteenth century, had been ordered to thin out their formations. The official bulletin, dated October 21, 1914, arrived too late, however, to have an effect on the First Battle of Ypres. By the time they received it, the young volunteers were already engaged in battle and retraining them, at least for the time being, was out of the question.[17]

A similar thinning out of formations and a replacement of columns with skirmish lines occurred in all German armies fighting on the western front. The two assumptions upon which the tactics of the *Drill Regulations of 1906* had been based—the need for officers to maintain personal control over their units and the need to mass rifle fire to achieve fire superiority—had been proved both false and costly. Despite the fears of some prewar officers, battalions and companies advancing in open order did not degenerate into purposeless masses of individuals trying to avoid combat. Although lieutenants could no longer control their platoons solely by voice command and captains could only see a fraction of their companies, German NCOs proved themselves capable of leading squads and half-platoons in the absence of the direct supervision of an officer. The "fire at will" of riflemen two or three meters apart from each other, moreover, was discovered to be as effective in many cases as the officer-controlled volleys of riflemen kneeling only inches away from each other.

ENVELOPMENT

The German skirmish line tactics of 1914 were further distinguished by a certain fondness for envelopment. Envelopment at the operational level had not only been popular but had been the very soul of German operational art for almost a century. Envelopment by divisions and regiments, likewise, had long been practiced. By the fall of 1914 German regiments and battalions were consistently sending out companies, and companies were sending out platoons to outflank an enemy in contact and, if possible, catch him in a crossfire.

The effect upon the enemy of such a maneuver was often devastating. On August 20, 1914, a French infantry company taking part in the seizure of a ridge in Alsace found itself at the foot of a small draw. As the Frenchmen moved forward up the draw, small groups of German riflemen infiltrated among the trees on either side of the draw. When the horseshoe was complete, the Germans opened fire. With his men dying around him, one of the French platoon commanders tried to attack into the ambush. He formed his men into a skirmish line and charged farther up the draw. The closer the Frenchmen got to the top of the draw, however, the more they exposed themselves to the German crossfire.

True to their peacetime training, the surviving Frenchmen knelt and began returning fire. After a few more minutes, however, the cohesion of the French platoon broke down. As a result of the predicament in which they found themselves, the unit of soldiers degenerated into a mass of individuals concerned more for their own survival than the accomplishment of their mission. Without orders, the French started to withdraw. Within a few minutes, the unauthorized withdrawal had turned into a rout. The young platoon commander found himself alone in the crossfire, thinking that not only the battle but the entire war was doomed to failure. "It was," he said to himself, "1870 all over again."[18]

NOTES

1. See, for example, Reichmann, *Observations,* pp. 6–17.
2. See, for example, Atteridge, *German Army,* p. 83.
3. There were 21 "ordinary" corps districts plus that of the Guard Corps.
4. For a detailed description of how this worked in practice, see Prince Kraft von Hohenlohe zu Ingelfingen, *Letters on Infantry, Letters on Cavalry, Letters on Artillery,* passim.

5.   G. F. Ellison, "Training of Recruits in the German Infantry," *Journal of the Royal United Service Institution,* Vol 33 (1889–1890), p. 255.

6.   "Each commander of troops, from the company commander upward, is responsible for the development, according to regulations, of those placed under his charge, and is to be allowed freedom in the choice of means." Prussia, Kriegsministerium, *Drill Regulations for the Infantry, German Army, 1906* (Washington, D.C.: Government Printing Office, 1907), p. 9, hereafter referred to as *Drill Regulations of 1906.*

7.   Balck, *Tactics,* p. 50.

8.   Wiegand Schmidt-Richberg, "Die Regierungszeit Wilhelms II." in *Handbuch zur deutschen Militärgeschichte 1648–1939* (Frankfurt am Main: Bernard & Grafe Verlag, 1968), pp. 85–87.

9.   Bernd F. Schulte, *Die Deutsche Armee, 1900–1914, Zwischen Beharren und Verändern* (Düsseldorf: Droste Verlag, 1977), pp. 171–184. See, for examples of this debate at the unit level, von Gottberg, *Geschichte des Hannoverschen Jäger Battalions Nr. 10* (Berlin: E.S. Mittler, 1903), pp. 349–50 and Freiherr von Hagen, *Geschichte des König l. Sächsichen 1. Jäger Battalions Nr. 12* (Freiburg in Sachsen: Verlag von Craz und Gerlach, 1909), pp. 203–4.

10.   The *Drill Regulations of 1888* had been translated into Japanese and adopted without a single modification by the Japanese Army. Despite having had plenty of opportunity, primarily during the Sino-Japanese War and the native pacification campaigns in Formosa, to make their own observations about infantry tactics, the Japanese authorities declined to make any changes to the manual, preferring to wait for the next German edition, which they also planned to adopt verbatim. Max Hoffmann, *The War of Lost Opportunities* (London: Kegan, Paul, 1924).

11.   *Drill Regulations of 1906,* p. 79.

12.   *Drill Regulations of 1906,* p. 5.

13.   Prussia, Kriegsministerium, *Field Service Regulations of the German Army, 1908* (London: Harrison and Sons, 1908), pp. 5–6.

14.   I do not have sufficient evidence to prove this contention, but it seems that units raised in places where class conflict was less pronounced—Hanover, Bavaria, and Württemberg, for example—were more inclined to adopt open order tactics than units raised in Alsace, Lorraine, or Silesia.

15.   Erwin Rommel (J.R. Driscoll, translator), *Attacks* (Vienna, VA: Athena Press, 1979), pp. 10–11.

16.   Wilhelm Balck, "Über den Infanterieangriff," *Militärwochenblatt,* September 4, 1919, pp. 562–66.

17.   In December of 1914 a training program was instituted within the Fourth Army to introduce an attack technique that was very similar to the Boer tactics described by German military writers of the period. Whether this was a conscious imitation of Boer techniques or a reinvention caused by similar circumstances is unknown.

18.   André Laffargue, *Fantassin de Gascogne. De mon jardin à la Marne et au Danube* (Paris: Flammarion, 1962), pp. 59–78. For more on André Laffargue, see Appendix C.

2

Fortress Warfare

> Covered by this fire, the infantry, accompanied by numerous parties of sappers, must work up to the enemy's position without a break. The night, too, must be used to secure the ground gained with earthworks, and dig covered communications ... machine guns must be brought up and entrenched during the night. This attack must press on irresistibly; losses must not be shirked ... artillery fire must accompany the infantry to the very last stage of the attack, and finally with common shell, even at the risk of inflicting losses on their own troops. The storming infantry must throw hand grenades inside the hostile position; the final bayonet charge must be delivered when close to the position, while the heavy howitzer shells continue to burst in and behind the position.
>
> *Gen. Friedrich von Bernhardi, 1913*

The combination of column and Boer tactics of the German infantry, as well as the German superiority in howitzers and heavy artillery and the overwhelming nature of maneuver at the operational level were sufficiently effective to permit the German Army to win the Battle of the Frontiers, the engagements with the Belgian Army at Liège and Antwerp, the battle of Mons, and, at least from a tactical point of view, the Battle of the Marne. Once the front solidified, however, even the "state of the art" Boer tactics, not to mention the already obsolete column tactics, ceased to be good enough. Continuous trench lines meant that there were no open flanks. Because neither operational nor tactical maneuver in the traditional sense was possible, all attacks would have to be frontal attacks.

Frontal attacks, moreover, would be more difficult in position warfare than in mobile warfare. Barbed wire severely limited opportunities for creeping up to an enemy in small groups. The fact that a defender could study the ground in front of him over a matter of days and even weeks meant that effective fire could be brought against the entries and exits to covered positions along an avenue of approach. Finally, the opportunity for the defender to integrate his machine guns and artillery into his defensive plans was far greater in position warfare. All these factors combined to make the dash across "no man's land," the few hundred meters that separated one side from the other, a very difficult proposition.

The inherent difficulties faced by the attacker in trench warfare did not, however, lead to a cessation of offensive action. When, in the fall of 1914, the armies had stopped moving, all had assumed that the war of grand maneuvers would soon resume. As a result, trenches were often dug with little consideration for such longer-term considerations as whether the enemy's being in possession of a hill gave him the ability to observe (and therefore accurately shell) the ground behind the trench, the same ground over which reinforcements and supplies would have to travel. To deny such advantages of terrain to the enemy, and to secure them for themselves, German corps and division commanders frequently ordered "attacks with limited objectives" *(Angriffe mit begrenzten Ziele).*[1]

Because they were oriented to the capture of a particular piece of ground rather than the destruction of a particular enemy force, attacks with limited objectives differed in many respects from the attacks that the German infantry had practiced before the war. The density of enemy forces, and the degree to which they had prepared the ground in their favor, were both greater in an attack with limited objectives than in an attack in the war of movement. The danger of an immediate counterattack once a position was taken was also greater. By far the greatest difficulty, however, was the fact that the enemy possessed a full complement of field guns which, but indirect or direct fire, could bring down an impassable barrage in "no man's land" and the assembly areas for the attack.

These tactical problems, however, were not entirely new to the German officer. Largely as a result of reports coming from the battlefields of the Russo-Japanese War, a bit of thinking had been done before the war on the subject of how best to conduct an attack with limited objectives against a fortified position. The method of taking a fortified position recommended by the *Drill Regulations of 1906* was essentially the same as that recommended for attacks in mobile warfare, although it differed in details. Somewhat more emphasis was placed on the artillery preparation—to silence enemy guns, to facilitate the crossing of "no man's land," and to inhibit the movement of counterattack forces. The firing line was to be built up at a position closer to the enemy, so that the assault with fixed bayonets could be delivered in one bound. As was the case with the attack in mobile warfare, it was this assault and the ensuing hand to hand combat that was seen as the decisive moment of the attack.[2]

According to the *Drill Regulations of 1906,* the main difference between the attack in mobile warfare and the attack against a fortified position was the degree of preparation required. The attack in mobile warfare was, of necessity, an ad hoc affair. The attack against a fortified position, on the other hand, was to be a systematic operation. Officers were to conduct a thorough reconnaissance of the objective and make sketches of both the ground and the enemy dispositions. Pioneers, troops who correspond to today's combat engineers, were to be brought up the night before the attack to clear barbed wire and other obstacles.[3]

To deal with problems peculiar to attacks against fortified positions, the German Army acquired, in the course of the ten or so years between the Russo-Japanese War and World War I, a number of special weapons. Trench mortars *(Minenwerfer)* and light (10.5cm) field howitzers[4] were included in the inventory to provide high angle fire to drop shells behind walls and other obstacles. The light field howitzers were crewed by field artillerymen, organized into batteries and battalions, and assigned to infantry divisions. At the beginning of the war, most first line German infantry divisions had a battalion[5] of 12 light field howitzers as part of their organic artillery brigade.[6]

Whereas the light field howitzer seems to have been inspired either by the British experience in the Boer War or the Turkish experience in the Russo-Turkish War of 1877–1878, the German trench mortars were definitely a product of the Russo-Japanese War. German observers at the siege of Port Arthur noticed how the Japanese pioneers had used improvised mortars made out of bamboo to launch relatively heavy explosive charges a short distance. It was these weapons, the German observers noted, that allowed the Japanese to breach the thick belts of obstacles that the Russians had placed in front of their trenches. In 1905, the German War Ministry asked the firms of Krupp and Ehrhardt to build prototypes that could throw a 50-kilogram charge at least 300 meters. The two firms responded to this requirement with enthusiasm and by 1914, the German Army had three standard trench mortars. The light (7.6cm) trench mortar could throw a 4.75 kilogram bomb out to 1050 meters. The medium (17cm) trench mortar, originally intended for use as a defensive weapon for fortresses, had a much heavier projectile (50 kilograms) and a somewhat shorter range (800 meters). The heavy (21cm) trench mortar, on the other hand, had a range of only 420 meters but a shell weighing a full 100 kilograms.[7]

The trench mortars were manned by pioneers, the "duty experts" in field fortifications and attacks against fortified positions. In keeping with the assumption that an operation against a fortified position would be an episode in a campaign rather than the principal tactical problem faced by the army, trench mortars had originally been assigned to the Siege Train *(Pionierbelagerungstrain),* a central pool of men and equipment for attacks on fortified positions and fortresses and the fortress pioneer battalions *(Festungspionierebataillonen)* that provided pioneers for the garrisons of the great fortresses that protected the German borders in many places. When it became evident that the German Army would be besieging one great fortress stretching from the North Sea to the Swiss border, the trench mortars were organized into independent battalions and assigned to divisions and corps on an "as needed" basis.

VREGNY PLATEAU

In January of 1915, near the town of Soissons on the Oise River northeast of Paris, the Third Corps (First Army) organized a large-scale attack with limited objectives conducted in accordance with prewar regulations on infantry and artillery tactics. The only innovation came in the organization of the two arms. The replacement of six infantry battalions by *Landwehr* battalions, as well as the attachment of a regiment's worth of companies, resulted in the 10th Infantry Brigade, the unit that carried out the main attack, having an infantry complement consisting mostly of provisional battalions and regiments.[8] The two field artillery regiments organic to the 5th Infantry Division were also "task organized." Heavy artillery batteries from the Third Corps artillery park were attached to pairs of field artillery batteries and formed into temporary groups which were assigned the same set of targets.[9]

The objective was the Vregny Plateau, a piece of high ground that allowed the French to overlook much of the ground behind the trenches occupied by the Third Corps and its neighbors. In keeping with their prewar regulations on field fortifications,[10] the French had fortified the plateau with three successive lines of resistance. These trenches, however, were not very deep, nor were they provided with any sort of bombproof dugouts. Thus, while the German fire would have to be spread over three positions, the French soldiers defending the plateau would have to crouch for over five hours with nothing more than their blue serge *képis* to protect them from the shells bursting only inches above their heads.[11]

The plan of attack against the plateau was complicated by a French attack against a neighboring division that began on January 8. This attack spilled over into the sector of the 5th Infantry Division, forcing the formation which Seeckt had held in readiness for his own attack to repel the French attackers and recover the lost ground recovered through counterattack. This process took five days. When, on the evening of January 12, it was completed, Seeckt was only two days away from January 14, the day he had originally set aside for the operation against the Vregny Plateau.

The High Command, however, cut down Seeckt's preparation time even further. Because a proportion of his artillery was to be withdrawn for refitting on the fourteenth, Seeckt had to launch his attack on the thirteenth or not at all. Seeckt decided in favor of the premature attack. Beginning at dawn, the German artillery began the systematic bombardment of the French positions while Seeckt feverishly completed the organization of the other half of the attack.[12] At noon, this work was completed, and the infantry moved forward against the first French position.

From the point of view of the infantry, the attack against the Vregny Plateau proceeded according to the *Drill Regulations of 1906*. Pioneers, equipped with wire cutters and hand grenades, led the attack. Creeping forward through gullies and other suitable avenues of approach, they cut lanes through the French wire, which was at that time still rather thin. Handgrenades prevented the French defenders, which included sharpshooting *Chasseurs Alpins,* from interfering with this work. Once the wire was cut, the infantry moved advanced in loose skirmish lines, rifles at the ready and bayonets fixed.[13]

The three French lines of resistance fell easily. The German artillery fire succeeded in "shaking" many of the French defenders. In many cases, the French simply dropped their rifles and ran away at the sight of the advancing rows of German riflemen,[14] making the heavy rain and the resultant mud more of an obstacle to the advance of some German units than the enemy. By 4:30 P.M., some German units had made it all the way to the south edge of the plateau.

Behind the third French position, however, was a maze of communications trenches that proved, in places, a far tougher nut to crack than the forward infantry positions. Here, among the woods, the Germans found batteries of 75mm field guns manned by gunners who had been trained to perfection in the art of direct fire and sharpshooters from two battalions of the elite French mountain infantry, the *Chasseurs Alpins.* Without the help of their own artillery, whose fire plans had apparently not taken this fourth position into account, the German infantry succeeded in taking these positions by assault, but at great cost. One company of the 52nd Infantry Regiment lost all of its officers.[15] The 1st Battalion of the 8th Life Guards Regiment lost half of its company commanders,[16] while Battalion Schultz, a temporary unit which captured two batteries of French artillery, had five officers and 25 enlisted men killed and 105 enlisted men wounded.[17]

These losses notwithstanding, the assault on Vregny Plateau was a success for the 5th Infantry Division. By nightfall, the assaulting infantry had cleared the entire objective. One detachment even pushed beyond the plateau to enter the north end of the town of Soissons. The booty was also enormous: 5650 Frenchmen marched off the Vregny Plateau into captivity, dragging behind them 35 field pieces and six machine guns.[18] The next day, the German infantry pushed even farther south. In places, they found small groups of wounded or dispirited Frenchmen.[19] In others, they found empty villages.[20] All units, however, reported that they saw French soldiers retreating over the Aisne, the river that ran just south of the Vregny Plateau.

The tactics of the systematic pulverization of the enemy position had worked. The Germans had succeeded in attaining their limited objective. However, had the attack been an attempt at a complete rupture of the French system with an aim to resuming the war of operational maneuver, the tactics would have proved insufficient. The patrols that the units of the 5th Infantry Division sent beyond the limits of the Vregny Plateau in the late afternoon of January 13 ran into masses of French troops that had just arrived by train. In the five or six hours that it took the slowest German unit to cross the two or three–kilometer-wide plateau, the French had been able to move their reserves scores of kilometers by rail.

The battle for the Vregny Plateau showed that, at least on the western front where rail lines existed in abundance, the defender had a distinct operational edge as well as a tactical advantage. Unless the attacker could break through the enemy position faster than the enemy trains could bring up reinforcements, he would achieve nothing. This, however, was not the lesson that von Seeckt drew from the operation. On the contrary, the report of the Third Corps on the battle of Soissons dealt primarily with the fact that the infantry tactics used by the German Army were in need of modification.[21]

Ironically, the French and British also concentrated on the tactical lessons of Soissons at the expense of the operational one. The French, having been on the receiving end of the German bombardment, were very impressed by it. For them, the success of the German attack at Soissons seemed to indicate that while position warfare would require major changes in the way that divisions and corps, as combined arms forces, would fight, infantry tactics at the regimental level and below would not have to change. In fact, the use of artillery as the primary means of obtaining fire superiority seemed to reduce the need for the infantry to provide its own suppressive fire. This latter belief was particularly tempting for the British, who, in the spring of 1915, were faced with the daunting task of trying to create an army out of a population that had had no direct experience with war since the Jacobite Rebellion of 1745.

CROSSING NO MAN'S LAND

Colonel von Seeckt was not the only German officer to discover that the techniques of 1914, even "state of the art" Boer tactics, did not serve them well in the conditions of 1915. Exercising a capacity for independent action that was the hallmark of the German officer of the time, a number of relatively junior officers came up with new methods for attacking a well dug in enemy.[22] These new methods built upon the precepts set down by the *Drill Regulations of 1906*—systematic preparation, the attainment of fire superiority, and the overwhelming infantry assault. The chief innovation, however, was the way in which the infantry moved across "no man's land."

An early solution to the problem of crossing fire-swept terrain was the use of *boyaux*, shallow ditches running across no man's land, that, because they had originally been dug as communications trenches, were roughly perpendicular to the fighting trenches. One such attack took place on February 28, 1915. Ensign August Hopp, a former student of theology at the University of Leipzig, led a group of 32 volunteers in single file through a *boyau* that ran up to (but not into) the enemy trench. According to Hopp's plan, the volunteers were to take the trench with cold steel once they got close enough to reach it in one bound. Hopp failed in his mission, however, because he and his volunteers found themselves trapped in the *boyau* between the rifle fire of Hopp's own regiment defending itself against a major French attack and the advancing Frenchmen themselves.[23]

Ensign Hopp's use of the *boyau* as an avenue of approach allowed him to get his group of volunteers close to the enemy without being seen. The weakness in his plan was the final assault. In order to take the objective in one bound, it would have been necessary for his group to form a line parallel to the trench. For a few brief moments, the assaulting Germans would have had to leave the security of the *boyau* and fully expose themselves to the full weight of enemy fire. To avoid this fire, the Germans would have to attack in single file, moving along the *boyau* until the point where it joined the trench and then entering the trench one by one. In such an attack, however, only one rifleman would be in a position to fire or use his bayonet. Other attackers could creep along the ground above the trench or stand behind the most forward man in the trench waiting to take his place when he fell.

THE GUARD RIFLE BATTALION

Despite its obvious limitations, this latter technique was used successfully on at least one occasion. In the Vosges, on December 30, 1914, the Guard Rifle *(Schützen)* Battalion, an elite light infantry unit,[24] was ordered to retake a section of the German trench line that had previously been captured by the French. In keeping with the German Army tradition of giving maximum discretion to the man on the spot, Major von Hadeln, the battalion commander, was merely told to take the trench. How he accomplished that mission was left entirely up to him.

Major von Hadeln was well aware that a frontal attack had little chance of success. He had been with the Guard Corps at Ypres and had seen the British rifle fire first decimate and then stop the advancing columns. More recently, an attempt by elements of the German 28th and 29th Infantry Regiments to take the French position by direct assault had failed. Von Hadeln therefore decided to use a new technique. Small detachments would enter the trench section at each end and work their way toward the center. Reaching the flanks would be made easier by the fact that each end of the French position was already occupied by German troops who had contained the French advance with a hastily built sandbag barrier.

Less than half of the Guard Rifle Battalion was to be used for the attack. A portion of the 1st Company was to attack on the right while a detachment of the 3rd Company, under the company commander Captain Willy Martin Rohr, was to move in on the left. The remaining portions of the 1st and 3rd Companies were echeloned behind the attacking detachments to serve as a back-up force. A further reserve was provided by the 2nd and 4th Companies, which Major von Hadeln ordered to stand by in the battalion assembly area.

At four in the morning on New Year's Eve, Major von Hadeln addressed his battalion. He had just taken command of the Guard Rifle Battalion and wanted to ensure that his troops shared his confidence in the new tactics they were about to use. Sneaking up to an enemy position in the early morning darkness, without the emotional release of the traditional "hurrah" and with strict orders not to shoot until the French opened fire, was not the way that these men had been taught to fight.

At 4:45 A.M. the attacking detachments began moving towards the French position. Within five minutes the detachment from the 1st Company was in the trench and had become engaged in fierce hand-to-hand combat. It took a few minutes longer for Captain Rohr's detachment to reach the French position. He and his troops had had to dodge a bit of French rifle fire on their way over. In less than ten minutes, however, the two detachments succeeded in clearing the trench of its occupants.

Minutes after the trench was taken, the men of the Guard Rifle Battalion found themselves facing a new challenge. In the woods to the west of the recently recaptured trench, French colonial infantry formed thick skirmish lines and moved forward in a determined counterattack. In a situation clearly foreseen by the writers of the *Drill Regulations of 1906,* the Riflemen of the Guard raised their Mausers and fired volley after volley of aimed fire into the French ranks. Despite the early morning darkness, the German bullets found their targets. In their closely packed formations, the attackers were almost impossible to miss. In the face of such losses, the French counterattack collapsed.

Shortly after dawn, the assault troops were relieved. Before they left, the Riflemen counted 120 dead Frenchmen in front of their recently captured position. Their own losses were slight by comparison. The detachment from the 1st Company had lost none of its men, although the company commander and one other man received flesh wounds. Captain Rohr's detachment lost 19 men, most of whom had been killed by French rifle fire before they reached the trench.[25]

HAND GRENADES

The weapons that the men of the Guard Rifle Battalion had used in "rolling up" *(aufrollen)* the French-occupied trench were the weapons of mobile warfare—rifles designed for long-range (up to 1000 meters) fire and bayonets designed to give the wielder an edge when bayonet fencing in an open field. The tactics used in the New Year's Eve attack, however, did not take advantage of the virtues of these weapons. Instead, the

Guard Riflemen had fought the way that they had in order to minimize the effect of similar weapons in the hands of the enemy. For the new tactic to come into its own, it required a new weapon.

The new weapon that soon became part and parcel of the German way of rolling up trenches was the hand grenade. As early as the second month of the war, German officers such as the Lieutenant of Pioneers Walter Beumelberg realized that a man with a bag full of hand grenades could systematically clear a trench more effectively and with less danger to himself than a man armed with a rifle and bayonet.[26] The advantage of the hand grenade was especially marked when the trench had been dug in a zigzag pattern rather than along a straight line. In a zigzag trench, the rifleman would have to expose his entire body to enemy fire every time he wanted to move from one section of trench to another. The grenadier, on the other hand, needed only to expose, at the most, a few inches of his hand in order to toss a grenade around a corner and clear a section of trench of any meaningful resistance.

The hand grenades used by the German Army in the first six months of the war consisted of two types. Ball hand grenades, produced in factories, had been kept in the storerooms of the great masonry fortresses that guarded Germany's borders for use in the defense of those fortresses. "Hairbrush" hand grenades were manufactured by pioneers from bulk explosives that each pioneer company kept in its wagons. Both types of hand grenade relied largely on blast effect to produce casualties.[27]

THE PIONEERS

In the early days of trench warfare, the only German troops trained to use hand grenades were the pioneers. At mobilization, each army corps of the German Army was assigned a Field Pioneer Battalion of three pioneer companies. This meant that there was one pioneer company for every 32 infantry companies, a ratio that spread the pioneers thin when the infantry discovered the usefulness of hand grenades and commanders started demanding that pioneers be assigned to their units. As a result, pioneers armed with hand grenades were assigned to infantry companies and platoons in small groups or even as individuals.

Hermann Balck,[28] who served as a second lieutenant in the 10th *Jäger* Battalion in the Argonne Forest in the fall of 1914, later recounted how a single pioneer would report to his platoon every night. The pioneer would be given a swig of schnapps and posted in the front trench with his hand grenades, there to await a French attack. Every morning, the pioneer would take his leave of the infantry and report back to the pioneer company from which he had come.[29]

It was not long, however, before word of the utility of these weapons reached the War Ministry in Berlin and various types were mass-produced and issued to the infantry. Two types became standard, the "egg" grenade *(Eierhandgranate)* that was only slightly larger than its namesake, and the now famous "potato masher" *(Steilhandgranate)*. Of these, the potato masher won the confidence of the front line troops. Its wooden handle allowed it to be thrown a considerable distance and it contained enough explosive to be effective against targets in the open. The egg grenade, on the other hand, was effective only in confined spaces such as dugouts.

SIEGECRAFT

The ingenuity of the German pioneers did not end with the hand grenade. Mines—explosives placed in a tunnel that had been dug under an enemy position—had been used in fortress warfare since the late Middle Ages. This ancient art was resurrected in the winter of 1914/1915. Though mines were occasionally used merely to produce casualties, they were chiefly used as a means of causing enough confusion among the enemy so that they were unable to interfere with the advance of friendly infantry. On December 20, 1914, German pioneers exploded a mine under a French position in the Argonne. The explosion killed those immediately above it and stunned those nearby. Two battalions of German infantry took advantage of the confusion and rushed in to take possession of the remnants of the French position.[30]

Although mine warfare had been started by German pioneers, both the French and the British countered by organizing soldiers who had been coal miners into special companies and conducting mining operations of their own. This led, in some areas, to subterranean warfare, with small bands of miners breaking into each others' tunnels and engaging in hand-to-hand combat.[31] On occasion, the various new forms of combat were combined. On January 29, 1915, a regiment of the German 27th Infantry Division conducted a hand grenade attack following the explosion of a German mine in a tunnel that had originally been dug by French miners.[32]

Another practice that had its origins in late medieval siegecraft was the digging of *saps*—trenches that were dug forward of and perpendicular to the most forward friendly trench. It was, of course, usually impossible to dig all the way to the enemy trench. A sap half- or three-quarters of the way across "no man's land," however, considerably reduced the time that the attacking infantry had to be exposed to enemy fire. Once the enemy position was captured, moreover, the sap could easily be expanded into a communication trench linking the newly captured trench to the other trenches in the attacker's system.

While it had the advantage of simplicity, digging one's way across (or under) "no man's land" was a time-consuming business. Preparations for an attack would have to be made weeks in advance. Worse still, the element of surprise was always lost when saps were involved and often lost when mines were dug. As a result, interest in such techniques waned as new means of crossing "no man's land" became available.

GAS

Perhaps the most terrifying weapons in the inventory of the German pioneers were chemical ones. The idea of using poison gas as a weapon predated World War I by more than half a century. Sending a cloud of chlorine gas into an enemy fortress had been proposed during both the Crimean War and the American Civil War. Half a century later, the delegates to the Hague Conventions of 1899 and 1907 had had sufficient faith in the possibility of gas warfare to take the trouble to outlaw it. These strictures, however, did little to inhibit an interest in the use of poison gas once the war of movement in the West had ended and members of the various high commands searched desperately for a means of restoring the war that they had been trained to fight.

The first major attempt by the German Army to use poison gas in combat took place at Ypres, on April 22, 1915. At four that afternoon, the German artillery laid a violent barrage on French positions on Pilckem Ridge, a piece of high ground the Allies had held since the First Battle of Ypres. At five, the valves on 5730 cylinders of chlorine gas were opened, forming a yellow-green cloud 300 or 400 yards wide and half a mile deep. A five-knot wind carried this cloud across "no man's land" and into the trenches occupied by French colonial (*zouaves* and *tirailleurs*) troops of the 45th Algerian Division and the middle-aged reservists of the 87th Territorial Division.[33]

Being heavier than air, the chlorine gas seeped into every dugout, crevice, and fold in the earth; the same places that had offered protection from artillery and machine gun fire now harbored the deadliest concentrations of the gas. This was too much for most of the French troops to take. Half-blind and choking, those that were not immediately struck down by the gas abandoned their trenches and ran for the rear, spreading panic as they ran.

A few hundred yards behind the gas cloud, the infantry regiments of three German divisions moved forward until they stood on top of Pilckem Ridge. Unknown to these Germans, the gas cloud that had cleared out the most forward French trench had also caused the abandonment of the French second and third lines. This wholesale evacuation had left a gap in the Allied lines at Ypres large enough to march a full army corps through. In ten minutes, 150 tons of chlorine gas had accomplished what the combined efforts of Division Winckler and the young War Volunteers had failed to achieve in almost a month of fighting the previous fall.

The German High Command had conceived of the attack on Pilckem Ridge as an attack "with limited objectives," the twin goals of which were the capture of the high ground itself and the testing of the new weapon. Because of these deliberately modest goals, the troops of the 51st and 52nd Reserve Divisions that had followed the gas cloud into the French positions stopped as soon as they reached their objective even though there were no enemy combat troops between them and the city of Ypres. As a result of this lack of ambition on the part of the Germans, the Canadians holding positions south of Pilckem Ridge were able to scatter small detachments across the gap left by the routed French. By the next morning, the gap had been completely sealed and the subsequent attacks of the 51st and 52nd Reserve Divisions failed to make any headway against the Canadians.

By the standards of an "attack with limited objectives," the gas cloud attack at Ypres was a resounding success. The villages of Pilckem and Langemarck, whose capture had eluded the War Volunteers in November of 1914, were in German hands. Two thousand Frenchmen and 51 guns were captured. And the losses of the two Reserve Divisions which had suffered such casualties the preceding fall were insignificant; in the 239th Reserve Regiment (52nd Division), a few men were killed at the very end of the day by stray French shells, but no one was hurt by direct fire from the French positions.[34]

Subsequent gas cloud attacks at Ypres and at other places on the western front did not have the dramatic effect of the first gas attack against Pilckem Ridge. News of the new weapon quickly spread to other parts of the front. Field expedient gas masks were speedily designed, manufactured, and issued. Although these were far from effective in keeping those in a gas cloud from eventually succumbing, their use reduced the short-term ability of gas to cause wholesale casualties and panic. The opportunity for a really decisive exploitation of gas cloud attacks had been lost.

The inability of all but the first of the German gas cloud attacks to clear an enemy position severely limited their tactical utility. German infantry following a gas cloud into the attack would either have to follow at a considerable distance, thus allowing the enemy a few vital seconds in which to recover his composure, or attack close behind the cloud, making it necessary for them to wear gas masks of their own. This latter option brought handicaps of its own. Never comfortable, the gas masks of World War I were incapable of letting in sufficient amounts of breathable air to allow the wearer to scramble over "no man's land" at anything like an acceptable pace for an attack.

Another limitation of gas cloud attacks was inherent in the technical means then available. The gas cylinders were heavy and bulky. Moving them to, and installing them near, the front line trenches was difficult, dangerous, and time-consuming work. Worse still from a tactical point of view, such activity was hard to hide from the watchful eyes of the enemy just a few score meters away. As a result, surprise was almost impossible to achieve.

Gas clouds were also limited by the weather. The attack on Pilckem Ridge had been delayed for ten days because of the lack of a favorable wind—the prevailing winds in northern France and Belgium blow from west to east. Other gas cloud attacks failed when a sudden shift in the wind blew the gas in the wrong direction, poisoning friendly troops in the process. Although German chemists made valiant attempts to improve the effectiveness of the gases used in gas cloud attacks, the limitations on the tactical use of such weapons remained.

After Ypres, the German scientists working on gas warfare concentrated on finding ways of delivering gas by artillery and trench mortar shells. These would not have any significant impact on tactics, however, until 1917. In the mean time, the German infantryman, having learned at Soissons and Ypres that neither weight of metal nor technological innovation would free him from the dirty job of crossing "no man's land" and clearing the enemy out of his trenches, focused once more on that task.

NOTES

1. The attack "with limited objectives" is a translation of the German *Angriff mit Begrenzten Ziel.* It was distinguished from other attacks by the lack of any intention to exploit success by pushing beyond the terrain objective and by the fact that the mission given to the commander of the attacking force was the taking of a piece of ground rather than the destruction of an enemy force.

2. *Drill Regulations of 1906,* pp. 84–85.

3. German pioneers were equipped with special wire cutters for the purpose of cutting lanes through barbed wire. More traditional obstacles (e.g., felled trees, sharpened stakes, ditches) were to be removed with hand tools and explosives.

4. For German weapons, I will use the German system of designating calibers in centimeters rather than millimeters. The 10.5cm howitzer, for example, is the same caliber as the U.S. 105mm howitzer used in World War II, Korea, and Vietnam (in fact, the latter is the direct descendent of the former).

5. Strictly speaking, the German *Abteilung* means "division." I use the term battalion, however, because German artillery *Abteilungen* correspond almost exactly in size, composition, and function to the artillery battalions of other countries at that time.

6. For most German Infantry Divisions, the artillery brigade consisted of two regiments of two battalions each, for a total of four battalions. The three battalions that were not equipped with the light field howitzer consisted of three batteries of six light field guns (7.7cm) each.

7. Bierman, "Die Entwickelung der deutschen Minenwerferwaffe," in Paul

Heinrici, ed., *Das Ehrenbuch der deutschen Pioniere* (Berlin: Verlag Tradition Wilhelm Kolk, 1932), pp. 482–84.

8. Von Seeckt mentions this transfer in his autobiography but doesn't explain the justification. Similarly, the regimental histories of the infantry units involved give detailed breakdowns of the ad hoc battalions and regiments into which their component companies were organized but don't mention any rationale. Hans von Seeckt, *Aus meinem Leben* (Leipzig: Hase & Koehler, 1938), p. 85.

9. *Der Weltkrieg*, Vol. 7, p. 25.

10. Ludwig Renn, *Warfare: The Relation of War to Society* (London: Faber and Faber, 1939), p. 137.

11. At this time, these were mostly what the Germans called "all purpose shell" *(Einheitsgeschoße)*, a projectile that contained more high explosive than a shrapnel shell of the same caliber but had a better fragmentation effect than a high explosive shell. Bruchmüller, Georg, *Die Deutsche Artillerie in den Durchbruchschlachten des Weltkrieges* (Berlin: E.S. Mittler und Sohn, 1922), p. 15, hereafter referred to as Bruchmüller, *Durchbruchschlachten.*

12. von Seeckt, *Aus meinem Leben,* p. 87.

13. My most detailed source for the tactics used by the Germans at Soisson is a poem written by one of the participants. The poem, which devotes a stanza each to both the pioneers and the artillery, as well as to each of the three French lines of resistance, was printed as an appendix to the regimental history of the 12th Grenadier Regiment. Ernst von Schönfeldt, *Das Grenadier Regiment Prinz Karl von Preussen (2. Brandenburgisches), Nr. 12 im Weltkriege* (Berlin: Gerhard Stalling, 1924).

14. von Seeckt, *Aus meinem Leben,* p. 85.

15. Martin Reymann, *Das Infanterie Regiment von Alvensleben (6. Brandenbg.) Nr. 52 im Weltkriege 1914/1918* (Berlin: Gerhard Stalling, 1923), p. 50.

16. H. Schöning, *Leib-Grenadier Regiment König Friedrich Wilhelm III (1. Brandenberg) Nr. 8* (Berlin: Gerhard Stalling, 1924), p. 122. The regimental histories of the 52nd Infantry Regiment and the 8th Life Guards do not separate the enlisted casualties for the assault on the Vregny Plateau from those incurred during the French attack of January 8 and the subsequent counterattack.

17. von Schönfeldt, *Das Grenadier Regiment,* p. 44.

18. von Seeckt, *Aus meinem Leben,* pp. 85–88.

19. F. Müller, *Brandenburgisches Jäger Bataillon Nr. 3* (Oldenburg i. O.: Gerhard Stalling, 1922), p. 24.

20. Reyman, *Das Infanterie Regiment,* p. 52.

21. von Seeckt, *Aus meinem Leben,* p. 88.

22. This attitude whereby the superior restricted his orders to the mission which his subordinate was to fulfill and gave the latter a great deal of discretion in his choice of means was known at the operational level as *Weisungsführung* (direction leadership). While there was no formal title for this attitude at the tactical level during World War I, it approximated what in World War II became known as *Auftragstaktik* (mission tactics).

23. A.F. Wedd, Editor, *German Students War Letters* (London: Methuen and Company, Ltd.), pp. 44–51. I use the term "ensign" to translate the German rank

of *Fähnrich*. A Fähnrich was an officer candidate serving in the field as an apprentice officer. He usually filled the billet of platoon commander.

24. The Guard Rifle Battalion, one of the few *Schützen* units left in the German Army at the time, was trained and organized as a *Jäger* battalion. (The Saxon Schützen Regiment "Prince George" was organized and equipped as a line infantry regiment.)

25. H.H. Alten et al., *Geschichte des Garde Schützen Battalions 1914–1918* (Berlin: Gerhard Stalling 1928), pp. 108–11.

26. Beumelberg may have been inspired by stories of similar tactics used by the Japanese in the Russo-Japanese War. See unsigned article, "Moderne Handgranaten," *Militär-Wochenblatt,* Nr. 163, 1915, pp. 3885–87.

27. Klietmann, "Beiträge zur Geschichte der deutschen Handgranate," *Der Feldgrau,* 1971, pp. 116–17.

28. Hermann Balck, a fourth generation professional officer, was the son of the tactician Wilhelm Balck. He later went on to become a company commander in the 22nd Reserve *Jäger* Battalion and leader of the *Jagdkommando* of the 5th Cavalry Division. In World War II he commanded a number of Panzer formations.

29. Balck, "Translation of a Taped Conversation with General Hermann Balck, 13 April, 1979" (Columbus, Ohio: Battelle, Columbus Laboratories, Tactical Technology Center, 1979), p. 22.

30. Rudolf Müller, *Das 3. Lotharingisches Infanterie Regiment Nr. 135* (Berlin: G. Stalling, 1922), p. 26.

31. Augustine, "Development of the Engineer Arm in the German Army during the World War" in Max Schwarte, ed. *War Lessons in Examples Taken From the World War.* (Unpublished manuscript, translation of *Kriegslehren, in Beispielen aus dem Weltkrieg,* located at U.S. Army Military History Institute, Carlisle Barracks, Carlisle, PA), p. 336, hereafter referred to as Schwarte, *War Lessons.*

32. Müller, *Das 3. Lotharingisches Infanterie Regiment,* p. 31.

33. This is one of the best documented engagements of World War I. The best account is given in L.F. Haber, *The Poisonous Cloud, Chemical Warfare in the First World War* (Oxford: Clarendon Press, 1986), pp. 34–35. See also Rudolf Hanslian, *Der chemische Krieg* (Berlin: E.S. Mitter & Sohn, 1937), *passim,* for detailed information about chemical warfare in World War I.

34. Schatz, *Geschichte,* pp. 41–42.

3

Special Assault Units

This kind of fighting seems made for the German, with his feeling for discipline and order, analogous, one might say, to the musical coordination of an orchestra.

Ernst Jünger,
Copse 125

Throughout the first winter of trench warfare, the ingenuity of the attacker found itself competing with the diligence of the defender. Each day that passed saw the defensive positions get stronger. A second trench and often a third were dug behind the forward trenches, joined together by communications trenches into a network. Behind the first network, additional defensive works—blockhouses, bunkers, second and even third trench networks—were added, their exact composition varying according to the terrain, the labor and materials available, and the wishes of the commander. Barbed wire obstacles as well as the more traditional *abatis* (felled trees with sharpened branches) and *chevaux aux frises* (pointed wooden or metal stakes), were installed and then extended. Hundreds of cannon and machine guns were stripped from ships, forts, and coastal defenses and sent to the front, where they were soon joined by thousands more as peacetime factories were converted to the production of weapons.

At the same time, the completion of the conversion to Boer tactics and the use of mines, saps, light howitzers, and trench mortars gave the German infantry the means of crossing "no man's land" without suffering the kind of casualties they had suffered at Ypres. By the end of the winter of 1914/1915, German infantry attacking with limited objectives in the West regularly succeeded in reaching the forward French or British trench. Clearing that trench remained a problem—as long as they relied on rifle and bayonet, the Germans had no particular advantage over similarly armed defenders.

If they succeeded in taking the first trench and started to push beyond, the German infantry found itself at a distinct disadvantage. As they entered into this unknown territory, the attacking Germans frequently lost contact with their supporting artillery and trench mortars. At the same time, they found themselves crossing ground that was covered by the fire of field pieces and machine guns that the enemy had placed behind his front line trench. Especially dangerous to the advancing Germans were machine guns that caught skirmish lines in the flank.

FLAMETHROWERS

One of the first of many possible solutions to this problem was provided by the German pioneers in the form of a special unit equipped with flamethrowers. On January 18, 1915, a Flamethrower Detachment *(Flammenwerfer Abteilung)* was formed of volunteers from various pioneer units. Ironically, many of the men who volunteered for duty with the Flamethrower Detachment were firemen in civilian life. Even the commander of the unit, a *Landwehr* captain by the name of Reddemann, was a fireman by trade, having been an officer of the Leipzig fire brigade before the outbreak of war.

Like other weapons in the arsenal of the German pioneers, the flamethrowers used by Reddemann's pioneers had been developed in the decade preceding the outbreak of war. Inspired by accounts of flamethrowing weapons used in the siege of Port Arthur during the Russo-Japanese War, Reddemann had begun conducting field exercises with simulated flamethrowers in 1907. In mock assaults on fortresses, he used water pumped by the horse drawn fire engines of the Posen fire department instead of burning oil. Later, he collaborated with Richard Fiedler, a Berlin engineer, to develop working prototypes of two models of flamethrower—one large and one small.

The large flamethrower was a direct descendent of the fire hoses that had taken part in Reddemann's peacetime exercises. Referred to by the Germans as the *"Grof" (Grosses Flammenwerfer),* it could spit fire out to a distance of 40 meters. The major drawbacks of the large flamethrower were its weight and the time it took to install it. It could only be used in carefully prepared attacks against enemy positions within 40 meters of the most forward German position—invariably a sap. A further limitation was the fact that the fuel tanks only carried enough fuel for one minute's worth of flame.

The back-pack model, called the *"Kleif" (Kleines Flammenwerfer)* was far easier to employ. It was normally operated by a crew of two men. One carried the apparatus on his back and the other handled the tube. The range of the small flamethrower was half of that of the large flamethrower, although it had the advantage of being light enough to carry across "no man's land." Despite the size difference, both models of flamethrower functioned the same way. Compressed nitrogen pushed flammable oil through a tube. Upon leaving the tube, the oil was ignited by a hand-held torch and burst into flame. Later versions of the small flamethrower used an igniter inside the tube that relieved the operator of the dangerous task of lighting his own flame.

The chief tactical effect of the flamethrower was the fear that it inspired in the hearts of enemy soldiers. Men who were brave in the face of invisible bullets recoiled instinctively from contact with burning oil. Against those foolhardy enough to stand against it, however, the flamethrower was capable of causing horrible physical damage. The streams of burning oil could infiltrate through the loopholes of a blockhouse or the embrasures of a bunker. Inside trenches and buildings, the oil could be "bounced off" a wall to burn an enemy hiding around a corner.

The first employment of flamethrowers in battle was during a German attack with limited objectives near Malancourt, a village in France just north of Verdun, in February of 1915. At a point in the German lines where "no man's land" was narrow, Captain Reddemann had his men install large flamethrowers in spas pushed to within 40 meters of the French forward trench. The attack began with the flamethrowers spitting 40-meter-long streams of burning oil into the French position. Even though most had not been burned by the oil, the defenders were too shocked to react when the German infantry attacked. Accompanied by pioneers with small flamethrowers on their backs, the infantry crossed the French forward trench and penetrated deep into the French position while suffering only light casualties.

As a result of the success at Malancourt and the patronage of Crown Prince William, the eldest son of the Kaiser and commanding general of the Fifth Army, the Flamethrower Detachment was enlarged. The expanded unit, designated the 3rd Guard Pioneer Battalion, was composed of six line companies (20 large and 18 small flamethrowers each), a battalion headquarters, a workshop detachment, and a small research staff.[1] As more flamethrowers became available and demand for flamethrower teams grew, additional companies were formed.[2] The 3rd Guard Pioneer Battalion as a whole was kept under the direct control of the High Command. Individual companies, however, were attached to the armies on the western front. Each army, in turn, attached flamethrower platoons and teams to units about to engage in offensive operations.[3]

THE FIRST ASSAULT DETACHMENT

The pioneers were not alone in thinking of solutions to the problem of machine gun nests and directly firing field guns deep in the enemy position. In the opinion of Lieutenant Colonel Max Bauer, an expert in siege artillery and one of the more influential officers serving with the General Staff,[4] the answer was to provide the attacking infantry with artillery of their own. The armaments firm of Krupp, with which Bauer had frequent dealings, had recently developed a lightweight (3.7cm) cannon that seemed suitable for this purpose. Bauer therefore proposed to the War Ministry that a special unit be formed to test this and other new weapons in combat.[5]

The use of actual combat units, rather than specialized testing agencies, to test new equipment was an old tradition in the German Army. It was thus that the old Prussian Army integrated the revolutionary Dreyse needle gun in the 1830s and 1840s. Bauer, however, may have had a purpose beyond the mere testing of a new weapon. His biographer, Adolf Vogt, believes that he was interested in forming "trailblazing" *(Bahnbrechende)* units to create a large enough gap in the trenches so that ordinary infantry could pour through and resume the war of movement.[6]

On March 2, 1915, the War Ministry ordered the Eighth Army Corps to form an Assault Detachment *(Sturmabteilung)* from men provided by pioneer units. In the course of the month of March, this unit, consisting of a headquarters, two pioneer companies, and an overgrown battery of 20 of the lightweight Krupp guns, was assembled at the artillery range at Wahn. The officer chosen to command this unit, Major Calsow, was a pioneer.

The Assault Detachment spent the months of April and May, 1915, developing techniques for using the Krupp guns, which were soon christened "assault cannon" *(Sturmkannone),* in combat. The men of the cannon battery were trained in the care, manipulation, and firing of the cannon themselves, while the men of the pioneer companies developed techniques for ensuring that the cannon got across "no man's land" and the first enemy trench in condition to take part in the fight. Besides brushing up on the traditional pioneer skill of clearing barbed wire and other obstacles, they practiced using portable steel shields to protect those clearing obstacles from enemy fire.

This training, however, was never put to use. The first combat mission of the Assault Detachment was the defense of a section of the German trench line in France. The pioneers were used as line infantry while the assault cannon were used like the very weapons that they had been procured to combat—as light field pieces positioned to the rear of the German front line trench. The cost of this improper employment was high. In the month of June the two pioneer companies had taken so many casualties from French artillery bombardments that they had to be consolidated into one understrength company.

The assault cannon proved to be unsuited to employment near the front line. Each time one fired, its pronounced muzzle flash made it easy for the French to determine its exact position. Once located, the assault cannon became the favorite targets of the French artillery. Needless to say, such a weapon soon became quite unpopular with the troops that had to serve in its vicinity.[7]

In August of 1915 Major Calsow was relieved of the command of the Assault Detachment despite his protest that the poor showing of his unit had been due to the fact that it had not been employed in accordance with the instructions of the War Ministry. In the eyes of Colonel Bauer, Major Calsow's main failing was that he did not see the true potential of the Assault Detachment. Calsow did not share Colonel Bauer's vision of the Assault Detachment as a laboratory where new techniques could be tried out and a school where they could be taught. Rather, he had been content to command a unit that provided other units with detachments of assault cannon and pioneers.

CAPTAIN ROHR

Major Calsow's replacement as commander of the Assault Detachment was the same Captain Rohr of the Guard Rifle Battalion that took part in the New Year's Eve attack described earlier in this chapter. A professional soldier who was also the son of a professional soldier, Rohr was born in 1877 in the fortress town of Metz. In 1891, two months short of his fourteenth birthday, he begun his military career as a cadet. After five years at various cadet schools, he was commissioned as a second lieutenant in the 66th Infantry Regiment. During his 16 years as a lieutenant, he served in a number of infantry and *Jäger* units, as well as at the Non-Commissioned Officers Academy at Potsdam, an institution that trained indigent teenagers for careers as NCOs, and the Infantry Marksmanship School. Following his promotion to captain in 1912, he served as a company commander in the 161st Infantry Regiment and the Guard Rifle Battalion.[8]

General Gaede, the commanding general of the formation *(Armee Abteilung Gaede)*[9] to which the Assault Detachment was attached in August, gave Rohr a free hand insofar as the training of his unit was concerned. His only instructions were to train his unit "according to the lessons that he had learned during his front line service" with the Guard Rifle Battalion.[10] This brief order, which was in keeping with the German Army tradition of granting a captain the maximum possible discretion in training his company, was to have a profound effect on the future of the Assault Detachment. In the next few months, Rohr was to transform his unit from an experimental pioneer unit into an elite infantry organization.

General Gaede's support was not limited to forbearance. He also provided Captain Rohr with a machine gun platoon (two model 1908 Maxim machine guns), a trench mortar platoon (four light mortars), and, from Captain Reddemann's command, a flamethrower platoon of six small flamethrowers. While General Gaede's reason for doing this was to give Captain Rohr a microcosm of a regiment or division so that he might experiment with new techniques of using these weapons, the assignment of so many supporting arms to a battalion-sized unit prepared the way for a new concept of how an infantry battalion should be organized and how it should fight. No longer the uniformly armed, deceptively symmetrical organization that had existed since the introduction of the bayonet at the end of the seventeenth century, the battalion was well on its way to becoming a team composed of different weapons, each with its particular virtues and vulnerabilities.

THE INFANTRY GUN

Immediately upon taking command of the Assault Detachment, Captain Rohr began to experiment with various ways of improving the capabilities of his unit. Looking for a replacement for the indiscreet 3.7cm assault cannon, he tested a number of light field pieces. The most suitable gun to provide the short range, direct fire that Rohr wanted turned out to be the Russian 76.2mm field gun, a large number of which had been captured in Poland and the Ukraine earlier in 1915. Captain Rohr had a number of these modified to optimize them for mobility. To save weight, barrels were cut down and long range sights, superfluous on a weapon expected to engage targets less than 1000 meters away, were removed. The carriage was lightened as well, although the steel shield was retained.

The 7.62cm infantry gun *(Infanterie Geschütz),* as the Germans rechristened the modified Russian field piece, allowed Captain Rohr to realize in the fullest possible sense the ideal of close coordination of artillery fire. Even the most accurate of indirect artillery fire would have to be shifted forward when friendly infantry got within a hundred or so meters of the falling shells. The chance that one or more of the shells would fall short of the target and kill some of the attacking troops was too great. An infantry gun firing directly at the target, on the other hand, might have its shells fall short by 10 or 20 meters, but never, except in the case of gross incompetence on the part of the gunners, 100 meters. This degree of accuracy made it possible for batteries of infantry guns to suppress an enemy position until the very moment that the attacking German infantry broke into it. It also made possible the destruction of point targets such as machine gun nests.

The infantry gun also made fire support more responsive to the immediate needs of the infantry. The field artillery brigade that provided indirect fire support to an infantry division was directly subordinate to the commanding general of the division and located thousands of meters away from the infantry. Fire plans for an attack had to be coordinated in advance "through channels" *(durch Dienstwege)* and, even if the field telephones were working and an artillery liaison officer was available at the right moment, it was difficult to shift fire onto new targets if the situation changed during an attack. Infantry guns, on the other hand, were directly subordinate to the Detachment Commander and moved forward in the attack with the foot soldiers.

SEMINAL EXPERIMENTS

In addition to artillery, Captain Rohr experimented with various kinds of body armor, to include the portable steel shields that were already in the inventory of the Assault Detachment and steel breastplates reminiscent of those of the late Middle Ages. Although the steel shields and breastplates were to remain standard equipment, Captain Rohr found that they did not fit in with the style of warfare that he was developing. Speed and violence of execution, Captain Rohr had discovered during his active service with the Guard Rifle Battalion, were far better protection than metal armor. The shields, Rohr believed, were only useful when the assaulting infantry could cross "no man's land" in a single bound or when there was a danger that the attackers would have to deal with flanking fire. The only piece of armor that Rohr adopted for all operations was the "coal scuttle" helmet *(Stahlhelm)* that was later to become the trademark of the German soldier of both world wars.[11]

The essential elements of the tactics that Rohr developed in the course of these experiments were (1) the replacement of the advance in skirmish lines with the surprise assault of squad-sized "stormtroops" *(Sturmtrupps* or *Stosstrupps)*,[12] (2) the use of supporting arms (machine guns, infantry guns, trench mortars, indirect artillery, flamethrowers) coordinated at the lowest possible level to suppress the enemy during the attack, and (3) the clearing of trenches by "rolling them up" with troops armed with hand grenades. In early October of 1915, the 2nd Pioneer Company of the Assault Detachment put these tactics to the test in an assault on a French position in the Vosges Mountains known as the *Schrätzmannle.*

At 5:29 on the evening of October 12, 1915, six large flamethrowers that had been built into saps opened fire on the French forward trench. From behind each flamethrower, a squad-sized stormtroop followed the jets of burning oil into a designated portion of the enemy trench, systematically clearing that section of trench with hand grenades. French field pieces and a machine gun firing on the stormtroops were quickly silenced by German trench mortars and artillery that had been standing by for such a task. After they had cleared the trench, the men of the stormtroops set about closing it off from the rest of the French position and building a breastwork. The stormtroopers were aided in this task by squads of men from an infantry unit who had followed them into the trench after it had been cleared.These latter carried tools and sandbags, articles that were too heavy for the stormtroopers to carry while crossing "no man's land" or fighting in the trench.[13]

TRAINING OTHER UNITS

Captain Rohr made the experiences of the battle for the *Schrätzmannle* the basis for the further training of the Assault Detachment, as well as for the training courses that he held for other units. The first of these courses for outside units was held in December of 1915 for selected officers and men of the 12th *Landwehr* Division. Because of the large number of students (43 officers, 351 NCOs and men) that attended this six-day-long course and the short time available, the Assault Detachment could do little more than make the attendees aware of their new methods of fighting.[14] Subsequent courses, however, lasted longer and were attended by fewer students. These factors allowed the Assault Detachment to conduct more thorough training.

The methods taught at Captain Rohr's courses constituted a radical departure from the tactics of 1914. Columns and skirmish lines were done away with. Squads were treated like tactical entities in their own right, moving as individual units toward their predesignated objectives as the stormtroops had at the *Schrätzmannle.* In the movement across "no man's land," no attempt was to be made to have the squads maintain any sort of connection with each other. "The objective," Rohr believed, "guaranteed unity of action." Neither was there to be any sort of predetermined formation within the squad. The men would move so as to best take advantage of the terrain.

In order to ensure that battle did not degenerate into a land navigation exercise, officers, NCOs, and men were oriented by means of large-scale maps (1:5000). To further ensure that all hands had a detailed knowledge of the battlefield and, in particular, the location and characteristics of squad objectives, a full-scale model of the enemy position to be attacked, complete with trenches and barbed wire, would be built in a training area behind the line and used for full dress rehearsals, some of which even included the use of live ammunition.[15]

The incorporation of the principle of individual squad movement into the tactics of the Assault Detachment "Rohr" was to have a profound effect on the role of NCOs on the battlefield. From the days of Frederick the Great the post of the German NCO had been behind the firing line, his chief duty being to ensure that no soldier left the firing line without authorization. Even the *Drill Regulations of 1906* placed the NCO behind the firing line, to push rather than to lead. When the squad became a tactical unit, however, the post of the squad leader changed. Thanks to Captain Rohr, he was now in front and in command.

The rehearsal of the attack on a model of the enemy position also constituted a "step up" for NCOs and ordinary soldiers. For almost a century, the German General Staff had used wargames as a means of training staff officers and testing operational plans. Later in the nineteenth century tactical wargames had been used to train regimental officers in the finer points of their battlefield duties. While rehearsing each individual squad on its role in an attack did not raise enlisted men to the level of general staff officers, it brought a form of wargaming to them. Furthermore, rehearsal drove home the point that each individual squad was no longer an anonymous group of men being fed into a firing line formed for a purpose unknown to its members. Instead, the squad had become an irreplaceable element in a plan that all of its members had studied and practiced.

The personal equipment of the men of the Assault Detachment was modified to meet the requirements of their new methods of fighting. The hobnailed heavy leather jackboots long associated with the German infantryman was replaced by lace-up half-boots and puttees of the kind used by Austrian mountain troops. To facilitate crawling, the field uniform was reinforced with leather patches on the knees and elbows. As the hand grenade had eclipsed the rifle as the chief individual weapon of the stormtrooper, the leather belt and shoulder harness that had supported the rifle ammunition pouches were discarded in favor of a pair of over-the-shoulder bags to carry hand grenades. The rifle itself was replaced with a Mauser carbine that had been designed as a personal defense weapon for service troops and pioneers. While the action on this weapon was identical to that of the service rifle, it was lighter and easier to handle.

HARTMANNSWEILERKOPF

The Assault Detachment was first used as a complete unit in an assault on the *Hartmannsweilerkopf,* a ridge in the Vosges mountains that had been fought over by *Jäger* troops and their French counterparts, the elite *Chasseurs Alpins,* since Christmas of 1914. Captain Rohr was familiar with this terrain; he and some of his men had participated in an attack there on October 15, 1915—an attack that had been carried out by the Guard Rifle Battalion and its sister unit the Guard *Jäger* Battalion.[16]

On January 10, 1916, in an attack on a much larger scale than the *Schratzmännle* operation, the entire Assault Detachment led two infantry regiments into the French position on the *Hartmannsweilerkopf* and cleared it with comparatively light casualties. The attack had all of the same elements as the assault on the *Schratzmännle*—a detailed rehearsal, individual squad movement, and the close coordination of flame-throwers, machine guns, infantry guns, and trench mortars.

Although Captain Rohr was an infantryman who spent much of his time giving the infantry the means of providing its own fire support, he did not dispense with indirect artillery fire on the *Hartmannsweilerkopf.* The artillery technique he employed in support of the assault was the direct descendent of that which had been used at Soissons in January of 1915. Suppressive fire on enemy batteries and a "box barrage" on the objective itself sealed off the battlefield. Preparatory fire facilitated the crossing of "no man's land." Unlike the German commanders at Soissons, however, Rohr avoided the seductive thought that artillery could do the infantry's work for it. The chief role of the artillery, like that of other supporting arms, was to suppress and paralyze the enemy so that the infantry could maneuver, to provide the anvil against which the hammer of the infantry would strike.

The artillery used on the *Hartmannsweilerkopf* and other attacks with limited objectives was usually restricted to the guns and howitzers already in the area. In 1915, a division would have as its organic artillery 12 light (10.5cm) field howitzers and between 36[17] and 54 light[18] (7.7cm) field guns. Heavier guns and howitzers belonging to the corps and army heavy artillery *(Fussartillerie)* might also be available. By the summer of 1916, the number of light field howitzers had remained the same while the number of light field guns had been reduced to 24.[19] Many more heavy pieces, however, were available. According to Wilhelm Balck, a typical division on the Western Front at that time had in its sector 12 heavy (15cm) field howitzers, four heavy (21cm) mortars, and eight heavy (15cm) field guns.[20] A further limitation on the use of artillery in attacks with limited objectives was shell rationing. Except when participating in a major offensive, each battery was given a daily allotment of shells that it could not exceed.

The limitation on the artillery support available for attacks with limited objectives had a salutary effect on the development of German infantry tactics. Unable to smother the entire enemy position with shells, Captain Rohr and other German infantry commanders had to use artillery as a complement to rather than as a substitute for other arms. By the end of the war it had become generally recognized in the German Army that artillery fire tended more to keep heads down than to tear them off. Accuracy and timeliness of fire, as well as the ability of the infantry to exploit its effects, came to be seen as more important than volume or duration of fire.

These tendencies notwithstanding, the fact that artillery accounted for most of the combat casualties in trench warfare led some to place faith in it as the chief solution to the deadlock of position warfare. Ignoring the law of diminishing marginal returns, many believed that if some artillery could kill some of the enemy, enough artillery could kill all of them. Among the Germans, this idea took hold in the mind of General von Falkenhayn, the same chief of the general staff who had ordered the Assault Detachment into being. While the Assault Detachment was working out a tactical system in which artillery would retain its prewar function of contributing to the attainment of fire superiority, Falkenhayn was working out a scheme in which artillery fire was to become an end in itself. In early February of 1916, the Assault Detachment entrained for Lorraine, leaving the relative peace of the Vosges for the charnel house of Verdun.

NOTES

1.   The workshop detachment manufactured and repaired all the flame-throwers used by the Reddemann's unit. The research staff continually improved the design. See Augustine, "Development of the Engineer Arm" (in Schwarte, *War Lessons*), p. 300. The fact that the workshop and research staff was co-located with the headquarters and the depot of Reddemann's unit provided a number of benefits. First, technical developments were given a high profile. Second, ideas for improving flamethrowers that originated with the actual flamethrower troops were readily available to the engineers. Third, ideas generated by the engineers of the research staff could be tested without delay by the "duty experts" in the employment of flamethrowers. As a result, Reddemann's flamethrower unit was able to design, test, manufacture, and field new weapons in less time than it takes many modern armies to write their "requirements documents."

2.   In April of 1916, the flamethrower unit consisted of 12 line companies and was consequently redesignated the Guard Reserve Pioneer Regiment. By the end of the war, the Guard Reserve Pioneer Regiment had become a force of 3000 men and over 300 flamethrowers.

3.   Reddemann, "Die Totenkopf Pioniere," and Schäwen, "Der Erste Flammenangriff" in Paul Heinrici, ed., *Das Ehrenbuch,* pp. 516–25 and Hermann Cron, *Die Organization des deutschen Heeres im Weltkrieg* (Berlin: E.S. Mittler und Sohn, 1923), p. 86.

4.   Bauer was considered to be the second most powerful man on the General Staff. It was he who, in 1916, demanded that General Falkenhayn be replaced as Chief of Staff. Walter Goerlitz, *History of the German General Staff* (New York: Praeger, 1953), p. 178.

5.   Max Bauer, *Der Grosse Krieg im Feld und Heimat* (Tübingen: Osiander, 1921), p. 87.

6.   Adolf Vogt, *Oberst Bax Bauer: Generalstabsoffizier im Zwielicht 1869–1929* (Osnabrück: Biblioverlag, 1974), p. 18.

7.   Hellmuth Gruss, *Aufbau und Verwendung der deutschen Sturmbataillone im Weltkriege* (Berlin: Junker and Dunnhaupt Verlag, 1939), pp. 15–21.

8.   Ibid., p. 20.

9.   An *Armee Abteilung* was a number of divisions detached from an army to perform a separate mission. Army Detachments Gaede and von Falkenhausen had been formed at the end of September to defend Alsace after the transfer of the Sixth and Seventh Armies.

10.   Gruss, *Aufbau und Verwendung,* p. 21.

11.   Ibid. Stormtroop units continued to wear the body armor when posing for

group photographs. Photographs taken during battle, however, show that the armor was left in the rest billets during actual operations.

12.   The German word *Trupp* (masc., pl. *Trupps*) means a small unit such as a squad, section, or platoon. The word *Truppe* (fem.), on the other hand, refers to a military unit of any size. *Truppen,* the plural of *Truppe,* can also be translated as "troops." Thus, the soldiers that serve in *Stosstrupps* were called *Stosstruppen.*

13.   Gruss, *Aufbau und Verwendung,* pp. 20–26. A German document dated December 12, 1915 and entitled "Instructions for the Employment of Flame Projectors" describes an ideal attack "with limited objectives" which seems to be modeled on this operation. The document was translated and printed in the *Infantry Journal* vol. 14, pp. 692–98.

14.   Gruss, *Aufbau und Verwendung,* p. 27.

15.   Ibid., p. 25.

16.   The October 15 attack on the Hartmansweilerkopf is described in the official histories of the Guard Rifle Battalion and the Guard *Jäger* Battalion. While the participation of Captain Rohr and his men, as well as the use of the large flamethrowers, is mentioned, the exact role played by Rohr's stormtroopers is not discussed. A clue to the tactics used by the *Jäger* troops during the attack is given by the following passage. "Corporal Groniger, one of the most dashing squadleaders, fell as he leapt out of the sap at the head of his assault squad *(Sturmtrupp)*." Of particular interest is the use, at this early date, of the word *Sturmtrupp* outside of the Sturmbataillon Rohr.

17.   Six batteries of six guns each or nine batteries of four guns each.

18.   Nine batteries of six guns each.

19.   Balck, *Development of Tactics,* p. 23.

20.   Ibid., p. 37.

4

Verdun

Infantry must cherish its inherent desire to take the offensive; its actions must be guided by one thought, viz, forward upon the enemy, cost what it may.

Drill Regulations of 1906

Throughout 1915, the German armies in the West had been, from a strategic point of view, on the defensive. Although battalions, regiments, and even divisions might undertake attacks with limited objectives, in the grand scheme of things Germany was content to hold the ground it had gained in France and Belgium while it concentrated its attention on the Eastern Front where the bulk of the forces of the Austro-German alliance were located. This strategy would be reversed in 1916. The Central Powers would go on the defensive in the east while they attempted to knock France out of the war.

Unlike the French and British generals, who sought to use their guns to blast a way to the "green fields beyond" and an opportunity to resume maneuver at the operational level, Erich von Falkenhayn, the German Chief of Staff, planned to use his artillery as a strategic weapon that would free him from the need to conduct war at the operational level. His guns and howitzers were to strike directly at what he saw as the weak point of the Anglo-French alliance, the unwillingness of conscripted Frenchmen to go on dying indefinitely for what Falkenhayn considered (and what German propaganda maintained were) the interests of Great Britain. He would use his artillery, proven superior in a year's worth of attacks with limited objectives that began with the assault on the Vregny Plateau at Soissons, to kill so many Frenchmen that they would give up the alliance with Great Britain and sue for a separate peace.

In order for this policy of attrition to work, Falkenhayn would need the cooperation of the French. He needed to find a place that the French would not give up easily, a magnet that would draw the French infantry within the range of the German guns. The place would have to have great military or symbolic value, preferably both. It would, moreover, have to be suitable to the employment of large amounts of artillery.

THE TERRAIN

The best location that Falkenhayn could find for his battle of attrition was the fortress of Verdun. In the march to the Marne in 1914, the advancing German armies had bypassed Verdun. As the lines stabilized, Verdun remained a salient, a bulge in the French line surrounded on three sides by the Germans. It was thus not only more vulnerable than a linear position to being cut off in a pincer movement, it was also potentially within the range of three times as much artillery.

The dominant feature of the terrain was the river Meuse, meandering from southeast to northwest. On either side of the river was a belt of gently sloping hills dotted with tiny villages and the dozen or so smaller forts that had been built to keep an enemy from approaching too closely to the citadel—the main fortress that sat astride the Meuse at the intersection of that river and the Paris road. Both the hills and the hollows between them were covered with trees, though in the hollows the trees grew closer together, forming the woods that would see some of the fiercest fighting of the battle.

The French did not occupy the citadel of Verdun itself so much as a ring of fortifications around it. After the fall of Liège, most Frenchmen believed that the stone walls built to withstand the siege artillery of the nineteenth century could not hope to stand against that of the twentieth. The French thus placed only token garrisons in both the citadel and the outlying forts and put the bulk of their troops and their faith in a series of trenches. Unlike the trenches in most French sectors, which, by German standards were rather shallow, the trenches around Verdun were well provided with deep dugouts and concrete machine gun nests. In the woods, where a centuries-old tangle of roots made the digging of trenches difficult, the French lines consisted of concrete blockhouses.

ARTILLERY

The artillery park that Falkenhayn concentrated at Verdun, despite the fact that it was less than the artillery staff of the Fifth Army had requested,[1] was unmatched by any in the history of the German Army up to that point. In the horseshoe around Verdun, the Germans packed 1612 artillery pieces.[2] About a third of these were light (7.7cm) field guns and light (10.5cm) field howitzers from artillery regiments[3] of divisions slated for the operation and divisions occupying neighboring sectors. The rest were considerably heavier weapons of what in earlier wars would have been called "siege artillery"—heavy guns in calibers up to 23cm and high angle weapons such as the 42cm heavy mortar. These were the weapons that Falkenhayn expected to do the bulk of the killing at Verdun.[4]

The senior artillery officer of the Fifth Army was General Schabel, an officer of the Heavy Artillery *(Fussartillerie)* with the title of "General of the Heavy Artillery at the Army High Command."[5] In keeping with the prewar manual on fortress warfare, Schabel divided the Fifth Army's area of responsibility into three artillery sectors, each of which corresponded to one of the three component army corps of the Fifth Army. The senior artillery officers of each of these corps thus became the artillery sector commander and was given control over all of the field artillery and most of the heavy artillery available to the Fifth Army. While this arrangement left only the heaviest pieces under Schabel's direct control, Schabel did not abdicate responsibility for the artillery battle as a whole. He retained the right to review the fire plans drawn up by each corps and was thus able to ensure that the first shells would fall at the same time, that the infantry would be able to step off into the attack at the same time, and that the entire front was adequately covered.[6]

As a supplement to its artillery, each German division at Verdun was well supplied with trench mortars. In the course of 1915, most German infantry divisions had acquired, as an organic unit, a trench mortar company consisting, as a rule, of two heavy, four medium, and six light trench mortars. These usually remained under the direct control of the commanding general of each division, although in some cases light trench mortars were attached to battalions.[7] In addition to the trench mortars organic to the divisions, each artillery sector was provided with a trench mortar battalion from the High Command reserve.[8]

The division of labor between the various indirect fire weapons was based on their peculiar characteristics. Trench mortars, light field guns, and light field howitzers, because of their short range and their subordination to divisions, were generally detailed to fire on the first French trench. Heavy mortars were also assigned targets in the first line.[9] The heavier howitzers were assigned targets in the second line. They also joined with the heavier guns in counter-battery work and what the Germans called "special missions" *(Sonderaufgaben)*—the shelling of villages, forts, roads, railroads, and the town of Verdun itself. For the suppression of the French artillery, the primary German weapon was a heavy howitzer shell full of *"T-Stoff,"* a nonpoisonous but highly irritating tear gas.[10]

Despite their mighty assemblage of indirect fire power, and despite the claims of many artillery officers that the infantry would be able to "goose-step" into the town of Verdun without firing a shot, the plans for the battle of Verdun were drawn up with a definite sense of the limitations of artillery and mortar fire. The two types of obstacles that the experience of 1915 had shown to be most deadly to advancing infantry—barbed wire and concrete machine gun nests—were given not to the artillery but to the pioneers to destroy. For creating lanes in the barbed wire, the traditional solution of pioneer teams armed with wire cutters and explosives was deemed sufficient.[11] To deal with the concrete machine gun nests, however, the Fifth Army assembled an unprecedented eight companies of flamethrower troops—almost all of the flamethrower troops then serving in the German Army. Against blockhouses and machine gun nests in the forwardmost French position, Reddemann's "firemen" used large flamethrowers built into saps. Squads armed with portable flamethrowers were assigned to battalions to deal with the concrete machine gun nests further to the rear.[12]

In some divisions, an additional means to combat machine gun nests was provided in the form of light field guns placed in the German jumping off positions. These guns were well protected by their steel shields and, given sufficient time and a sufficient number of rounds to zero in on a target, could be reasonably sure of eventually achieving a direct hit on a machine gun nest.[13] Although the batteries that provided these guns were beginning to be called "accompanying batteries" *(Begleitbatterien),* they do not seem to have followed the infantry into the attack. The guns were too heavy to manhandle quickly over "no man's land" and horses would have been too conspicuous in all but the most secure areas.

THE INFANTRY

Nine infantry divisions, all belonging to Crown Prince William's Fifth Army, were detailed for the operation at Verdun (see Illustration 3). In Falkenhayn's conception, the role of the infantry regiments of these divisions was to be subsidiary to that of the artillery. Their main job was to present a sufficiently credible threat so that the French would feed as many troops as possible into the killing zone. The attacks conducted by the German infantry at Verdun therefore were attacks with limited objectives, seizures of little pieces of *la Belle Patrie* that the French would try to recapture regardless of the cost in lives.

Most of the units sent to fight at Verdun had been on the western front throughout 1915. It is not surprising, therefore, that units destined to take part in the operation were assembled in the villages and towns behind the lines for a number of weeks before the attack and were given time to train. Although the training of the infantry of the divisions detailed for the attack was not carried out according to any master plan, it generally began with the building of dummy trench systems, followed by the rehearsal of companies, battalions, regiments, and, in at least one case, the entire division. At the same time, specialists such as field

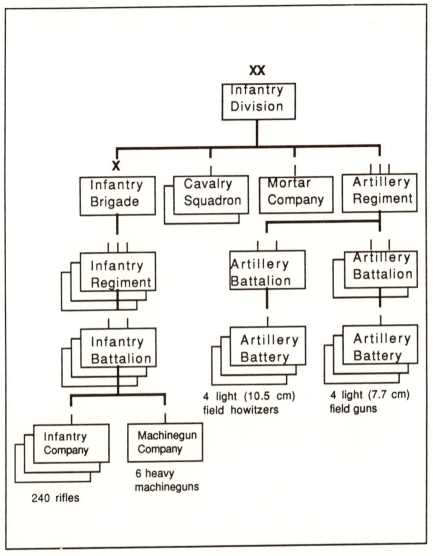

Illustration 3
Combat Units of a German Infantry Division, Verdun, 1916

telephone operators, runners, trumpeters, machine gunners, and infantry-pioneers (men drawn from the ranks of infantry units who assisted the pioneers in the work of cutting wire, blowing up dugouts, etc.) were designated and trained.[14]

During this training period, storm troops patterned after those of the Assault Detachment "Rohr" were formed in many units. These improvised assault squads were assigned particular tasks for the first day of the offensive—the capture of a certain blockhouse or machine gun nest, for example. In other units, a portion of the troops were trained as hand grenade throwers and formed into special squads. In either case, the first wave of the attack at Verdun would contain men armed primarily with hand grenades whose task it would be to clear out trenches and strong points—the difference in nomenclature between a hand grenade squad *(Handgrenatentrupp)* and a stormtroop *(Sturmtrupp)* being due more to the role that the Assault Detachment played in training the unit than actual function in the battle.

FIRST AND SECOND DAYS

The German offensive at Verdun began early on the morning of February 21. At 8:12 A.M. Crown Prince William gave the order for the artillery to open fire. With the exception of a few pauses to allow patrols to ascertain the damage, the bombardment lasted all day. The patrols usually reported seeing caved-in trenches, destroyed barbed wire obstacles, and groups of French soldiers running to the rear. The patrols also reported that they had received little or no fire from the enemy positions; the only German casualty of the day was an artillery liaison officer hit by a splinter from a short round. In some cases, the patrols even managed to take prisoners. Pilots of reconnaissance aircraft confirmed the reports of widespread destruction. They described railroad tracks that had been torn up by the shells of the German heavy artillery and reported that fires had broken out in the town of Verdun.[15] So far, the plan was working.

On the second day, the mission of the artillery changed from destruction to suppression. Between eight A.M. and midday, each of the nine infantry divisions of the Fifth Army conducted a series of attacks with limited objectives to capture the forwardmost French position in front of its sector. Field artillery and trench mortars, operating under the direct control of division, regimental, and in some cases even battalion commanders, supported these attacks by laying barrages on the French positions.

The hand grenade squads and stormtroops of the first wave, thoroughly rehearsed in the rear, often moved right up to the barrage,[16] risking the occasional casualty from a short shell in order to be able to fully exploit the effects of the fire. Because of this practice, the improvised stormtroops often found that they were able to take possession of a trench within a few seconds of the barrage being lifted. The French, still trying to gather their wits about them after being on the receiving end of 30 to 50 shells per hour from every German field piece,[17] were caught in their dugouts and therefore unable to offer any coordinated resistance.[18]

Although the attack order of Crown Prince William only specified the composition of the first wave of the attack,[19] leaving the organization of subsequent waves to subordinate commanders, the second wave of German infantry generally consisted of riflemen deployed in skirmish lines. The primary role of these riflemen was the defense of the trenches that the grenade throwers had captured. The experience of attacks with limited objectives had made German commanders aware that the moment of greatest danger in an attack was the few minutes after the enemy position had been taken. Exhausted and disorganized grenadiers with empty grenade sacks were easy prey for counterattacking enemy reserves. So that the counterattackers would find themselves faced with equally fresh riflemen, the bulk of the infantry attacking at Verdun was assigned to the second wave.

Following the riflemen was a third wave of carrying parties with ammunition, pioneer tools, and materials for improving the captured trenches. As they were not expected to meet any resistance, the carrying parties generally moved forward in columns. In case they were needed to reinforce the riflemen of the second wave, the men of the carrying parties carried rifles and hand grenades. The six machine guns assigned to each battalion at this time moved forward with the third wave. Machine guns had been used in attacks with limited objectives to suppress targets in the enemy positions since late in 1914. Such was the German confidence in their artillery in the early days of the battle for Verdun, however, that, as a general rule, the machine guns were only brought into action once an enemy position was taken.[20]

Against the forwardmost trenches of the French lines, these tactics were generally effective. Every German division reached its objectives on the second day of the operation and a few units, commanded by officers who took advantage of unexpected weaknesses, were able, after a pause of a few minutes to request permission from Fifth Army Chief of Staff General Schmidt von Knobelsdorf,[21] pushed a few hundred meters beyond their assigned objectives. The promise made by German artillery officers that the infantry would be able to goose-step across "no man's land" was rarely fulfilled. The 24-hour bombardment had certainly torn up the ground forward of the German line and caused unprecedented destruction. That same bombardment, however, also served to animate in a handful of survivors a fanatical spirit of resistance that could only be overcome in close combat.

A CHANGE OF FOCUS

On the third day of battle, the German attacks began to acquire characteristics that were not in keeping with Falkenhayn's strategy. Forgetting that the goal of the attack at Verdun was the killing of as many Frenchmen as possible while economizing on German lives, the commanding general of the 6th Infantry Division ordered his infantry regiments to attack the French positions in a woods known as the Herbebois "without regard to casualties."[22] As the Brandenburgers who filled the ranks of those regiments pushed farther into the woods, they met stiffer and stiffer resistance. French reinforcements had arrived the previous evening and had taken up positions in shell holes and piles of rubble. With no trenches to provide certain boundaries between opposing forces and with the skeletons of trees hindering the observation of artillery liaison officers, the German infantry found itself relying more and more on its own resources the further it pushed into the woods.

The type of fighting experienced by the men of the 6th Infantry Division in the Herbebois was to become the pattern for most of the fighting at Verdun. Falkenhayn's conception of attrition did not fit in with the way that most German officers felt about battle. In peacetime, they had been taught to move forward "cost what it may." In the course of 1915, they had learned how to take small pieces of real estate despite the advantages that repeating rifles, machine guns, and barbed wire gave to the defender. At Verdun, the force of Falkenhayn's concept of the operation could not compete with this almost instinctive desire to push forward and capture terrain. Thus, the Fifth Army found itself trying to capture the fortress of Verdun.

As each day passed, however, this task grew more difficult. The deep penetrations made by some German units early in the offensive soon became a thing of the past as the French put a machine gun in every shellhole and a rifleman behind every tree stump. During the week of February 21–27, the Germans had advanced by leaps and bounds. The high point of that week was February 25, when three companies of the 6th Infantry Division captured the almost undefended Fort Douaumont ten kilometers beyond the line of departure that they had crossed on the twenty-first. After February 27, however, the pace of German progress slowed down markedly. The primary tactical events were still attacks with limited objectives, but the scale was much different. During the first week of the battle, a German attack could push the German lines a kilometer or more forward. During March, April, and May, however, daily progress began to be measured in scores of meters.

The factors that contributed to this slowing down of the battle were many. The first was the increasing strength of the French defenders. In keeping with their general policy, the troops that had been assigned the task of holding Verdun were mostly from territorial units, that is to say, they were older men considered unfit for the exertions of active campaigning. Units consisting of younger men were generally kept in reserve, for offensive work or for counterattack. On the afternoon of February 24, the first regiment of these latter regiments arrived in the village of

Douaumont, just northwest of Fort Douaumont. By the time the Germans attempted, on the twenty-sixth, to take that village, an entire French corps had been entrusted with its defense.[23]

The increased numbers of the French dramatically changed the effect that the woods and villages had on the battle. During the first week of fighting, when French forces could not occupy these features in depth, woods and villages had provided cover and concealment for German units pushing deep into the French position. Once the French had the manpower to occupy these features properly, however, the Germans were not only denied passage through them, but found that the more open ground was well covered by flanking fire from these positions.

Between February 26 and 28, the 5th Infantry Division made three attempts to capture Douaumont Village. With each successive attack, the German artillery bombardment lasted longer and included a larger number of artillery pieces. (The third attack followed a five-hour bombardment that included the fire of 30.5cm and 42cm "super heavy" mortars.) Each time the bombardment was lifted, however, the French riflemen and machine gunners in the woods to the west of the open ground that the German infantry had to cross to get to Douaumont Village were able to stop the attack with enfilading fire.[24] Those attacking Germans who were shielded from this machine gun fire by bends in the woods suffered just as badly from the effects of French artillery shells exploding among the treetops[25] and the French machine gunners and riflemen in the village itself.

Many of the junior officers of the infantry battalions that took part in the three assaults used imaginative tactics. A lieutenant of the 12th Grenadier Regiment had his platoon crawl through the snow to reach a French strongpoint, cut through the wire with wire cutters, and clear out the blockhouses with grenades. *Stosstrupps* of the same regiment, reinforced with flamethrower teams, attempted a surprise night attack against Douaumont Village. While the attack against the strongpoint succeeded, the night attack on the village failed. In the latter case, the *Stosstrupps* came upon a thick barbed wire obstacle that had not been marked on their maps.[26]

Above the regimental level, however, the attacks against Douaumont Village were conducted very much like the attack that the 5th Infantry Division had carried out against the Vregny Plateau a little more than a year before. The artillery preparation had been substantial, but not closely coordinated. There was thus a space of some minutes between the time that the German artillery stopped firing on the forward French positions and the time when the German infantry were scheduled to be upon those positions. As a result, the French riflemen and machine gunners, sheltered by their concrete blockhouses or the masonry basements and rubble of the village, were able to bear the bombardment with few losses.

In fact, the only machine gun that seems to have been knocked out by the preparatory bombardment was the one destroyed when a German shell scored a direct hit on the belltower of Douaumont's church.[27]

THE ROLE OF THE ASSAULT DETACHMENT

In this sort of fighting, the qualities fostered by the Assault Detachment—initiative on the part of individual soldiers and ferocity in close combat—were at a premium. Beginning on February 22, stormtroops from the Assault Detachment joined the grenade throwers in the first wave of many attacks. In most cases, only one to four stormtroops were assigned to a battalion. Where French resistance was expected to be especially tough, however, as in the case of a line of well defended pill boxes in the Herbebois, a whole company of the Assault Detachment, supported by flamethrowers, heavy machine guns, light trench mortars, and infantry guns, led the attack of an infantry battalion of the 6th Division.

From the point of view of Captain Rohr, the most effective way for the commander of an infantry battalion to use the stormtroops assigned to his unit was to imitate the techniques that Rohr had developed in the Vosges. The destruction of each strong point (e.g., pillbox, blockhouse, machine gun nest) had to be prepared by a thorough reconnaissance, planned in detail, and thoroughly rehearsed. Many of the German battalion commanders at Verdun, however, were ignorant of Rohr's methods. Detailed reconnaissance, planning, and rehearsals were often dispensed with. The leaders of the stormtroops were often reduced to reconnoitering the objective the night before the attack, seeing it only in the light of day after it had become too late to change the plan. Worse still was the commander who thought that the stormtroopers assigned to him should work as ordinary pioneers and used a machine gun platoon that had been sent to support the stormtroopers to replace one of his organic machine gun platoons after the latter had been wiped out.[28]

In early March, the Assault Detachment, which had never been sent into battle at Verdun as a complete unit, was withdrawn to safe billets in Beauville, a town near Verdun that was to serve as its "home" for most of the rest of the war. At Beauville, the Assault Detachment spent the bulk of the battle training the replacements for the men that it had lost during the first month's fighting and conducting courses for officers and men from other units. Throughout the course of the six-month-long battle, however, the Assault Detachment continued to provide *Stosstrupps* and heavy weapons teams to support the attacks of other units.[29]

Far more common than the stormtroops of Assault Detachment "Rohr" in the first wave of any German attack at Verdun were the flamethrower teams of Captain Reddemann's Guard Reserve Pioneer Regi-

ment. The eight flamethrower companies that were attached to the Fifth
Army for the first day of the Verdun operation stayed throughout the
course of the battle. The heavy flamethrowers supplemented the
artillery—they helped the infantry break into a position. The portable
flamethrower teams, on the other hand, were a substitute for, as well as a
complement to, the men armed with hand grenades. Like the hand grenade, the portable flamethrower was a weapon that could kill an unseen
enemy. Its flames could reach around corners and seep into the embrasures of blockhouses. Portable flamethrowers proved especially useful in
the subterranean battles that took place in the long corridors of forts such
as Vaux and Douaumont.[30]

DEFENSE IN DEPTH

The steady pressure of the German attacks at Verdun, the advance of a
few hundred meters each day, made it increasingly difficult for the
French to build proper trenches. The longer the battle continued, the
more the French relied on a more or less ad hoc defense of forests, shell-
torn fields, and the basements of ruined houses. Small groups of riflemen
and machine gunners, while physically isolated from each other, created a
zone wherein an attacker would be faced by fire from all directions. In
doing this, the French created, wittingly or unwittingly, a much stronger
defense than they had at the beginning of the battle when their infantry
defended carefully prepared positions. This informal "defense in depth"
proved quite resistant to attacks by infantry battalions in skirmish lines,
even if it was preceded by a wave of grenade-throwing storm troops. A different approach was needed.

The response of the artillery was to change the way that it shifted its fire
from one set of targets to another. For the first two years of the war, the
German artillery fired primarily upon known targets. For most guns and
howitzers, this meant known enemy trenches. As the advancing German
infantry approached a trench being bombarded, artillery observers, either those positioned on high ground overlooking the battlefield or those
advancing with the infantry, would signal their batteries to shift fire to
the next trench line. This system worked well at Soissons, Gorlice-
Tarnow,[31] and other battles where the enemy kept to his trenches. When,
however, the positions of the enemy could be located anywhere in a given
zone, artillery firing on known trench lines would miss the bulk of the
defenders.

The solution to this problem was found in the "rolling barrage." Recognizing that the most significant tactical effect of artillery fire is the temporary suppression of enemy troops rather than the destruction of any
particular target,[32] German artillerymen at Verdun started placing fire on
the ground *between* enemy trenches. The artillery support of the attack-

ing infantry would thus begin with a standing barrage in "no man's land." At a predetermined time—what we would now call "H-hour"—the barrage would "jump" forward one or two hundred meters. Simultaneously, the attacking infantry would leave their jumping off positions and start moving forward. The barrage would then jump forward another one or two hundred yards every two to four minutes according to a prearranged schedule until it lay beyond the infantry's final objective.

If everything went according to plan, the exploding shells of the rolling barrage would keep enemy troops from using their weapons until a few seconds before the Germans were on top of them. In other words, the Germans would be able to repeat, against a well dispersed enemy, the success they had enjoyed on the first day of the battle of Verdun against Frenchmen who, as a rule, had kept to their dugouts and trenches. The difficulty with the rolling barrage, however, was coordinating its movement with that of the infantry. Artillery officers and NCOs serving as forward observers still advanced with the first waves of the attacking German infantry and were equipped with means with which to communicate orders to slow down a rolling barrage that was advancing. The signal rockets, telephones, and, on occasion, messenger dogs and homing pigeons, that the artillery forward observers used, however, were not very reliable. As a result, the rolling barrage that "got away" from infantry that was advancing too slowly or, conversely, held up infantry that was moving more rapidly than had been expected, were far more common than the attack where infantry and artillery fire advanced at the same pace.[33]

Because of these difficulties in coordination, the rolling barrage could not be expected to do for the German infantry of 1916 any more than the standing barrages of Soissons and Gorlice-Tarnow had done for the German infantry of 1915. The bulk of the work of fighting through a defense in depth remained the job of the attacking infantry, and in order to succeed against decentralized defensive tactics they would have to further decentralize their own offensive tactics.

One aspect of this further progress of decentralization was what the French called "infiltration."[34] The *Stosstrupps* of the first wave, as well as the rifle squads and machine gun teams of subsequent waves, pushed deep into the French positions wherever they could without insisting that the units on their flanks be able to make the same progress. These small units, led by NCOs and junior officers, were able to strike at groups of Frenchmen from the flanks or rear, and, in the case of machine guns, interdict the movement of men and supplies within the French defensive zone. The Germans, who seem to have done this naturally and without much discussion, had no name for this breakdown of the skirmish line.

Despite the lack of a German name, the tactics of bypassing strong points, pushing deep into an enemy position and attacking the enemy on his flanks and rear were regularly taught to units coming into the battle for the first time by officers and NCOs from units that had already fought at Verdun. Like the formations that were at Verdun at the beginning of the battle, reinforcing divisions were given time to train before being sent into battle. While some of this training included traditional subjects— bayonet fighting, for example—the bulk consisted of putting to use the lessons recently learned.

The Bavarian Life Guards Regiment, one of the three regiments of the Alpine Corps, an elite mountain division that was transferred to the Fifth Army on May 1, 1915, spent that entire month training for Verdun. The program began with the training of individual guardsmen as grenade throwers, moved to the work of "rolling up" trenches, attacking strong points from the flanks and rear, and the rapid occupation and rebuilding of captured enemy trenches to live fire exercises of battalions, regiments, and finally the whole division on elaborate dummy trench systems.[35]

FLEURY

The Life Guards put this training to work on June 23, 1916, when they took part in an attack of the reinforced Alpine Corps against French positions centered on the village of Fleury, an attack that was part of a six-division attack that was the most ambitious operation of the whole Verdun campaign. Encouraged by the delivery of large amounts of "Green Cross" ammunition—shells containing the very poisonous diposgene gas which the French masks could not, at that time, filter out—the Fifth Army headquarters planned an advance of all six participating divisions on a front of five and a half kilometers to a depth of as many as six kilometers. The major defect of the plan, however, was that the Green Cross ammunition could only be used against the rearward positions of the French. Thus, while it could be used with good effect to suppress the French battery positions, it was of no help in breaking through the zone of the French infantry.[36]

The bombardment of the Alpine Corps' objective, a one-kilometer-wide hill anchored on the right by the Chapitre Woods[37] and on the left by two small forts, began on the morning of June 22. In the sector of the Alpine Corps alone, 26 batteries of heavy artillery reinforced the division's organic field artillery regiment, firing a mixture of high explosive and Green Cross poison gas shells both on the objective and on the "no man's land" between the objective and the German lines.[38] At seven on the morning of the 23rd, the intensity of fire increased, the gas gave way entirely to high explosive, and the fire that had filled "no man's land" was shifted forward to provide a rolling barrage to lead the Life Guards across "no man's land." At the same time, a portion of the heavy guns and howitzers continued shelling Fleury.[39]

At eight, the Life Guards advanced with three battalions (the 2nd, the

3rd, and an attached *Jäger* battalion) in line and a fourth (the 1st) in reserve. The 2nd Battalion of the Life Guards, in the center of the first line, was reinforced by two *Stosstrupps* from the Assault Detachment "Rohr" and 20 pioneers. The two other battalions of the first line were each reinforced with one *Stosstrupp* and 20 pioneers while the reserve battalion had a full platoon of pioneers and four light trench mortars attached. The 24 or so available machine guns—from the machine gun company of the *Jäger* battalion, the regimental machine gun company of the Life Guards, and an independent machine gun detachment attached to the Life Guards—were, with the exception of six or so that were kept with the reserve battalion, distributed among the rifle companies.[40]

The first obstacle in the path of the advancing Life Guards was a pair of French machine guns so located as to be able to enfilade the attacking skirmish lines. Unlike the Brandenbergers of the 5th Infantry Division, however, the Bavarians had equipped their first wave with the means of dealing with such a threat. An NCO moving forward with the first wave quickly brought two machine guns into position and succeeded in suppressing the French fire until the Life Guards had passed through. Other French machine guns, these located in the "no man's land" that had felt the brunt of the German preparatory bombardment, showed themselves long enough to kill a handful of Germans before they too were silenced by the Life Guards of the first line. By 8:30, the Life Guards had reached the railroad track that marked the northern edge of the village of Fleury.

Once upon the objective, however, the Life Guards ran into a far more powerful hindrance—a curtain of heavy artillery fire set down by their own guns. The plans for the operation had called for the Life Guards to signal, by means of colored rockets, their readiness to have the barrage shifted to the rear. The small rockets that they fired could not be seen through the dust and smoke and the firing apparatus for the high altitude rockets had been lost in the fighting in "no man's land." The Life Guards were stuck for the better part of an hour until one of the men detailed to carry a high altitude rocket launched it from his hand. The barrage lifted and the Life Guards began the battle for the village itself.[41]

A large number of Frenchmen, extraordinarily well equipped with machine guns that had come fresh from the factory into the battle, sheltering in cellars beneath the ruins of the village, survived the German bombardment. To clear the cellars of Fleury, the Life Guards broke up into small teams and used a modified version of the "rolling up" technique they had practiced so often in May. Although sometimes they could rely on a friendly machine gun to suppress a known French position, most of the time the *Stosstrupps,* official or ad hoc, relied on the skillful movement through the rubble to protect themselves from the very machine guns they were hunting.[42]

At about ten in the morning, the ability of the German guns assigned to counter-battery work to keep the French battery positions "stoked" with gas was waning rapidly. At the same time that the Germans were running low on gas shells, the day was growing hotter, causing a more rapid dissipation of the diphosgene into the atmosphere than had been planned for.[43] By 10:30 the French artillery was back in action, filling the one-kilometer-long trail between the German jumping off points and the village of Fleury full of explosions that took a great toll of the reserve battalion that the commander of the Life Guards had sent to occupy the village.[44]

Although the Life Guards managed to take complete control of Fleury, the failure of the German artillery to maintain fire superiority and the failure of other German units to attain the same degree of success left them exposed on the top of a hill surrounded on three sides by the French. The machine guns and ammunition that they captured at Fleury, however, were put to good use in the defense of the village against French counterattacks that took place over the next three weeks. Despite French harassing fire and the fact that there were still a number of active French machine guns in the Chapitre Woods, the reserve battalion with its trench mortars and machine guns was able to join the rest of the regiment for the long defensive battle.[45]

ASSAULT GROUP IN RESERVE

An interesting variation on these tactics was used by the Bavarian Ersatz Division in the late spring and summer of 1916. Companies deployed in thin skirmish lines moved forward until they ran into a strong point that they could not easily reduce themselves. The company commander would then call forward an "assault group," an improvised unit consisting of one to three infantry squads, portable flamethrower teams, pioneers armed with explosives, machine guns, and light trench mortars. The assault group would then use techniques developed by the Assault Detachment "Rohr" to systematically reduce the strong point. This job completed, the skirmish lines would move forward again and the assault group would return to its position in the rear of the attacking battalion.

This method was first used in May of 1916. On July 7 of that year, following an artillery bombardment that lasted only 75 minutes, the Bavarian Ersatz Division captured a position with a front of 1800 meters. In 25 minutes the attacking infantry had overrun the four lines of resistance that the French had established in the sector. The certainty that bypassed strongpoints would be reduced by the assault groups permitted the riflemen to push deep into the French position wherever the French were weak. The attack was only stopped when the Bavarians encountered counterattacking French troops that had been effected neither by the artillery preparation nor the shock of finding themselves cut off, bypassed, and surrounded.[46]

The practice of putting the bulk of a unit's combat power into an "assault group" that followed rather than preceded a light skirmish line does not seem to have become standard at this time. The depth to which a German unit was expected to penetrate into any enemy position—three or four hundred meters at most—and the opportunities for detailed reconnaissance, made it possible to select before the attack the most likely enemy strong points and detail *Stosstrupps* to reduce them far ahead of time. There were occasions, as somebody in the Bavarian *Ersatz* Division obviously recognized, where it would be impossible to discover an enemy strongpoint until its garrison actually started firing. In those cases, the job of the skirmish line was not to consolidate the gains of the *Stosstrupps* but rather to carry out a "reconnaissance in force."

OVERVIEW

The attack of the Bavarian *Ersatz* Division on July 7 was one of the last major attacks of the German offensive. On July 11, Crown Prince William ordered his divisions to cease all offensive actions. The British were attacking on the Somme and all available resources would be needed for the defensive battle there. In terms of attrition, Falkenhayn had achieved his immediate strategic objective of bleeding the French. 400,000 Frenchmen who were in the ranks of the French Army at the beginning of the battle were either dead, wounded to the point where further military service was impossible, or prisoners of war. It had not been the German artillery alone that achieved this, however, but the German infantry. And to achieve such gains, they had to expose themselves to the fire of the French artillery, which was just beginning to supplement its field guns with howitzers. As a result, for every three Frenchmen rendered hors de combat, the Germans had lost two of their own soldiers.

The reason was not any failure of German tactics, which had made a great deal of progress since the early months of the war, but rather of Falkenhayn's inability to execute his strategy of attrition. Beginning with Crown Prince William and his chief of staff, the leaders of the Fifth Army never fully understood Falkenhayn's concept for the battle. The operations order drafted by Schmidt von Knobelsdorf and signed by William converted the operation into a series of attacks with limited objectives, the ultimate goal of which was the elimination of the French salient.[47] While these leaders of the Fifth Army realized that artillery was to do most of the work and that they should economize their infantry,[48] they failed to grasp that the ultimate objective was killing Frenchmen rather than seizing terrain. Thus, on the second day of the battle, Schmidt von Knobelsdorf enthusiastically gave permission for some units to push beyond the first day's objective, even though that advance did nothing to further Falkenhayn's strategy.

Given Falkenhayn's inability to communicate with Crown Prince William and Knobelsdorff, it is not surprising that four echelons of command below Falkenhayn's High Command and three below William's Fifth Army division commanders, like that of the 6th Infantry Division, should revert to the terrain-dominated fighting of 1915 and order the seizure of the day's objective "cost what it may." The same can be said for regimental and battalion commanders. Even more so than the division commanders, these officers had spent a year specializing in the taking of ground. Although they did it well, tactical skill could not take the place of strategy.

In the larger scheme of things, then, Verdun must be counted as a German defeat. Although France might take two generations to recover culturally from the losses suffered at Verdun, it's military recovery was almost immediate. The French and British Empires provided more than enough replacements for those lost at Verdun whereas the German soldiers that fell at Verdun could only be replaced by the marginally fit, the very young, and slackers combed from previously exempted occupations.

Insofar as the technique of taking an enemy trench was concerned, little new had been learned at Verdun. The attacks with limited objectives of 1915, being interspersed with periods of rest and retraining, had provided a far better laboratory for new tactics than the continuous fighting at Verdun. At the squad and company level, Verdun simply confirmed what "state of the art" German officers already knew, that the key to success in attacking a trench was close coordination of heavy weapons at the lowest possible level and excellence in close combat on the part of squads capable of moving and fighting as independent units. The training period that preceded each infantry unit's introduction to combat at Verdun, however, exposed a large number of German infantrymen to the techniques of the Assault Detachment "Rohr." Those that survived the fighting at Verdun provided their units with an organic cadre of officers, NCOs, and men proficient in Rohr's method.

At a slightly higher level, however, where the techniques of the *Stosstrupp* were strung together into a tactical system for pushing deep into an enemy position, Verdun provided the German Army with many valuable lessons. The greatest of these was a refined sense of the capabilities and limitations of artillery fire. While there were occasions when artillery fire alone succeeded in causing the occupants of a strong point to raise a white flag or run to the rear, in most cases French soldiers survived bombardments of unprecedented ferocity with their ability and will to fight intact. At the same time Verdun gave German soldiers an understanding of the ability of artillery fire to suppress enemy action until the point where the advance of German infantry made that action impossible.

More so than other engagements, the attack against the Fleury heights provided insights into what happens to a battle when one unit pushes far deeper into the enemy position than others. The first insight was that such an operation was possible. While the French machine guns in the woods were certainly a nuisance, they were quickly suppressed by German machine guns moving with the second wave and thus failed to prevent the Life Guards from accomplishing their mission. The second insight was the limitation of centralized artillery fire. The three battalions of the Life Guards that took Fleury were armed with nothing more than rifles, machine guns, and hand grenades. That the Life Guards could have done a lot more if they had more control over their artillery fire—either through closer coordination of indirect fire or the provision of a direct fire capability in the form of infantry guns—was a point not lost on them.[49]

Another noteworthy innovation was the "assault group" technique used by the Bavarian *Ersatz* Division. This was the precursor to the tactics of late 1917 and 1918, where small infantry units equipped with the means of providing their own fire support bypassed strong points in order to attack deep in the enemy position, or at the very least took those strong points from the flanks or rear. While nothing that the "assault groups" of the Bavarian *Ersatz* Division did would have been a surprise to someone who had served with the Assault Detachment "Rohr" during the latter half of 1915, the mere fact that such tactics were being practiced by ordinary infantry was indicative of a trend that would continue.[50]

After Verdun, the German Army in the West returned to the defensive posture of 1915. Once again offensive actions were restricted to small scale attacks "with limited objectives" and trench raids. While these actions did little to effect the eventual outcome of the war, they did provide another two years "in the laboratory" for the German infantry, and, in particular, for the Assault Detachment.

NOTES

1.   Konrad Krafft von Dellmensingen, *Der Durchbruch. Studie an Hand der Vorgänge des Weltkrieges 1914–1918* (Hamburg: Hanseatische Verlagsanstalt, 1937), p. 346. Hereafter referred to as Krafft von Dellmensingen, *Der Durchbruch*.

2.   Germany. Reichskriegsministerium. *Die Operationen des Jahres 1916 bis zum Wechsel in der obersten Heeresleitung* (Berlin: E.S. Mittler, 1936), p. 61. This work, the tenth volume in the official series *Der Weltkrieg 1914–1918* prepared by former members of the Historical Section of the German General Staff who were

hidden after the Treaty of Versailles in various civil bureaus, is hereafter referred to as *Der Weltkrieg 1914–1918,* vol. 10.

3.   Beginning in February 1915, the German War Ministry reorganized the German infantry division. One infantry regiment and one light field gun battalion were removed from existing divisions and used to form new formations. At the same time, the number of guns in a light field gun battalion were reduced from 18 to 12. This left the typical German infantry division with three infantry regiments and one artillery regiment of two light field gun battalions and one light field howitzer battalion. von Kuhl, *The Execution and Failure,* p. 112.

4.   *Der Weltkrieg 1914–1918,* vol. 10, pp. 60–62.

5.   From an administrative point of view, the heavy artillery was totally separate from the field artillery. It had its own inspector who reported directly to the Kaiser, its own regiments, and its own school system. In the field, however, units of the two branches were directly subordinated to the senior artillery officer of the division, corps, or army. For more on the history of the German heavy artillery, see Georg Bruchmüller, *Die Deutsche Artillerie in den Durchbruchschlachten des Weltkrieges* (Berlin: E.S. Mittler und Sohn, 1922) passim, hereafter referred to as Bruchmüller, *Durchbruchschlachten.*

6.   Krafft von Dellmensingen, *Der Durchbruch,* p. 346.

7.   H. Schöning, *Leib-Grenadier Regiment,* p. 159.

8.   *Der Weltkrieg 1914–1918,* vol. 10, p. 62.

9.   I assume this was possible because the extremely high angle of fire of these weapons made "short" rounds less probable. While the German literature of World War I is full of references to "short" shells from light field guns and howitzers, I have yet to find an incident where a heavy mortar shell caused "friendly" casualties.

10.   Krafft von Dellmensingen, *Der Durchbruch,* p. 346.

11.   See, for example, Karl Witte, *3. Rheinisches Pionier-Bataillon Nr. 30* (Berlin: Gerhard Stalling, 1928), pp. 112–25.

12.   Krafft von Dellmensingen, *Der Durchbruch,* p. 346.

13.   One gun in the Caures Woods required 20 rounds worth of "near misses" to achieve a direct hit on a single machine gun nest. H. Kurz, "Geschütz und Maschinengewehr," in Albert Benary, ed., *Das Ehrenbuch der Deutschen Feldartillerie* (Berlin: Verlag Tradition Wilhelm Kolk), pp. 373–74.

14.   Cordt von Brandis, *Der Sturmangriff. Kriegserfahrungen eines Frontoffiziers* (n.p., 1917), p. 3.

15.   Ludwig Gold, *Die Tragödie von Verdun 1916 I* (Berlin: Gerhard Stalling, 1926), pp. 53–54.

16.   I have yet to run into a source that tells me how close "right up" to a barrage is. I would guess that any closer than 30 or 40 meters from the point of impact would result in the attacking infantry being hit by a large number of splinters. In a German training film from the early days of World War II, pioneers are shown advancing so closely behind a barrage that clumps of earth thrown up by the exploding shells fall on them.

17.   The trench mortars and heavier guns had a much slower rate of fire.

18.   Reports of these largely bloodless victories filtering back to the French High Command led to speculation that the German infantry had "infiltrated"

into the French positions. The idea that the German infantry were infiltrating is ridiculed in an unsigned article, "Die Deutsche Taktik bei Verdun," *Militär-Wochenblatt,* Nr. 66/67, 1916, pp. 1610–12.

19.   Crown Prince Wilhelm, "Befehl für die Angriffskorps: 27/1/16," reprinted in Gold, *Die Tragödie von Verdun,* pp. 258–59.

20.   U.S. Army War College, *Notes on Recent Operations No. 2* (Washington, DC: Government Printing Office, 1917), p. 35.

21.   When Crown Prince Wilhelm, who was generally considered to be less than a serious soldier, took over command of the Fifth Army, the Kaiser gave him strict instructions to heed the instructions of Schmidt von Knobelsdorf: *"Was er dir rät, mußt du tun!"* Crown Prince Wilhelm, "Befehl für die Angriffskorps," p. 4.

22.   Adolphe Goutard, "Verdun 21 Février—4 Mars 1916: Le contraire d'une ruée," in *Verdun 1916. Actes du colloque international sur la bataille. 6–7–8 Juin 1975* (Verdun: Association Nationale de Souvenir de la Bataille de Verdun, University de Nancy II, 1975), p. 85.

23.   Ibid., pp. 103–06.

24.   Reymann, *Das Infanterie Regiment,* p. 93.

25.   During the first of these attacks, the 1st Battalion of the 8th Life Grenadier Regiment was "morally broken down" by such artillery fire and had to be pulled out to serve as the division reserve battalion. Schöning, *Leib-Grenadier Regiment,* p. 167.

26.   Schönfeldt, *Das Grenadier Regiment,* pp. 77–78.

27.   Ibid., p. 166.

28.   Gruss, *Aufbau und Verwendung,* pp. 28–29.

29.   Ibid., pp. 29–31.

30.   It was Verdun that provided the scene for almost all of the 150 attacks involving flamethrowers that had taken place between the introduction of the weapon and July 1916.

31.   See Chapter 7.

32.   The exception here, of course, is the effect of the "super heavy" artillery, particularly the heavy siege mortars. Capable of gouging a hole in the earth large enough to shelter a platoon, these were used by the Germans throughout both World War I and World War II to destroy point targets. See, for example, their use at Verdun on June 1, 1916, described in von Cochenhausen, "Artillery Preparation Fire in Trench and Open Warfare" in Schwarte, ed., *War Lessons,* pp. 115–16 and 130–31.

33.   von Cochenhausen, "Artillery Preparation Fire," in Schwarte, ed. *War Lessons,* passim.

34.   Unsigned article, "Die Deutsche Taktik bei Verdun," *Militär-Wochenblatt,* Nr. 66/67, 1916, pp. 1610–12.

35.   Ritter von Reiß et al., *Das Königlich Bayerische Infanterie Leib Regiment im Weltkrieg, 1914–1918* (Munich: Max Schick, 1931), pp. 147–50.

36.   Krafft von Dellmensingen, *Der Durchbruch,* pp. 371–74.

37.   These had been under attack by *Jäger* battalions reinforced by flamethrowers and *Stosstrupps* from the Assault Detachment "Rohr" since June 21 but were not fully cleared by the twenty-third. *Reserve-Jäger-Bataillon Nr. 4,* p. 167.

38.   This artillery fire came so close to the German jumping-off positions that it caused casualties among the German infantry.

39.   This was one of the first German uses of Green Cross shells. Von Reiß et al., *Das Königlich Bayerische Infanterie Leib Regiment*, pp. 161–62. See Chapter 5 for a detailed description of German gas shells.

40.   Ibid., pp. 161–64.

41.   Ibid., pp. 165–66.

42.   Ibid., p. 166.

43.   Krafft von Dellmensingen, *Der Durchbruch*, pp. 374–75.

44.   Von Reiß et al., *Das Königlich Bayerische Infanterie Leib Regiment*, pp. 165–66.

45.   Ibid., pp. 165–66.

46.   Balck, *Entwickelung*, p. 99.

47.   Krafft von Dellmensingen, *Der Durchbruch*, p. 344.

48.   "During this bombardment the attack troops of the corps . . . are to be deployed so as to limit to the greatest degree possible damage to the infantry," Crown Prince Wilhelm, "Befehl für die Angriffskorps" (in Gold, *Die Tragödie von Verdun)*, p. 258.

49.   The regimental history of the Life Guards makes this point in emphasized type. Von Reiß et al., *Das Königlich Bayerische Infanterie Leib Regiment*, p. 167.

50.   The use of a light skirmish line ahead of the main striking force was also a direct ancestor to the "surface and gap" *(Flächen und Lückentaktik)* tactics used so effectively by the German infantry in World War II. "Surface and gap" tactics are also called "reconnaissance pull" tactics because the focus of the attack is not determined during the planning phase but rather in the course of the battle as the light forces leading the attack discover more about the enemy disposition. See Michael D. Wyly, "Fundamentals of Tactics" in William S. Lind, *Maneuver Warfare Handbook* (Boulder, CO: Westview Press, 1985), pp. 73–80.

5

Expansion

It is no contradiction that we like to call ourselves condottieri and feel a strange affinity with those adventurous spirits who had so much blood in their veins that any pretext and any flag was a proper excuse for spilling it.

Ernst Jünger,
The Storm of Steel

The experience of the Assault Detachment during the early part of the battle of Verdun not only demonstrated the value of the tactics that it had developed but also underlined the inherent difficulty of the unit's double assignment. The use of the Assault Detachment as a combat unit interfered with its responsibility for training other units in its methods. The War Ministry's first response to this problem, undoubtedly brought to its attention by Colonel Bauer, was to increase the size of the Assault Detachment. The number of pioneer companies was raised to four and the machine gun platoon was traded for a machine gun company of six heavy machine guns. Still more firepower was provided in the form of a mountain gun battery equipped with Ehrhardt 7.5cm mountain guns. On April 1, 1916, the larger unit was redesignated Assault Battalion "Rohr" (see Illustration 4).

Concurrently with the expansion of the Assault Detachment, four *Jäger* Battalions were to be converted into Assault Battalions on the model of Captain Rohr's unit. This would be a relatively easy process. Because the *Jäger* Battalions were free-standing units,[1] their conversion would not disrupt the organization of any regiment or division. The *Jäger* Battalions, moreover, already possessed an organic machine gun company of 12 machine guns and four rifle companies. All that would have to be added in the way of troops would be men needed to fill the trench mortar, infantry gun, and flamethrower units.

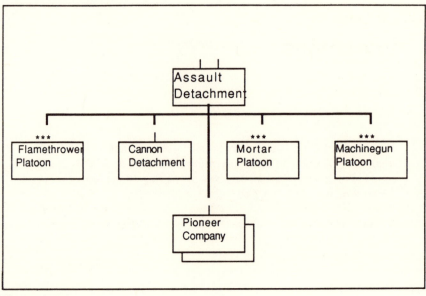

Illustration 4
Assault Detachment "Rohr," September 9, 1915

More important than organizational convenience was the natural pre-disposition of the *Jäger* troops toward stormtroop tactics. The *Jäger* Battalions had their home garrisons in the mountainous and wooded areas of Germany. For centuries, *Jäger* officers had sought to recruit hunters, foresters, and other outdoorsmen into their units. (The very word *Jäger* means "hunter".) While the onward march of civilization and the expansion of the number of *Jäger* Battalions made it difficult to completely exclude farmers and even city dwellers, the influence of the mountaineers and the woodsmen remained strong until the end of the war.

The tactics of the *Jäger* Battalions, building on the spirit of self-reliance of the *Jäger* troops themselves, tended to be more open and fluid than those of the line infantry. In the eighteenth and early nineteenth centuries *Jäger* units had been armed with rifles and trained to fire aimed shots at a time when other foot soldiers carried muskets and were considered mere cogs in a "walking battery." This tendency towards open order tactics had been reinforced by the guerilla warfare experience of the many *Jäger* who took part in the American War of Independence. Captain Rohr, who had served with both *Jäger* and line infantry units, was certainly aware that the traditional *Jäger* virtues of self-reliance and fluid movement on the battlefield would facilitate the conversion of *Jäger* battalions into Assault Battalions.

REPLACEMENTS

From the point of view of the War Ministry, which was responsible for the organization of the German Army and would issue the orders for the conversion of the *Jäger* units into Assault Battalions, the most important consideration in the decision was the question of personnel replacements. Each permanent unit (regiment or independent battalion) in the German Army was associated with a certain town or district from which it drew recruits. In wartime, a small cadre of officers and NCOs would remain in this home district to conduct basic training for new recruits and refresher training for reservists and men returning from hospitals and agricultural leave. This depot system ensured that replacements sent to units at the front spoke the same dialect as the troops beside whom they would be fighting and were at least partially socialized.

Not being a permanent unit, the Assault Detachment had to draw its replacement personnel from the depots of other units. As a result, it had often been used as a dumping ground for men that other units were only too happy to be rid of. Needless to say, these men were rarely suitable candidates for membership in what was supposed to be an elite assault unit. Weeding out these misfits and molding the rest into a cohesive unit had taken a great deal of time and effort. By building the new Assault Battalions on the foundation of old *Jäger* Battalions, this problem could be avoided.

The Assault Battalion "Rohr" set up a training course at Beauville, a town east of Verdun that served as its home for most of the war, for officers and selected NCOs[2] of the four *Jäger* Battalions that had been chosen by the War Ministry for conversion. The curriculum for the two-week-long training course was similar to that which Captain Rohr had used to train officers and NCOs of other units. Before the course ended, however, Rumania had entered the war on the side of the Allies and a force had to be hastily assembled to reinforce the hard-pressed Austro-Hungarians. Three of the four *Jäger* Battalions were withdrawn from the conversion program and shipped to the Rumanian front. The remaining unit, the 3rd *(Brandenburg) Jäger* Battalion was redesignated the 3rd *Jäger*-Assault Battalion (*Jäger-Sturm-Batallion*) on August 4, 1916.

In the course of becoming the second assault battalion, the 3rd *Jäger* Battalion had transferred out 500 officers, NCOs, and men who were considered physically unfit for duty as stormtroopers. They were replaced by a draft of younger men who could more easily submit to the rigorous two-month training program that the graduates of Captain Rohr's course set up for the entire battalion. The chief feature of this training program was repeated live fire exercises on a dummy trench system that had been built in the battalion training area. As had been the case with the first assault battalion, the Mauser rifles (M1898) that had equipped the old *Jäger* battalion were replaced with Mauser carbines, the jackboots were exchanged for mountain boots and puttees, and the steel helmet became the standard headgear for battle.

The organic supporting arms of the new Assault Battalion consisted of an infantry gun battery (six converted Russian field guns), a trench mortar detachment (eight light trench mortars), and a flamethrower platoon (six light flamethrowers). In addition, the battalion was provided with five trucks, rare and precious items in those largely horsepowered times. These would allow detachments from the Assault Battalion to remain fresh until a few hours before they began their assault.[3]

LOWER ECHELON ASSAULT DETACHMENTS

Increasing the number of Assault Battalions from one to two was hardly sufficient to meet the needs of the German Army for instruction in trench warfare. General von Falkenhayn recognized this and, on May 15, 1916, he ordered the Second, Third, Fourth, Sixth, and Seventh Armies, as well as Army Detachment Strantz, to each send two officers and four NCOs to Assault Battalion "Rohr" for training. Upon their return, these officers and NCOs were to train company and platoon-size elite assault units within their respective divisions and regiments. The existence of these units would give each army the ability to form ad hoc assault detachments by bringing them together and providing them with machine guns, flamethrowers, trench mortars, and infantry guns from each army's reserve.

While these provisional units would be used in attacks with limited objectives, they would find most of their employment in trench raiding—nocturnal forays into enemy trenches in order to gather information, capture prisoners, destroy fortifications, avenge an enemy raid, or just "shake things up." Organized trench raiding seems to have been introduced by men of the 1st and 2nd Battalions of the Garhwali Rifles, units of the Indian Corps serving with the British Expeditionary Force in France. Fierce mountain men who had been trained from childhood to sneak into enemy camps and cut throats, the Garhwalis were troops of such high quality that they were traditionally brigaded with Ghurkhas. Other British Empire contingents, particularly those of the "White Dominions",[4] soon picked up the practice. By the end of 1914, the Germans and the French had also begun raiding across "no man's land."

The practice of forming special units for trench raiding did not originate with General von Falkenhayn's order of May 15, 1916. In the second half of 1915 and the first half of 1916, a number of regiments and divisions had formed such units on their own initiative. The impetus for the formation of these units seems initially to have come from the view that the hand grenade, the chief personal weapon of the trench raider, was a specialist's weapon. In December 1915, the commanding officer of the

3rd Battalion of the 235th Reserve Infantry Regiment ordered the formation of a six-man hand grenade team (*Handgrenatentrupp*) in each platoon. These men, who were to be "courageous and expert handgrenade throwers" were given a distinctive badge to wear.[5]

Although these units often used methods similar to those developed by Captain Rohr,[6] they had a variety of names. Most popular were names that included the word "assault" (*Sturm*)—"assault company" (*Sturmkompagnie*) or "assault troop" (*Sturmtrupp*). Some names stressed the instructional role of the unit—"assault school" (*Sturmschule*) or "instruction detachment" (*Lehrabteilung*). While others—"hunting commando" (*Jagdkommando*)[7] and "raid troop" (*Patrouillentrupp*)—reflected the fact that the units were concerned primarily with raids across, and patrols within, "no man's land." Regardless of the name by which the units were known, the men belonging to them were usually referred to as "stormtroopers" (*Stosstruppen*).[8]

In some divisions, the elite assault units were controlled directly by the commanding general. On others, control was left in the hands of regimental and battalion commanders. The size, equipment, training, and status of the various assault units also differed greatly one from the other. Some assault units, particularly those at the division level, were permanent formations. The 400-man Assault Detachment (*Sturmabteilung*) of the Naval Corps[9] and the Assault Squadron (*Sturmeskadron*) of the 4th Dismounted Cavalry Division, for example, were close copies of the Assault Battalions. The men lived and trained apart from other units, received special rations and other privileges, and were often distinguished by special insignia.

The majority of assault units, however, were brought together only for missions and training. When the raid or the exercise was over, the men were returned to their parent companies. This practice prevented the loss of aggressive and energetic men from the line companies. The man who had the courage to cross "no man's land" night after night in search of hand-to-hand combat, after all, was not the kind of man a company commander wanted to lose.

THE STORMTROOPER SPIRIT

In most cases, the men who made up the elite assault units were volunteers. In other instances, particularly in those formations (*Landwehr* and *Landsturm*) made up mostly of older married men, the men for the assault units were chosen because of their youth, fitness, or bachelor status. Regardless of how they found their way into the assault unit, the young stormtroopers invariably developed a spirit that was at odds with that of the line infantry.

Trench warfare had turned the ordinary infantryman into a species of laborer. Most days were spent installing barbed wire, digging trenches, and carrying supplies. Nights were devoted to guard duty and the often unsuccessful attempt to find a suitable spot within the trench where one could catch a few hours of sleep. This routine was interrupted only by machine gun and artillery barrages, stray shells, and snipers—impersonal killers that denied the ordinary soldier the satisfaction of facing his enemy "man to man."

The stormtrooper, on the other hand, became an almost romantic figure. Like the fighter pilot or the U-boat sailor,[10] he could raise himself above the seemingly purposeless suffering of the trenches to strike directly at the enemy. While the ordinary soldier grew weary of the war and was kept in the ranks by a mixture of patriotism, coercion, and his own unwillingness to evade his duty, the stormtrooper often developed a lust for battle that the writer Ernst Jünger, himself the leader of a regimental *Stosstrupp,* equated with that of renaissance mercenaries.

The fact that some commanders formed stormtroop units on their own initiative as well as the enthusiasm with which many commanders executed the orders from higher echelons to form additional elite assault units suggests that "command interest" on the part of General von Falkenhayn was not the only motivation at work here. Something in the common experience of a number of different commanders in a number of different areas suggested to them that ordinary soldiers organized into ordinary units should not be used for the most demanding tasks of trench warfare. Using only the most aggressive men for the job of closing with the enemy and killing him at close range may have been necessary because of the fact that not all soldiers were capable of this sort of duty. Even regiments with no previously established elite assault units formed ad hoc units of their most aggressive men for the execution of a particularly difficult assignment.

Throughout the last century and a half, a number of observers have noted that the modern battlefield gives the soldier who does not wish to fight ample opportunity to avoid combat. During the Franco-Prussian War, one of the first conflicts where both sides were armed with breach-loading rifles, the German military writer Captain Fritz Hönig described the bunches of stragglers and shirkers that formed behind every attacking skirmish line. Those who had lost the will to fight hid behind trees; whole groups of leaderless men huddled together in hollows and depressions.[11]

In World War I this phenomenon manifested itself in the form of trench truces. Once the initial enthusiasm for the war died down, the troops in the trenches on both sides of "no man's land" tended to become more concerned with their own creature comforts than with killing the enemy.

In a quiet position everything is done to maintain, if at all possible, the calm. If one knocks out the opponents' bunkers or blockhouses, the other does the same, and both lay exposed under the open sky and no one has won anything. For this reason, orders for patrols to take prisoners find little approval and few volunteers. The opportunity is too slight and life seems too precious for such pettiness.[12]

The most blatant example of this policy of "live and let live" was the unofficial Christmas Truce of 1914, when British and German soldiers in the Ypres sector met in "no man's land," exchanged addresses, family photographs, and liquor and played soccer. Most expressions of the common sense pacifism of the front line troops, however, took less obvious forms. Patrols would go out to a safe spot in "no man's land" and sit. Shots would be fired at unoccupied positions and warnings would be given before artillery bombardments ordered by higher commands were to commence.

One way to interrupt these unseemly episodes of peace in the middle of a world war was to conduct raids using troops that were not part of the trench garrison. The "imported" raiders would feel no kinship with their victims, neither did they have any incentive to minimize damage out of fear of reprisal. On the contrary, the elite assault troops would be on their way back to their rest billets long before the retaliatory bombardment or "revenge raid" was launched.

Raiding units also helped to relieve the frustration felt by soldiers serving in an army on the strategic defensive. The news of a successful raid reported in a frontline newspaper,[13] passed at formation, or heard through the "grapevine" made the average soldier feel a certain vicarious satisfaction. At least someone was hitting back at the largely unseen forces that made his daily life both miserable and dangerous.

HIGH LEVEL SUPPORT

Until the fall of 1916, Colonel Bauer's chief ally in boosting the Assault Battalions had been Crown Prince William. In February of 1916 the Crown Prince had invited Captain Rohr to visit him at his headquarters and in March he observed a tactical exercise involving the entire Assault Detachment. On October 5 he even went so far as to write an order requiring that all infantrymen and pioneers under his command be trained as stormtroopers. His eventual goal was to make the elite assault units superfluous by bringing all infantry and pioneer units up to their standards of aggressiveness, physical fitness, and tactical skill. In the meantime, however, the Assault Battalion "Rohr" was his favorite unit.[14]

In September 1916, however, the assault units acquired a new patron, a man even more powerful than the son of the Emperor. While visiting the Crown Prince at his headquarters in Montmedy, General Erich Ludendorff reviewed a company of the Assault Battalion "Rohr" that was serving as an honor guard. Having served on the eastern front for almost two years, Ludendorff was largely ignorant of the tactics being developed in the West. At Montmedy he saw, for the first time, the steel helmets, the puttees and mountain boots, and the leather-patched uniforms of the stormtrooper. Intrigued, Ludendorff inquired about the nature of this new unit and soon began to see the possibilities of their style of fighting. Within a few days, he was converted to the idea that the stormtroopers should become the model for the rest of the German infantry.[15]

Like most officers trained in the German General Staff, General Ludendorff was a devotee of both tactical and operational maneuver. In his battles on the eastern front he had always sought the open flank and the opportunity to defeat the enemy by surrounding him, hitting him in many places, and convincing him that there was no alternative to surrender. This approach had brought him victory after victory against the Russians, national recognition, and quick promotion.

On August 29, 1916, a few days before his discovery of the Assault Battalion, Ludendorff had taken de facto command of the entire German Army.[16] Unlike his predecessor General von Falkenhayn, Ludendorff believed that the onset of trench warfare did not mean the end of the possibilities for operational maneuver in the West. The existence of the Assault Battalion "Rohr" further strengthened Ludendorff's belief that better tactics could lead to the rupture of a section of the Allied trench system and thus bring a return to the war of grand maneuvers. Influenced no doubt by this belief, Ludendorff signed an order on October 23, 1916, authorizing the formation of an assault battalion within each army on the western front.

By February 1917, 15 assault battalions[17] and two independent assault companies had been formed. Some of these had been formed by consolidating lower echelon assault units. Others were built up from scratch.[18] Like the two already existing assault battalions, the new units were to serve primarily as training schools for officers and men from line units, although all regularly contributed detachments for trench raids and attacks "with limited objectives."

While the strength of new Assault Battalions varied widely, they were all organized on the pattern of the first two assault battalions. Two to four assault companies were supported by one or two machine gun companies, a light trench mortar company, and infantry gun battery, and a flamethrower platoon. The infantry gun batteries were equipped with either mountain guns or the converted Russian 7.62cm field pieces. These batteries, which were part of a series of 50 independent infantry gun batteries, were initially trained by the infantry gun battery of the Assault Battalion "Rohr." The flamethrower platoons were likewise nominally independent units (they were detached from Major Reddemann's

Guard Reserve Pioneer Regiment) permanently attached to the assault battalions.

The two independent assault companies each consisted of three assault platoons, a machine gun platoon, and a light trench mortar platoon. Full-fledged army-level assault battalions in everything but size, they were numbered 13 and 18 in the same series as the assault battalions. (The assault battalions numbered 1, 4, 5, 6, 7, and 9 were assigned to armies bearing the same numbers. The 2nd Assault Battalion was assigned to the Third Army while the 3rd *Jäger*-Assault Battalion was assigned to the Second Army. The other assault battalions and companies were assigned to armies and army detachments that were designated by names rather than numbers.)

TECHNIQUE

Guidelines for the new assault battalions and lower echelon elite assault units were available in the form of *Instructions for the Employment of an Assault Battalion,* a short manual written by Captain Rohr and published on May 27, 1916. The *Instructions* stated that an assault battalion would habitually support infantry attacks by attaching assault teams (*Sturmtrupps*), consisting of four to eight stormtroopers under the command of an NCO, to infantry regiments and battalions. The task of each assault team was to lead infantry platoons and companies across "no man's land" and through the enemy wire, break into the enemy trench, roll it up with hand grenades, and destroy bunkers and machine gun nests with "ball charges."[19] Small infantry units—squads, half-platoons, and platoons would follow in irregular columns directly behind the assault teams. The use of skirmish lines was discouraged because of their vulnerability to enfilade fire from machine guns.

The main task of the supporting arms was to facilitate the movement of the attackers across "no man's land." Infantry guns fired on known machine gun and field piece positions. Machine guns protected the flanks of the attack and also attempted to suppress enemy machine guns. Trench mortars, grenade launchers,[20] and part of the supporting artillery provided the barrage on the enemy front line to suppress enemy riflemen, while the rest of the indirectly firing artillery laid a box barrage to isolate the objective and suppressed enemy guns and howitzers. The only supporting arm that moved up with the Assault Teams were the light flamethrowers, which were used to clear trenches. Because of the vulnerability of the fuel tank on the back of the flamethrower operator, however, Captain Rohr cautioned against using flamethrowers to lead an attack.

The barrage on the enemy front line was lifted at a predetermined moment. Within a few seconds of the detonation of the last shell, the Assault Teams would enter the enemy position as the designated points and begin clearing the trenches. The following infantry took possession of each trench as soon as it was cleared, despatched pockets of resistance, escorted prisoners and booty to the rear, and prepared to defend against the inevitable counterattack. Immediately behind the line infantry, the organic trench mortars and grenade launchers of the Assault Battalion would move forward to positions from which they could support the further prosecution of the attack.

A paraphrase of Captain Rohr's *Instructions* was incorporated into the December 1916 version of the *Training Manual for Foot Troops in War,* the first attempt by the War Ministry and the General Staff to replace that portion of the *Drill Regulations of 1906* which dealt with tactics.[21] *The Training Manual for Foot Troops in War* also contained, for the first time, the beginnings of official recognition that the column and skirmish line tactics of the prewar period were unsuited for trench warfare. Officers at the front, of course, had known this for two years or more and had trained their troops accordingly. Official recognition of this fact, however, meant an improvement in the training of recruits.

Since the beginning of the war, the basic training of recruits was conducted at the regimental depots in Germany by retired or convalescent officers and NCOs. Because these instructors often lacked experience or energy, the training that they imparted was antiquated and formalistic—lots of close order drill, to include goose stepping, bayonet fighting, and the line and column formations of the *Drill Regulations of 1906.* Recruits reporting to the front were often so badly prepared for conditions there, that divisions set up Field Recruit Depots. The instructors at the Field Recruit Depots were fresh from the trenches and were therefore able to pass on some of their experience. Replacing the *Drill Regulations of 1906* with the *Training Manual for Foot Troops in War* meant that recruits would start preparing for trench warfare before they left Germany.[22] This made the job of the Field Recruit Depots and the Assault Battalions somewhat easier, although the fact that the training areas in Germany were often in densely populated areas meant that the kind of dummy trench systems that were often set up at the Field Recruit Depots could not be erected near the regimental depots.[23]

PLANNED OBSOLESCENCE

Once the rest of the German infantry had been recreated in their image, the Assault Battalions would become redundant. Because of this, they were organized as provisional units, with no home barracks, no district from which to draw recruits, no connection to a particular locality, no genealogy like those which linked many other units in the German Army to eighteenth and even seventeenth century regiments,[24] and no colors. Home bases were provided in occupied France, Belgium, or Russia. The not insignificant losses suffered by the Assault Battalions were made up by calling for volunteers from other units. This "planned obsolescence," however, did not prevent the Assault Battalions from acquiring all of the trapping of elite units.

In March of 1917, the men of the Assault Battalions received the right to be addressed as "Grenadier."[25] Along with this title came the right to wear the "Guard braid" (*Gardelitzen*)—the twin roman numeral "I's" on the collar that hitherto had been the exclusive insignia of the Prussian Guard. The men of Assault Battalion "Rohr" received additional distinction in the form of a crown embroidered in silver thread on the lower left-hand sleeve of the jacket.[26]

More tangible recognition came in the form of double rations—not an inconsiderable privilege in the last two years of the war—and a liberal leave policy. The fact that they were always busy training also meant that the men of the Assault Battalions were freed of the fatigue and sentry duties that filled the days of the ordinary German soldier. To those familiar with Norse mythology, the world of a stormtrooper must have seemed like Valhalla—mock battle during the day and feasting at night.

The training programs of the Assault Battalions were quite different from those of the ordinary infantry. Close order drill, one of the mainstays of the prewar curriculum and the chief means by which the soldier was accustomed to obeying the voice of his officers, was largely though not entirely dispensed with. Its place was taken by exercises that cultivated rather than suppressed the initiative of the men. Half of each training day was usually devoted to sports. Some of these were "civilian" sports; running, gymnastics, and soccer were quite popular. Other sports had a more martial aspect; these included obstacle courses and grenade throwing contests.

The other half of the day was spent in the practice of various battle drills—crossing "no man's land," breaching barbed wire obstacles, clearing trenches, cooperating with flamethrowers, following closely behind a barrage, and the like were all practiced. These battle drills were often supplemented by live fire exercises, dress rehearsals for battle with reduced charge grenades and the frequent admonition to aim high. Needless to say, this sometimes resulted in casualties.

ELITE ASSAULT UNITS IN OTHER ARMIES

The conditions that had led to the formation of elite assault units were not unique to the Germans. The prewar tactics of all belligerents were manifestly unsuited for trench warfare in general and trench raiding in particular. In January of 1917, the French Army formed assault troops known as *grenadiers d'élite* or *groups francs.* In August of that year, the Russian Army formed a "Shock Battalion" in each division.[27]

Of all the countries allied against Germany, the Italians went the furthest to develop elite assault troops. As had been the case with the Germans, this development began with a single unit. In 1915, a single *compagnia di volontari della morte* (Company of the Volunteers of Death) was formed. In imitation of this unit, many infantry regiments formed *reparti di soldati arditi* (Detachments of Fearless Soldiers). By the end of 1916, each army, corps, and infantry regiment had a detachment of *arditi,* as did some battalions. After their defeat at the hands of the Germans and Austrians trained in stormtrooper tactics at Caporetto, the Italian Army decided to form an entire army corps of elite assault units.

While the enemies of Germany were often forced to discover for themselves the techniques of the German stormtroopers, Germany's allies could benefit from more direct tutelage. Beginning in September of 1916, Austro-Hungarian officers and NCOs regularly attended training courses offered by the assault battalions. In November of 1916, an Austro-Hungarian assault company was formed and attached to each of the German assault battalions on the eastern front.[28] Officers, NCOs, and stormtroopers trained this way provided the cadre for the assault companies that were formed in 1917 in most infantry regiments and mountain brigades of the Austro-Hungarian Army. For larger undertakings requiring expertise in stormtrooper tactics, the regimental assault companies were formed into an assault battalion directly subordinate to the division commander. In addition to the regimental assault companies, the division assault battalion usually contained an infantry gun platoon, a trench mortar section, and a grenade launcher section.[29]

There were many cases where the non-German assault units attained the same standard of efficiency and ferocity as their German counterparts. The effect of non-German assault units on the tactics of the ordinary infantry of their respective armies, however, was negligible. While the French *grenadiers d'élite* were conducting trench raids not unlike those of German stormtroopers, the ordinary French infantry was learning to rely more and more on week-long bombardments. The same can be said for the Italians, who copied the French doctrine of attrition while ignoring the experience of their own *arditi.*

NOTES

1. In peacetime, one *Jäger* Battalion was directly subordinate to each army corps. In war, *Jäger* Battalions were attached to cavalry divisions to perform such duties as the clearing of woods and villages, to infantry divisions to serve as extra battalions, and to inexperienced formations for "stiffening."

2. Each *Jäger* Battalion sent its commander, a captain, two lieutenants, and 12 NCOs.

3. Gruss, *Aufbau und Verwendung,* pp. 40–43.

4. Canada, New Zealand, Australia, South Africa. Troops from Rhodesia also developed reputations as fierce raiders, although, technically speaking, Rhodesia was a colony rather than a dominion.

5. Although the order for the formation of these teams indicates that the commander of the 3rd Battalion was more concerned about the use of hand grenades in defense rather than offense, the technique used—the "rolling up" of a trench—was applicable to both.

6. See Appendix A for a detailed description of a trench raid conducted by a lower echelon elite assault unit at this time.

7. "Hunting commandos" had been formed by the Russians during the Russo-Japanese War, a fact that was widely reported in the German military press of the time. The German use of the term seems to reflect a conscious imitation of the Russian practice.

8. The term *Stosstruppen* was coined by Captain Reddemann for the men of his light flamethrower teams. It was soon taken over, however, by the grenade-throwing members of elite assault units as a replacement for the earlier term *Sturmtruppen.*

9. The Naval Corps (*Marine Korps*) was composed of volunteers from the Navy led by naval officers and NCOs detached from the Army. The *Sturmabteilung* of the Naval Corps served both as a training unit and an elite assault unit. Bernard Ramcke, *Vom Schiffsjüngen zum Fallschirmjäger-General* (Berlin: Verlag der Wehrmacht, 1943), pp. 91–92. Later in the war, the *Sturmabteilung* of the Naval Corps was used as an NCO school. Privates who had taken part in a number of raids with the *Sturmabteilung* were promoted to the rank of corporal (*Gefreiter*) and detached for service with the assault detachments of line companies. U.S.A., General Headquarters, AEF, 2nd Section, General Staff. *Summary of Intelligence,* No. 69 (March 21, 1918).

10. It is worthy of note that while the German war bond posters of 1914, 1915, and 1916 used a knight on horseback to symbolize the German Army, a stormtrooper with a steel helmet, bloodshot eyes, and a bag full of hand grenades served as the "poster child" for the 1917 campaign.

11. The U.S. soldier and journalist S.L.A. Marshall documented a similar problem among U.S. servicemen in World War II. See S.L.A. Marshall, *Men Against Fire: The Problem of Command in Future War* (Gloucester, MA: Peter Smith, 1978).

12. Franz Schauwecker, *Im Todesrachen, Die Deutsche Seele im Weltkrieg* (Halle: Heinrich Diekmann, 1921), p. 264, translated and quoted in Eric J. Leed, *No Man's Land: Combat and Identity in WWI* (London: Cambridge University Press, 1979), p. 89.

13. One of these newspapers was even called *Der Stosstrupp* and had a regular feature titled "Stormtrooper Spirit" (*Stosstruppgeist*).

14. *Lieblingstruppe*—literally "darling unit."

15. D.J. Goodspeed, *Ludendorff, Genius of World War I* (Boston: Houghton, Mifflin Company, 1966), p. 194.

16. General Paul von Hindenburg succeeded to Falkenhayn's title of Chief of the General Staff. Ludendorff, with the custom-made title of First Quartermaster, made most of the decisions however.

17. Assault Battalion "Rohr," assigned to the Fifth Army, was numbered as the 5th Assault Battalion, while the 3rd *Jäger*/Assault Battalion retained its number even though it was assigned to the Second Army.

18. The task of training cadre for the new assault battalions was shared between the 3rd *Jäger*/Assault Battalion and the Assault Battalion "Rohr."

19. *Geballte Ladungen*—the heads of six "potato mashers" tied around a seventh complete "potato masher."

20. Referred to as "priests," the grenade launchers were short-range light spigot mortars that threw a small bomb a few hundred yards. They were organic to the Assault Companies.

21. Beginning in early 1916, the War Ministry and the General Staff collaborated on a series of manuals dealing with trench warfare. The first of these, *Mine Warfare,* dealt with subterranean warfare. Edgar Graf von Matuschka, "Organizationsgeschichte des Heeres, 1890–1918," *Handbuch zur Deutschen Militärgeschichte* 5 (Frankfurt am Main: Bernard and Graefe Verlag für Wehrwesen, 1968), p. 232.

22. The *Training Manual for Foot Troops in War* of December 1916 also contributed to Ludendorff's goal that all German infantrymen be retrained as stormtroopers. "As many officers and NCOs as possible," the manual stated, should undergo one of the training courses given by an Assault Battalion.

23. Matuschka, "Organizationsgeschichte," p. 232.

24. With the exception of some of the older Prussian and Bavarian regiments, these genealogies were somewhat artificial. Many of the German states, such as Hannover, that had fought against Prussia in 1866 found that, after their defeat, their armies were disbanded and the lineage of their regiments assumed by new units formed under Prussian officers.

25. The men of the Assault Battalion "Rohr" and the 3rd *Jäger*/Assault Battalion retained their old titles of "*Pionier*" and "*Jäger,*" respectively.

26. The men of the Flamethrower Platoons, because they retained their affiliation with the Guard Reserve Pioneer Regiment, continued to wear the insignia of that regiment—the silver skull and crossbones.

27. The major impetus for the formation of "Shock Battalions" may have been political rather than tactical. At this time, three months before the Bolshevist coup, the Russian Army was literally disintegrating.

28. For example, an assault battalion was formed within the Army Group of Archduke Charles, a mixed German and Austro-Hungarian formation. Numbering as the 17th German Assault Battalion, this unit was likewise composed of subjects of both the Hapsburg and Hohenzollern empires. The supporting arms companies and the 1st Assault Company contained Germans, while the 2nd Assault Company was Austro-Hungarian.

29. Franz Böltz, "Österreich-Ungarn 1914–1918: noch Organisation 1917–1918–Infanterie," *Der Feldgrau* 6, 1957, p. 122.

6

Organization and Technology

The hardiest sons of the war, the men who lead the stormtroop, and manipulate the tank, the aeroplane, and the submarine, are pre-eminent in technical accomplishment; and it is these picked examples of daredevil courage that represent the modern state of battle. These men of first-rate qualities with real blood in their veins, courageous, intelligent, accustomed to serve the machine, and yet, its superior at the same time, are the men, too, who show up best in the trench and in the shell holes.

Ernst Jünger,
Copse 125

The men of the assault battalions did not work in a vacuum. While they refined and taught their new tactics, other parts of the German Army did not stop their efforts to solve the riddle of trench warfare. Some of these solutions were evolutionary developments of techniques already in the German Army's repertoire or new uses for old weapons. Others resulted from the introduction of new weapons. Whatever their causes, these developments largely complemented and occasionally duplicated the work of the assault battalions. Thus, with each passing year of the war, the principles of independent action by small units and the coordination of supporting arms at the lowest levels became rooted ever more deeply in the German conception of the infantry attack.

The battles in the Argonne and the Vosges that so greatly influenced Captain Rohr's tactical thinking also had an influence on other officers in other units. Perhaps the most famous of these was First Lieutenant Erwin Rommel of the 124th (*Württemberg*) Infantry Regiment. In June 1915 he participated in an attack "with limited objectives" in which the tactics greatly resembled those of then as yet unformed assault battalions. The assault troops proper—those who would break into the enemy trench and clear it of the enemy—were distinguished from those soldiers detailed to follow the attack carrying ammunition and entrenching tools. The former were sent to the rear for a few days of rest and training so that they might be fresh for the attack, while the latter remained in the front lines as defensive troops.

As this attack was made before the introduction of infantry guns, and before large numbers of machine guns, flamethrowers, and trench mortars were available, artillery was the primary supporting arm in the attack. A box barrage was used to isolate the objective, while a curtain of fire was placed on the French front trench until the moment when the assault troops were ready to move into that trench. At that point, the fire was shifted to the second trench. Once the first trench was cleared, the process was repeated with the artillery being shifted to the third and last French trench.

Another attack conducted by the 124th Infantry Regiment that same summer was conducted using techniques even more similar to those of the assault battalions. The attacking troops were divided into small assault teams, each of which had a definite objective. Although these assault troops would begin their attack in a skirmish line, there was no requirement that they maintain that formation once the attack started. On the contrary, each team was commanded to push on to its objective regardless of the progress of the other teams.

At least one of the companies detailed for the attack, the one commanded by Lieutenant Rommel, had spent some time in the rear rehearsing the operation on a mock-up of the enemy position. This rehearsal allowed the assault teams to move in concert with the supporting artillery barrage.

The last shells struck close ahead of us, and, before the smoke cleared, our three assault teams rose noiselessly from their trenches and dashed for their objective on a front of 280 yards. The attack moved through the smoke and noise of the battlefield with the same precision shown in the rehearsals of the past few days.

Had these two attacks taken place in 1917 or 1918, they would not have been considered remarkable; in fact, they would have been something less than "state of the art." The fact that they took place in the summer of 1915, at a time when the first Assault Detachment was still concentrating its efforts on the 3.7cm assault cannon, however, indicates that Captain Rohr's ideas about tactics, while advanced for the time, were not entirely idiosyncratic. In the absence of evidence of significant contact between Captain Rohr or even the Guard Rifle Battalion and the 124th Infantry Regiment at this time (e.g., training courses, pamphlets, exchange of liaison officers, participation in the same battle), we must conclude that at least two separate units developed similar techniques independently of each other.

This evidence of parallel development also indicates that the same spirit of hard-headed analysis and innovation that animated Captain Rohr was also present in other German officers. This fits in with the way that German officers were trained. Rather than being asked to memorize prefabricated techniques or procedures, a student of tactics was placed in command of imaginary forces, presented with tactical dilemmas, and required to formulate his own orders. Each solution was judged, not against a preselected "school solution," but rather according to the keenness of the student's observations and the soundness of his thought process.

DEFENSIVE TACTICS

That more units did not develop their own solutions to the thorny tactical problems presented by position warfare is due more to lack of opportunity than lack of inclination. Until late 1917, the German Army was involved in two types of campaigns. In the east, it fought campaigns of operational maneuver. In the west, it was on the strategic defensive. In the former, where the concentrations of guns, machine guns, fortifications, and men that were common in the west rarely had the opportunity to form, there was little pressing need for better tactics. In the latter, the chief tactical problem was the defense rather than the taking of ground.

The assault battalions played only a minor role in the great defensive battles of 1916 and 1917. They were either in the rear areas training troops or somewhere else conducting a raid or attack "with limited objectives." The ordinary German infantry defending the trenches was therefore on its own. Nevertheless, in the course of these years, the German infantry developed a system of defensive tactics that placed emphasis on the same set of military virtues that were valued by the assault battalions.

The defensive tactics that the German Army took to war in 1914 paralleled the offensive tactics of the time. The key considerations were firepower and control. As many rifles as possible were to be placed in the firing line and kept under the close control of an officer. As holding ground was considered to be a matter of honor, this firing line was required to be inflexible in the face of the enemy. A commander might order a local withdrawal in the case of a heavy bombardment, but he was required to reoccupy his former positions the moment that the bombardment stopped.

In the winter of 1914–1915, the Germans, like the other belligerents, added depth to their defenses. Machine Gun Sharpshooter Detachments, their weapons often protected by concrete bunkers, were placed in a second line a thousand meters behind the first line. The effect of this simple expedient on an attacker could be devastating. On September 25, 1915, near Loos, a town not far from Ypres, two British infantry divisions broke through the first German line and ran into the second line. Caught between a battery of six light field guns and a handful of machine guns sited to catch an attacker in the flank, the British lost 8000 men. It was, to German observers, the Massacre of the Innocents in reverse. This time the British advanced in their antiquated formations and the German sharpshooters mowed them down.[1]

As the depth of the German defenses increased and the cost of defending the front line grew greater, the emphasis in German defensive tactics changed. Instead of trying to hold on to a piece of terrain whatever the cost, the key feature of the German defense became the timely counterattack to destroy the attacker at the moment when he was most off balance. By the end of 1917, the long thin trenches filled with riflemen standing shoulder to shoulder at parapets had been replaced with a checkerboard system of concrete bunkers and small forts that sheltered individual platoons, squads, and machine gun teams.[2] Additional squads, platoons, and companies were sheltered in larger bunkers behind the front line in readiness to mount small counterattacks against local breakthroughs. Like stormtroop leaders, the NCOs in command of these small forts often had to make decisions in the absence of orders. "The position of the NCO as group [squad] leader," wrote Ludendorff in his memoirs, "thus became more important. Tactics became more and more individualized."

The bulk of the defender's combat power, however, lay not in the concrete forts but rather remained thousands of meters to the rear of the forward positions. There, battalions, regiments, and even divisions would remain outside of the range of the attacker's artillery until they were called upon to make a decisive strike against the attacking infantry. As more and more of the troops involved in the defensive battle found themselves in the counterattack forces, the distinction between attack and defense blurred. The techniques taught by the assault battalions were as likely to be used in the counterattack as in the attack proper.

SUPPORTING ARMS

The defensive battles of 1916 and 1917 not only provided an atmosphere generally hospitable to the tactics of the assault battalions, they also resulted in a profound change in the way that the German infantry was organized (see Illustrations 5 and 6). With each passing month, the German infantry division gained supporting arms (artillery, trench mortars, and machine guns) while losing riflemen. At the outbreak of the war, the German infantry division might properly have been called a "rifle division." Each of the four infantry regiments had 12 infantry companies, every combatant of which was armed with a rifle, but only one machine gun company (of six machine guns)[3] and no other organic supporting arms.

Early in 1915, six more machine guns were issued to each regiment, allowing the formation of a second regimental machine gun company. In 1916, yet another six machine guns were given to each regiment. This gave the regiment the means to form three machine gun companies, one of which was permanently assigned to each battalion. Thus, by the end of 1916, the proportion of machine gun to infantry companies within each regiment had been increased from 1:12 to 1:4. By the last year of the war,

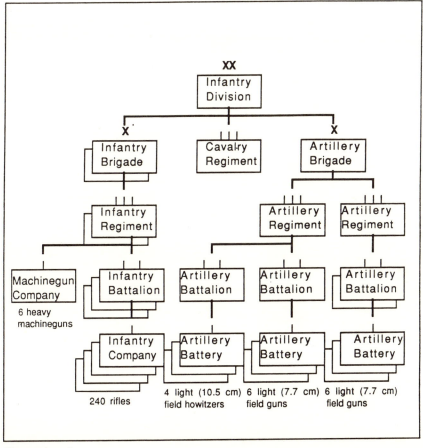

Illustration 5
Combat Units of a German Infantry Division, August 1914

when manpower shortages forced one rifle company per battalion to be disbanded, the ratio was reduced to one machine gun company to three rifle companies.

If the division as a whole is considered, the ratio became even more heavily weighted toward the machine gun company. Independent machine gun platoons and companies, and, after the summer of 1916, battalion-sized machine gun sharpshooter detachments (three companies of six machine guns each) were attached to many divisions.[4] In divisions with two attached machine gun sharpshooter detachments, a not uncommon phenomenon by early 1917, the ratio of machine gun companies to rifle companies was more than 1:2.

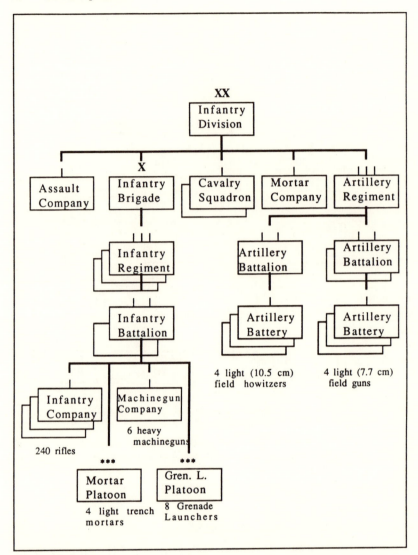

Illustration 6
Combat Units of a German Infantry Division, January 1917

Trench mortars enjoyed a similar increase in their numbers. In February of 1915, each division's pioneer company was given six light trench mortars. By the end of that year, each division was allotted a trench mortar company of two heavy, four medium, and six light trench mortars. In the course of 1916, the number of light trench mortars was increased to 12. In early 1917, the allotment of light trench mortars was again increased so that a platoon of two light trench mortars could be formed in each infantry battalion.

The placing of both machine guns and trench mortars directly under the control of the infantry battalion commander was an important step that moved the ordinary infantry farther along the trail already blazed by the assault battalions and, to a lesser extent, the *Jäger* battalions. It also meant that the German Army, in particular the War Ministry, recognized that the machine gun and light trench mortar were no longer special weapons to be attached to the infantry in unusual circumstances but rather that they were part and parcel of modern warfare, mobile as well as static. This trend coincided with the introduction of a light tripod mount for the Maxim machine gun and a wheeled carriage for the light trench mortar, both of which developments made these weapons easier to move on the battlefield.

The same reform that removed an infantry regiment from each division also removed a field artillery battalion. Each division's organic artillery was thus reduced from 12 batteries, nine of light (7.7cm) field guns, and three of light (10.5cm) field howitzers, to nine batteries, six of light field guns, and three of light field howitzers. The loss in field artillery, however, was more than compensated for by an increase in the proportion of heavier pieces. As a general rule, each division in a "quiet" sector was given two batteries of heavy howitzers and one battery of 10cm guns.[5] For major offensives, additional heavy batteries would be allocated.

The movement toward a higher proportion of supporting arms within the infantry division was accelerated in 1917 by the introduction of the grenade launcher (*Priesterwerfer*) to the infantry companies. A less deliberate contributor to this trend was the inability of the War Ministry to provide enough recruits to fill the ranks of infantry units. Even when, in 1917, the authorized strength of the infantry company was reduced from 240 to 180, company commanders had to make do with far fewer men than they were entitled to get by the official tables of organization.

By the end of 1917, as a result of the changing composition of the German infantry, the rifleman had become, within the infantry division, the infantry regiment, and even the infantry company, a member of a minority. This was a profound constraint on the tactical options available to a German commander. With fewer riflemen to go around, it became more and more difficult for an attacking infantry unit to fill its sector with even a thin skirmish line. The death blow to the skirmish line as a tactical formation was not dealt, however, until the introduction of large numbers of light machine guns to the German infantry.

THE LIGHT MACHINE GUN

While the German Army was one of the first armies to see the potential of the heavy machine gun, it was one of the last major belligerents of World War I to issue a standard light machine gun to the infantry. The British and the Belgians had both adopted the U.S.–designed Lewis gun before the outbreak of the war, while the French adopted the infamous *Chauchat* late in 1915. The Germans, on the other hand, did not start the large-scale issue of light machine guns to ordinary infantry units until the middle of 1916. It is not surprising, therefore, that the first light machine guns used by the German ground forces were weapons that had been captured from the enemy.

The first attempt to make systematic use of captured light machine guns was the formation of the *Musketen* Battalions. Each of the three companies that made up each *Musketen* Battalion was further divided into ten four-man teams. The principle weapon of each of these teams was the *Muskete,* a modified Madsen light machine gun. The Madsen, made in Denmark, was an air-cooled, magazine-fed, bipod mounted weapon capable of firing single shots as well as bursts of automatic fire.

Germany acquired these Madsens as booty. In the decade preceding the outbreak of war in 1914, Russia had bought a number of Madsens for issue to their cavalry squadrons. In the spring and summer of 1915, the German armies advancing in Galicia and Poland captured hundreds of Russian Madsens. Officials of the War Ministry saw the potential of this weapon, which, weighing only 21 pounds, was one of the lightest machine guns in the world at the time. The War Ministry had the captured Madsens converted to the standard German rifle cartridge (7.92mm) and, in August of 1915, ordered the Military District of Mainz to form two *Musketen* Battalions.

Starting in the early fall of 1915, the *Musketen* Battalions were sent to the Western Front. Although they were sometimes used merely to reinforce defending infantry units,[6] they served primarily as a mobile reserve of machine guns that could be used in a "fire brigade" role. If, during the course of an offensive, the enemy succeeded in piercing the line of machine gun nests that supported the front line position, a *Musketen* Battalion would be sent to establish an emergency barrier of automatic fire in front of the advancing enemy. This assignment proved quite dangerous. By the summer of 1916, the *Musketen* Battalions had used up the entire stock of Madsens in the German inventory.

The solution to the shortage of Madsens was found in the British Lewis gun. Many of these "automatic rifles" had been captured in the course of 1915 and 1916 and, like the Madsens, converted so as to be able to use standard German ammunition. Heavier than the Madsen (31 pounds), the Lewis gun was nevertheless quite popular with German troops. Even after the introduction of German manufactured light machine guns, some German troops, particularly those in elite assault units, preferred to use Lewis guns.

The *Musketen* Battalions used Lewis guns until April of 1918. By that time, ordinary infantry battalions had become, for all practical purposes, light machine gun units and there was no longer any need for a unit that had neither the flexibility of an infantry battalion nor the sustained firepower of a machine gun unit. The *Musketen* Battalions were therefore re-equipped with heavy machine guns and converted into Machine Gun Sharpshooter Detachments.

MODEL 08/15

German-made light machine guns did not appear on the eastern front until 1916, when independent Light Machine Gun Platoons were formed and attached to infantry units. Each platoon was equipped with nine Model 1915 "Bergmann" light machine guns. Not to be confused with the more successful Model 08/15 light machine gun, the Bergmann was developed as a private initiative by the firm of Theodor Bergmann. However, unlike the other major "private initiative" light machine gun of the war, the Lewis gun, the Bergmann was not a very reliable weapon. The air-cooled barrel of the Bergmann overheated after 30 or 40 rounds had been fired and the mechanism had a tendency to jam.

These problems were solved by the introduction of the Model 08/15 light machine gun in December of 1916. The 08/15 was a slightly modified Maxim heavy machine gun (Model 08) equipped with a wooden shoulder stock and mounted on a bipod. Many of the characteristics of the heavy Maxim were retained, including the water-cooled barrel. While this resulted in a weapon that was far heavier than other contemporary light machine guns (43 pounds), it also resulted in a weapon that retained many of the virtues of the heavy Maxim. The 08/15 was capable of firing a series of long bursts in a short period of time with little danger of the mechanism jamming and no danger of the barrel overheating.

As had been the case with the *Muskete* and the Bergmann, the War Ministry had introduced the 08/15 with the intention that the light machine gun be used primarily as a defensive weapon. The heavy Maxim that had proven its worth behind the first trench line, had been found to be too heavy for effective employment in the front line itself. There had been many occasions during British and French offensives where German machine gun crews had not had enough time between the end of the enemy bombardment and the time that the enemy infantry reached the German front lines to exit their dugouts, set up their machine guns, and begin firing.[7] A lighter machine gun, the War Ministry hoped, would not take so long to set up in such a situation.

The initial allotment of 08/15s was two to each infantry company. This number was soon increased to three and then four. By the end of 1917, some companies on the western front had six light machine guns, although companies on the eastern front often had to make do with one or two.[8] Production of the 08/15 was facilitated by the fact that most components of the weapon were identical to components of the heavy Maxim machine gun, reducing drastically the need to develop additional capacity in the already over-strained German economy. By January of 1918, 37,000 08/15s had been built in Germany[9]—enough to provide each of the 9000-odd infantry companies in the German Army at the time with at least four light machine guns each.

TACTICAL EMPLOYMENT

When the 08/15 was first introduced to the German infantry, it was considered to be a specialists' weapon. Light machine gunners were segregated from the riflemen of the company by the practice of placing them in the fourth platoon—the company "pool" of trench warfare specialists such as snipers, grenade launcher operators, and the company stormtroop. This was feasible as long as there were only one or two light machine guns per company.

As the number of light machine guns per company increased, however, it became necessary to parcel them out to the rifle platoons. This development, made necessary by the sheer numbers of light machine guns being issued to the infantry, combined with an increase in the number of stormtroopers to produce a radical transformation in the organization and capabilities of the infantry platoon. Instead of being composed entirely of riflemen, it was now composed of three types of squads—the light machine gun squad, the rifle squad, and the storm troop.

The creation of two new types of infantry squads provided the platoon commander[10] with the means for a new variation on the prewar tactics of fire and maneuver. Suppressive fire from the light machine gun squad permitted the rifle squads and stormtroops to maneuver to a position on the flank or the rear of an objective (such as an isolated machine gun nest) and attack it with rifle fire or hand grenades. In the "rolling up" of trenches, the fire of the light machine gun could sweep the ground above the trench being cleared by men from the rifle squads or stormtroops.

This combination of fire and maneuver sometimes even occurred within the light machine gun squad. To ensure that the light machine gun should never want for either a gunner or sufficient ammunition, the light machine gun squad had an authorized strength of eight men. Only one man, albeit a strong one, was needed to carry the machine gun itself. Two or three others followed him carrying ammunition and water. Four or five supernumerary machine gunners armed with carbines or rifles and hand grenades followed the "first string" machine gun team. Although the regulations governing the use of the light machine gun did not foresee the practice, this "second string" team could serve as a small rifle squad maneuvering under the covering fire of the light machine gun.

From the almost incidental use of supernumerary machine gunners for rifle and grenade work it was a short step to what the Germans later were to call the "unit squad" (*Einheits-Gruppe*), a hybrid squad consisting of a light machine gun team and a four-to-eight-man rifleman/grenadier team. While this arrangement didn't make it into the German training manuals until well after the war, it seems to have been practiced in some German units as early as the winter of 1917–1918. As the number of light machine guns in the German Army increased and as the number of infantrymen decreased, few commanders could afford the luxury of separate rifle and light machine gun squads.[11]

TYPICAL INFANTRY COMPANIES

A look at the tables of organization used by two different infantry companies of the Bavarian Life Guard Regiment in 1918 gives an idea of the transformation of the infantry company and platoons that took place in the course of the war. One company is divided into five platoons—three identical "battle platoons" (*Kampfzüge*), an "expansion platoon" (*Erganzungszug*), and a reserve. The "battle platoons" are composed of two "unit squads" (*Einheitsgruppen*) and an assault squad (*Stossgruppe*), the reserve contains two specialist squads, a small reconnaissance squad and a grenade launcher squad. The "expansion platoon" contained four spare NCOs and 16 spare men as well as the company armorer.[12]

The other company has only four platoons. The three "line" platoons are similar to each other—each has two rifle squads and two light machine gun squads. The first of the three platoons, however, has a grenade launcher squad while the third has an assault squad. The company headquarters platoon has another, albeit smaller (four men instead of eight) assault squad and a small reconnaissance squad.[13]

The light machine gun did to the German platoon, and in some cases, the squad, what the heavy machine gun and trench mortar had done to the battalion and regiment and what the grenade launcher had done to the company. By the end of 1917, all pretense that any infantry unit was uniformly armed with rifle and bayonet had been dropped. Every infantry unit down to the platoon was a combined arms force, capable of supporting its maneuver with its own fire.

The idea that the battlefield was a place where infantry regiments and battalions fought for general fire superiority and then clashed with each other as complete units was gone forever. In its place grew the conception that the attack of a regiment or battalion was really a series of much smaller combats, where each platoon and squad attempted to obtain a very local fire superiority and then exploit that with very local movement. The lesson that had been learned by the assault battalions in the course of trench raids and taught by them behind the lines was being reinforced by the light machine gun. The regimental and battalion commanders could bring their units to the battlefield, but the control of the actual fighting had devolved to the lieutenants and the sergeants.

GAS SHELL

Realizing the inherent limitations of gas cloud attacks, the War Ministry had ordered the concurrent development of artillery and trench mortar shells capable of delivering various types of gas. These were of little tactical value, however, until German chemists developed gases that were deadly in small quantities, so that the few cubic centimeters of gas carried within a projectile would have the desired effect on the enemy. The first gases to meet this requirement were "K-Stoff," a chemical that asphyxiated those effected far more effectively than chlorine, and "T-Stoff," a strong but nonpoisonous irritant. The chief tactical uses of these gas shells in trench raids and attacks "with limited objectives" was counterbattery fire and the building of "box barrages" to isolate positions.

By 1917, German artillery pieces and trench mortars were regularly firing three types of poison gas shells. Those shells known as "Yellow Cross" contained mustard gas, a heavy, oily substance that would cause painful boils on the skin and temporary blindness a few hours after contact. The slowness with which mustard gas acted, as well as the fact that it took days to dissipate, dictated the way in which it could be used on the battlefield. Mustard gas was employed primarily to attack forces on the flanks of an area being attacked, so as to reduce their ability to participate in a counterattack. It was not used against the position that was to be attacked itself, as that would expose the attacking troops to the effects of the gas.

"Green Cross" shells carried diphosgene, an especially effective asphyxiating agent that was to serve as the primary killing gas of the last two years of the war. By the time that diphosgene was introduced, however, gas masks had been sufficiently improved so as to be proof against it. To solve this problem, the Germans used Green Cross shells in combination with Blue Cross shells containing both high explosive (75%) and diphenylchlorarsine (25%), a chemical that could penetrate all but the best gas masks. Although the gas was deadly only in very high concentrations, it cooperated with diphosgene by causing the victim to sneeze violently. This sneezing forced the victim to tear off his gas mask, thus exposing himself to the deadly effect of the diphosgene.

The combination of Green Cross and Blue Cross shells was used in trench raids and attacks "with limited objectives" to attack enemy artillery positions as well as to build "box barrages." Blue Cross shells alone were used in the barrages that suppressed the enemy infantry defending their trenches against German infantry attack. In this role, Blue Cross was almost as effective as conventional high explosive in throwing debris into the air to keep heads down while providing an additional distraction in the form of the uncontrollable sneezing caused by the gas.

ATTACKS WITH LIMITED OBJECTIVES—1917

In the spring of 1917 the French "Nivelle Offensives" gave the German Army in the west yet another opportunity to demonstrate its tactical skill. Attacking in the vicinity of the river Aisne, the French failed to break through the entire defensive position but succeeded in capturing key terrain. This gave them certain advantages over the German troops in the area once the offensive stopped and "normal" trench warfare resumed. In the course of the summer of 1917, regiments of the German Seventh Army[14] launched a series of attacks "with limited objectives" to remedy this situation by retaking some of this lost terrain.[15]

As had been the case with earlier attacks "with limited objectives," the attacking troops of the Seventh Army used the methods of the assault battalions. The troops detailed for each attack were pulled out of line and intensively trained on dummy positions for two to four days. Even though most attacks were carried out by full-strength battalions and even regiments, the emphasis was placed on the maneuver of squads.

Every man knew his place of departure, his objective, his mission; Every [machine gun] battery chief, every commander of *Stosstrupp* or *Kampftrupp* received a sketch marked according to the flags used in rehearsal and showing the itinerary to be followed.[16]

The artillery barrages used to prepare these attacks were invariably short—the attack carried out by battalions of the 13th and 15th Reserve Infantry Regiments against the Cerney Plateau on July 31, 1917, was preceded by a bombardment that lasted only five minutes.[17] While the loss of duration was often compensated for by an increase in the number of artillery pieces available to support the attack, there were some cases where the short preparatory bombardment consisted only of trench mortar fire. Four companies (two from the 53rd Infantry Regiment and two from the 260th Reserve Infantry Regiment) supported by a detachment from the 7th Assault Battalion carried out a surprise dawn attack on June 1, 1917, after three minutes of trench mortar fire on the enemy position.[18]

The standard operating procedures of the assault battalions were modified, however, by a heavy reliance on gas shells to neutralize enemy batteries, the mounting of diversionary attacks to confuse the enemy and force him to fire his defensive barrage on empty ground, and the equipping of the assaulting infantry with light machine guns. These changes served primarily to reinforce rather than to change the foundations of stormtrooper tactics. The use of gas shell reinforced the tendency to use artillery primarily as a means of paralyzing the enemy rather than as a tool for attrition. The use of diversionary attacks contributed to a trend toward a style of fighting that was as much concerned with confusing enemy commanders as with physically destroying their soldiers. Most important of all, the light machine gun finished the trend toward the self-projecting squad that had started with the experiments in Boer tactics during the first decade of the twentieth century.

Although the attacks "with limited objectives" of the Seventh Army rarely pushed more than 400 meters into the enemy position, the infantry tactics that were used in the first phase of the assault were the tactics that the German infantry would use until the end of the war and, for all practical purposes, throughout World War II. All that was needed to convert the stormtrooper tactics of the Seventh Army into the "infiltration tactics" of 1918 was a solution to the problem of the "intermediate zone"—the belt of machine gun nests behind the first line of trenches. In other words, the techniques developed between 1915 and 1917 to cross "no man's land" and take the enemy forward trench would have to be extended to deal with a somewhat more fragmented though certainly no less formidable obstacle.

NOTES

1.   One German machine gun crew reported having fired 12,500 rounds that day. It is also said that when the British started to retreat, the Germans stopped firing out of pity. The battle is often referred to in German sources as the "Corpse Field of Loos" (*Das Leichenfeld von Loos*).

2.   U.S. Army War College, "German Experiences in Flanders and at Lens" (A translation of Chief of the General Staff of the Field Army Bulletin Nr. 62865, 22-8-18, signed Ludendorff) (Washington, DC: War Department, 1918).

3.   Beginning in 1916, the number of machine guns per machine gun company was increased to 12.

4.   The period of attachment was often quite short. The 22nd Machine Gun Sharpshooter Detachment was attached to 24 different formations during the course of its 26 months of existence. Hans Brauns, *Maschinen-Gewehr-Scharffschützen-Abteilung Nr. 22* (Berlin: Gerhard Stalling, 1923), p. 16.

5.   See Appendix B for a more detailed description of the artillery available to a division in a quiet sector.

6.   Alexander Kaiser, *Paderborner Infanterie-Regiment (7. Lothr.) Nr. 158* (Berlin: Gerhard Stalling, 1924), p. 70.

7.   See Ludwig Renn, *Warfare* (London: Faber and Faber, 1939), p. 111.

8. An order of the War Ministry, dated December 12, 1916, set the goal of three light machine guns per company by February 1917. Army War College, *Notes on Recent Operations No. 2* (Washington: Government Printing Office, 1917), p. 46.

9. Great Britain, *War Office,* General Staff, German Army Handbook, April, 1918 (New York: Hippocrene Books, 1977), p. 56. This book, a reprint of the original published by the War Office, is hereafter cited as *German Army Handbook.*

10. By this time, most platoon commanders were staff sergeants (*Vizefeldwebel*), temporary officers (*Offizierstellvertreter* or *Feldwebelleutnants*), or very junior second lieutenants. Most companies were commanded by second lieutenants, while most battalions were commanded by captains.

11. A British intelligence document dated April 10, 1918, quotes Ludendorff as preferring, in the case of a shortage of men, the elimination of rifle squads rather than light machine gun squads. Great Britain, War Office, *Notes on Recent Fighting,* April 10, 1918.

12. The regimental history of the Bavarian Life Guards unfortunately gives no indication of the purpose of this platoon. Ritter von Reiß et al., *Das Königlich Bayerische Infanterie Leib Regiment im Weltkrieg, 1914–1918* (Munich: Max Schick, 1931), p. 392.

13. Ibid., Appendix VIII.

14. The Seventh Army consisted of three groups (*Gruppen*), temporary formations consisting of two to four divisions commanded by a *Generalkommando*—the commanding general of a corps and his staff. Because the attacks carried out by Gruppe Vailly (commanded by the *Generalkommando* of XI Corps) were recorded in a memorandum that was distributed to the entire German Army, it is sometimes believed that only Gruppe Vailly took part in the attacks with limited objectives to recapture ground lost to the French in April and May of 1917. As a matter of fact, all three of the Gruppen of the 7th Army took part in these attacks.

15. *Der Weltkrieg 1914–1918*, Vol. 12., pp. 391–93.

16. U.S. Army War College, *German and Austrian Tactical Studies* (Washington, DC: Government Printing Office, 1918), p. 106.

17. Ibid., p. 107.

18. Hans von Troilo, *Das 5. Westfälische Infanterie Regiment Nr. 53 im Weltkrieg 1914–1919* (Berlin: Druck und Verlag von Gerhard Stalling, 1924), p. 89. This attack was distinguished by the use of indirect machine gun fire to form a barrage *behind* the objective in order to cause casualties among those Frenchmen attempting to fall back to their second position.

7

The Eastern Front

On the Eastern Front we had for the most part adhered to the old
tactical methods and the old training that we had learned in the days
of peace.

Erich Ludendorff[1]

In the west, the war of grand maneuvers ended with the First Battle of
Ypres. The combination of skirmish line tactics and field artillery was
rarely able to break through trench systems that got deeper with each
passing month. On those few occasions where gaps were made by an attack, the defender was always able to use railroads and motor transport to
move reinforcements to the threatened area and plug the gap.

In the east, the war of grand maneuvers never ended completely. Instead, position warfare alternated with maneuver at the operational
level. The territory over which the war in the East was fought—the forests of Lithuania and the vast plains and swamps of Poland, the
Ukraine, and Russia—proved too large to fill with men and guns. (In
the winter of 1916–1917 German divisions in the east held sectors 20 to
30 kilometers wide.[2] The same space in Flanders could be filled with as
many as eight divisions. Even the relatively quiet areas such as Alsace
required a division for every ten kilometers or so.) As a result, corps and
army commanders on both sides found that they did not have the resources to defend their sectors in the manner of their counterparts on
the western front.

Against such thin defenses, which were much more like those imagined
in the decade before the outbreak of war, the open order "Boer" tactics of
1914 proved to be quite adequate.[3] Even when the Germans had to attack
a Russian trench line head on, Russia's relative lack of machine guns, the
poor marksmanship on the part of the Russian infantry, and the inability
of the Russian artillery to work closely with their own infantry, as well as

the dispersion of the attacking Germans, ensured that there would be no massacres on the scale of the First Battle of Ypres. When the Germans added their overwhelming superiority (qualitative as well as quantitative) in artillery to the equation, they were in a position to guarantee victory with minimal losses. In short, there was a far less pressing need for the Germans to rethink their tactics in order to cross "no man's land" and take enemy trenches.[4]

It was only occasionally that the tactical conditions on the eastern front resembled those of the western front. Here and there, however, a few acres of land were often fortified in a manner reminiscent of position warfare in the West, forming strong points as difficult to take as any trench system in France or Belgium. The Germans first encountered this phenomenon in the foothills of the Carpathian mountains—a range that forms the juncture of Hungary, Poland, Romania, and the Ukraine. There, along a 50-kilometer-wide front between the Polish towns of Gorlice and Tarnow in what was then the Austrian province of Galicia, the Germans attempted their first breakthrough of the Russian line.[5]

The strategic goal of the operation was relatively modest—to relieve pressure on Germany's Habsburg ally. The Russian capture of the fortress of Przemysl and their success in the Carpathians threatened to bring about the collapse of the Austro-Hungarian effort against Russia. Having, in the course of the first nine months of the war, proved its inability to make inroads against the Russians or even subdue tiny Serbia, Austria-Hungary was no longer able to defend its own border. If successful, a breakthrough between Gorlice and Tarnow, a hilly region that connected the Carpathian Mountains to the south with the flat Polish heartland to the north, would split the Russian forces along a natural "faultline." A breakthrough also brought with it the opportunity for a battle of encirclement on the Polish plain.

The main attack was assigned to the Eleventh Army, a recently formed force composed of both German and Austro-Hungarian units.[6] The German troops, eight infantry divisions' worth, were drawn mostly from the western front. The four Austro-Hungarian infantry divisions and the exclusively Hungarian cavalry division, on the other hand, were taken from other parts of the eastern front. The bulk of the artillery (about 250 out of 352 field guns or light field howitzers and 110 out of 144 heavy pieces over 10.5cm caliber) and all of the trench mortars (96 of all calibers) were German.[7]

Despite its polyglot composition, the command of the Eleventh Army was exclusively German. The commanding general, August von Mackensen, was an old cavalryman who usually wore a hussar's dolman and pelisse in preference to the more sedate frock coats or tunics favored by other German generals of the time. The chief of staff was the same Colonel Hans von Seekt who had planned the attack "with limited objectives" at Soissons in January 1915. Later to become famous as the post-war rebuilder of the German Army, Seekt was already, in the words of Gordon Craig, "recognized by his colleagues as one of the more outstanding soldiers of his generation."[8]

The three of the four German formations of the Eleventh Army—the Guard Corps, the Forty-first Reserve Corps, and "Combined Corps Kneußl" (119th Infantry Division, and the 11th Bavarian Infantry Division)—had been pulled back from the front lines during the Winter of 1914–1915 to prepare for a planned (but never executed) spring offensive in northern France and Flanders.[9] Billeted in quiet towns miles behind the trenches, these troops avoided the debilitating routine of trench maintainance, artillery duels, and housekeeping under fire. Instead, they practiced the skills of war, route marching in particular, in open terrain.[10] The troops of the Austro-Hungarian Corps were likewise unskilled in the tactics that were just then being developed in the west.

The separation of these troops, and their tactical leaders, from the trenches, however, had an effect that lessened, rather than increased, their readiness for combat. The time that these units were away from the front was also the time when the front was innovating at its most rapid pace. Attacks with limited objectives and early trench raids provided an opportunity for German units to learn ways of coping with their new tactical situation. At a time when there were neither assault detachments nor even field manuals to serve as teachers of trench warfare, the absence from the front of the troops who were to fight at Gorlice-Tarnow would cost them in blood during the first four days of the battle.

THE DEFENSES

By the standards of the eastern front, the Russian defenses at Gorlice-Tarnow were quite well prepared. The foothills of the Carpathians provided the framework for the Russian position—a series of low hills that the Russians turned into earthwork bastions. Connecting these hill forts were ordinary trenches, more deeply dug than was the rule in the Russian Army at the time and providing some protection against overhead fire. Both hill forts and trenches were well protected by "Spanish riders," a primitive form of barbed wire obstacle that could be easily mass produced behind the lines under the supervision of the few qualified combat engineers available to the Russians.

While the trenches would be easier to take than the better built and garrisoned hill fortresses, their possession would provide little advantage to the attacker. The field batteries of the Russian artillery, trained to prefer direct over indirect fire and equipped with the excellent 7.6cm field piece, were so positioned in the hill forts as to be able to enfilade the shallow valleys. As a result, any force that wished to move through those valleys was obligated to first seize the heights.[11]

As had been the case at Soissons on the western front, the German advantage at Gorlice-Tarnow lay chiefly in the possession of a better artillery park, particularly large numbers of high-angle of fire weapons—howitzers, heavy mortars, and trench mortars. About three-quarters of the artillery of the Eleventh Army (352 pieces) came from the organic artillery regiments of the divisions. The other quarter (144 pieces) consisted of heavier weapons placed at the disposal of corps commanders. No artillery was kept under the direct control of the Eleventh Army.[12]

The 96 trench mortars detailed for the operation were not used, as they were beginning to be in the west, to provide a barrage immediately in front of attacking infantry. Instead, they were used for the purpose for which they had originally been introduced into the German Army's inventory—destructive, rather than suppressive, fire. Still organized in battalions manned exclusively by pioneers, the trench mortars were employed no differently from the howitzers, light and heavy, that provided most of the destructive power of the German artillery. The only concession to their special characteristics was their location along the front. Because of their short range relative to howitzers, the trench mortars were concentrated opposite westward-facing salients that the Russians had driven into the Austro-Hungarian lines before the arrival of the Germans.[13]

THE ATTACK

The bombardment began at nine—a short while after sunset—that evening of May 1. At first the guns, howitzers, and trench mortars fired at their "sustained rate"; rounds were shoved into the breechblocks and lanyards pulled at a slow and steady pace that preserved the artillery pieces from overheating and the crews from exhaustion. Twice during the night—from ten to eleven on the evening of the first and from one to three in the early morning of the second—the German artillery ceased firing. In addition to giving the artillerymen an opportunity to rest, it gave forward observers a chance to ascertain the damage, confused the Russians as to the nature of the bombardment, and enticed Russian machine gunners to open fire, thereby revealing their exact locations.[14]

Between four and six on the morning of May 2—the exact time varied from corps to corps—the German artillery focused its attention on the forwardmost Russian line and increased its rate of fire. Between 9:00 and 9:30, the tempo of the bombardment increased again to the maximum rate that the guns and the gunners could tolerate. One hour later—again the exact time depended on the corps commander—the fire shifted to targets behind the forward Russian trenches and the German infantry rushed forward in the thick skirmish lines of 1914.[15]

In most places, the Russians responded to the approaching wall of bayonets by fleeing. The sheer weight of the bombardment—the heavier pieces fired 200 shells each while the light field howitzers fired 300—had convinced many Russians that there was no point in resistance. The experience of Queen Augusta Regiment of the Guard Corps was typical. Formed in three waves, it crossed "no man's land" at a cost of two or three casualties. Four and a half minutes after it had crossed the line of departure, this unit was in undisputed possession of the first Russian trench and hundreds of Russian soldiers who had thrown away their weapons.[16]

Two neighboring regiments, however, suffered casualties comparable to those which they had suffered at Ypres the previous fall. Of the 3000 or so men who advanced in the ranks of the Kaiser Alexander Regiment, which had the misfortune to attack a sector defended by Siberian Riflemen, 12 officers and 290 men died while an equal number were seriously wounded.[17] The Queen Elizabeth Regiment experienced similar damage. Particularly hard hit was the 12th Company, which ran into Russian machine guns that had survived the bombardment. Sixty-six members of that company died in the first few minutes of the assault and 37 were wounded. After the battle, the regimental surgeon noted that most of the dead had been hit by at least two bullets each.[18]

The tactics of the Austro-Hungarian Infantry were essentially the same as those of the Germans. When the artillery fire shifted, they rose from their trenches, formed skirmish lines on the double, and rushed forward into the smoke, yelling their battle cries in a dozen languages.[19] Where the Russian will to resist had already been broken by shell fire, the skirmish line was as good a formation as any to move the Austro-Hungarian battalions into their new trenches. The Austro-Hungarian XIV Corps, however, had the misfortune to run into one of the few groups of Russians that refused to be intimidated by the heavy guns. Despite the fact that some of their component infantry companies lost three-quarters of their men and all of their officers, the two infantry divisions of that corps failed to get beyond the "Spanish riders" the Russians had set up in "no man's land."[20]

Fortunately for the Austro-German offensive, the sectors where the Russians surrendered en masse greatly exceeded those where the attackers were held up or massacred. As a result, the breakthrough attempted on May 2 was a resounding success and the battle turned into a pursuit that lasted for 11 days. When the marching was over, 140,000 Russian prisoners were in the hands of the Central Powers, almost all of Poland had been cleared of Russian troops, and the danger of a Russian invasion of Hungary was completely eliminated.

BRIDGEHEADS

The Gorlice-Tarnow campaign changed the shape of the Russian front. The northern sector, with which the Germans were principally concerned, moved into eastern Poland, the Ukraine, western Russia, Lithuania, and southern Latvia—flat lands whose major terrain features, at least from an operational point of view, were the broad rivers that flowed into the Baltic. After each of the many campaigns in which the Germans tore a corps or army-sized gap out of the Russian line and sent those of their enemies who escaped death or capture fleeing to the east, one or more of these rivers permitted the Russians the time to reestablish their defenses and even economize on forces needed to hold ground.

To leave open the option of resuming offensive action, as well as to prevent the Germans from gaining control of the few good bridges that were available, the Russians made a practice of occupying and fortifying bridgeheads on the "German" side of rivers. To reduce these bridgeheads, the Germans often conducted attacks "with limited objectives." The chief characteristic of these attacks was the use of huge concentrations of artillery. In the west, the constant threat of British and French attacks prevented any one division or corps commander from giving up a portion of his artillery to support an attack "with limited objectives" conducted by a unit belonging to another formation. In the east, while there was less artillery to go around, what was available could be brought together for even relatively minor operations. The same wide rivers crossed by few bridges that made it necessary for the Germans to attack the fortified bridgeheads also made it far less dangerous to "strip" the artillery from divisions holding ground in "quiet sectors." As a result of this phenomenon, a German infantryman attacking "with limited objectives" in the east could often count on more artillery support than his counterpart in the west.

In an attack on the Witonitz bridgehead on November 1, 1916, the three infantry regiments of the 121st Infantry Division were supported by 156 artillery pieces and 49 trench mortars. Four months later, 300 field pieces and 100 trench mortars supported the attack of the 1st Landwehr Infantry Division against the bridgehead at Toboly. In both attacks, the ratio of artillery to attacking infantry was higher than that of the first day of the attack at Verdun, where, on average, an infantry division was supported by 94 guns and 60 trench mortars. The bombardments in support of German attacks on bridgeheads, moreover, were shorter and thus more intense than those of the first day at Verdun. The latter bombardment lasted over 24 hours. At Witonitz, on the other hand, the artillery fired for five hours and 15 minutes. At Toboly, the bombardment lasted five hours and 45 minutes.[21]

BRUCHMÜLLER

The coordination of the artillery effort in many of the German attacks on Russian bridgeheads was accomplished by Lieutenant Colonel Georg Bruchmüller. Bruchmüller, who had retired from active service before the war, had been recalled to active duty and placed in command of the artillery of a *Landwehr* Division. In April of 1916, in his execution of the artillery support for the counterattack of the three divisions of the German X Corps near Lake Narocz, he demonstrated a talent for "knowing, as if by instinct, the exact quantity of ammunition that was necessary to discharge on any single point to render it ready to be stormed."[22]

As a result of the success of the battles for which he prepared the artillery plan, Bruchmüller acquired a reputation as a skillful organizer of artillery. Not only generals but the very troops who were to follow the last volley into the enemy trench gained confidence in Bruchmüller's ability to coordinate artillery fire. "The troops," wrote General Max Hoffmann, the de facto commander of German forces on the eastern front for the last two years of the war, "also noticed that an attack that had previously been prepared by artillery under Bruchmüller's command was a sure thing, and they advanced with sure confidence in the success of any undertaking that had been prepared by Bruchmüller and his staff."[23]

One of the principle features of the bombardments organized by Bruchmüller at Witonitz and Toboly was a "rolling barrage" (*Feuerwaltz*) similar to that used at Verdun during the late spring and summer of 1916. As Captain Rohr emphasized in the west, Bruchmüller stressed in the east that the key to the "rolling barrage" was the closeness with which the infantry followed the barrage.[24] The first element in ensuring this was the fire discipline of the artillery—getting the batteries to work together to ensure that not only would the barrage move according to schedule, but that short rounds would be kept to the absolute minimum. The second element was convincing the infantry that following 50 meters or less behind a curtain of exploding shells was a good idea.

Rohr achieved this level of confidence by having his stormtroops practice their attacks with live artillery fire. Bruchmüller, having to deal with significantly larger units, made a practice of giving lectures to the officers, including NCOs serving as platoon commanders, of the infantry units which would take part in one of his attacks. In these lectures, he described in detail the artillery plan he had put together, the effect he intended the artillery fire to have on the enemy, and coordination measures such as signal rockets, liaison officers, and forward observers.[25]

The other forms of artillery fire used in the reduction of bridgeheads on the eastern front, like the rolling barrage, had as their aim the attainment of fire superiority. Although a great deal of physical destruction was bound to occur, the purpose of artillery fire was not to destroy physically the enemy. Rather, the high explosive, shrapnel, and gas that was dropped on the enemy kept him from moving his reserves, effectively firing his artillery, machine guns, and rifles, or doing anything else that might interfere with the movement of the German infantry.

Thus, the light field guns, light field howitzers, and the trench mortars provided the rolling barrage. The heavier guns and howitzers, firing a mixture of shrapnel, high explosive, and gas at longer ranges, served to suppress the Russian artillery. The heavier batteries also provided box barrages that blocked the path of reinforcements and prevented the defenders of the bridgeheads from retreating in good order.[26] Only the heavy mortars were assigned the job of destroying (rather than neutralizing) specific targets such as known command posts or concrete bunkers.

RIGA

Bruchmüller's greatest bombardment on the eastern front was that which preceded the capture of the city of Riga in September of 1917. The bombardments at Witonitz and Toboly had been aids to the advance of solitary divisions. The bombardments in East Galicia and at Lake Narocz had as their aim the support of a single army corps. At Riga, however, Bruchmüller's guns would participate in an offensive carried out by a much larger force—the 13 divisions of General Oscar von Hutier's Eighth Army.

The strategic purpose of the attack at Riga was the trapping of the Russian forces guarding the Baltic Coast. The operational means by which this was to be achieved was the classical battle of encirclement that had served the Germans so well everywhere but in the west. General von Hutier had much experience in this style of warfare. Before taking command of the Eighth Army, von Hutier had taken part in a number of encirclement battles on the eastern front as commanding general of the XXI Corps.

The greatest obstacle in the way of von Hutier's planned maneuver was the broad Dvina, the river that had held up the German advance for over two years (see Illustration 7). In the neighborhood of Riga, the Russians occupied the entire north bank of the Dvina, most of the sandbar islands in the river, and that portion of the south bank closest to the Baltic Coast. The Russian commander expected that any German attack in the vicinity of Riga would fall on the south bank of the Dvina, where the larger part of the Russian garrison defended the only modern bridges that spanned the river, to include the only railroad bridge across the river within a hundred-mile radius.

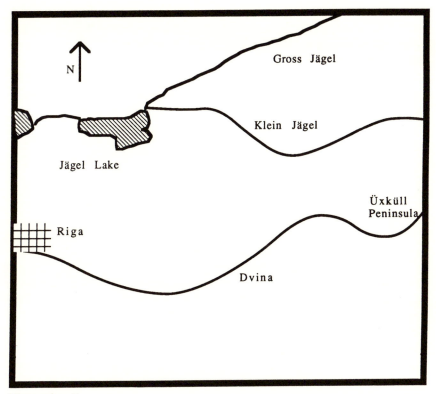

Illustration 7
The Dvina River between Riga and the Üxküll Peninsula

Von Hutier did not plan, however, to attack where an attack was expected. In order to achieve a measure of surprise, he chose to cross the Dvina at another point. Thirty kilometers east of Riga, a bend in the Dvina formed the Üxküll Peninsula. In the river south of the peninsula were three large islands. Von Hutier's intention was to build three pontoon bridges connecting this peninsula to the south bank. Across each of these three bridges, von Hutier intended to march three infantry divisions. With these nine divisions on the north bank, von Hutier would be able to march north in force, cutting off the garrison of Riga from the rest of the Russian Army.

PREPARATIONS

Before the pontoon bridges could be built, however, German troops would have to cross the river by boat and secure both the islands and a bridgehead on the north bank. Such an operation would bear a close resemblance to an attack "with limited objectives," although the fact that "no man's land" was a river required certain alterations to established procedures. The protection of the troops crossing 300 or 400 meters of water—interrupted only by the islands that provided the Russians holding them with excellent fields of fire—was to be provided by a hurricane bombardment similar to that used by Bruchmüller at Toboly, Witonitz, and in East Galicia.

On the north bank of the river there were two Russian positions. One, of three and four trench lines, followed the trace of the beach. The other, of two lines, occupied the wooded high ground four to five kilometers north of the beach. Between these two positions was a mixture of pine forests, meadows, and bogs—terrain with which German soldiers who had fought on the eastern front were quite familiar. Bruchmüller's bombardment would fall on both of these positions, as well as on the Russian-occupied islands.

Preventing the Russian troops occupying the first position from interfering with the crossing was a job assigned to the trench mortars. In the woods behind the trenches on the German side of the river, 100 heavy, 130 medium, and 320 light trench mortars were emplaced. All of these, with the possible exception of some of the light trench mortars, were organized into a Trench Mortar Brigade whose commander reported directly to Colonel Bruchmüller.[27]

Behind the trench mortars were the light field guns and howitzers of the field artillery. With high explosive and gas, the light field howitzers were to bombard the Russian second position. Some of the light field guns were assigned the task of closing the left and right sides of the "box" that Bruchmüller intended to use to isolate the Russian position. Other light field guns were directed to shell the communications trenches that connected the various trenches that made up the Russian first position. The heavier batteries—the giant mortars, the 10cm–long range guns, and the heavy howitzers—were assigned individual targets such as crossroads and the villages of Gut Üxküll and Oger-Galle. The latter village was fired upon with incendiary shells to prevent the Russians from using the houses as observation posts.[28]

The infantry regiments detailed for the river-crossing operation were given special training far behind the German lines. Most of this training consisted of learning how to use the wooden boats that would take the first waves of infantry across the Dvina, with lakes serving as substitutes for the river. The regiments designated to cross the river by means of the pontoon bridges also spent a few days practicing the crossing. The distance between the training areas and the area of operations, as well as the thick forests that covered that part of Latvia, prevented the Russians from learning about these preparations.[29]

Similar forests on the south bank of the Dvina hid the movement of men, guns, and material into the German jumping-off positions. The German trenches on the Dvina and the woods behind them soon became filled with the infantrymen, pioneers, and artillery liaison teams of the first wave. Additional pioneers were present to clear lanes through the German wire, to serve as crews for the trench mortars, to man the boats for the first wave, and to build the bridges that would carry the follow-on forces.[30]

BOMBARDMENT

At 4:00 A.M. on the morning of September 1 the bombardment began with the gassing of the Russian artillery emplacements and the second infantry position. In the course of two hours, a total of 20,650 gas shells, the same combination of "Blue Cross" and "Green Cross" shells that had recently proven so effective in attacks "with limited objectives" on the western front, fell on the defending Russians.[31] Some of the Russian gunners, lacking confidence in the ability of their gas masks to protect them, deserted their posts as soon as the gas shells started to fall. Others remained at their guns until they succumbed to the effects of the gas.[32]

At 6:00 A.M., the German guns, howitzers, and trench mortars that had hitherto remained silent opened fire with high explosive and shrapnel shells along a front of over 120 kilometers. The bulk of the artillery fire, however, was concentrated on the peninsula where the landings were to be made. Smaller concentrations of fire were placed on targets on the Russian-occupied positions south of the Dvina, where the Germans had planned supporting and diversionary attacks. Even though many of the German batteries had not had the opportunity to register their guns properly, the fire was sufficiently accurate to have the desired effect.

At 9:10 A.M., the infantry squads of the first wave lifted their boats on their shoulders and carried them across the forward trench, through recently cut lanes in the German wire, and into the water. Jumping into its boat in one leap, each squad rowed as fast as it could across the 300 to 400 meters of water that separated it from the enemy shore—no one wished to be caught in a watery "no man's land" totally devoid of any sort of cover.

Fortunately for the attacking German infantry, the trench mortars were doing a first-class job of suppressing the Russian defenders of the peninsula. The boats crossing the Dvina received little fire from the trenches on the north bank. A few of the infantrymen of the 2nd Guard Infantry Division were hit by stray shells—whether they were Russian or German is unknown. Otherwise the crossing was uneventful.

On reaching the Üxküll peninsula, German infantry commanders fired their green rockets into the air. At these signals, the German rolling barrage began moving forward, providing a vanguard of explosions behind which the German infantry fixed bayonets, formed skirmish lines, and moved forward into the Russian position.

Resistance on the beach was light—the handful of flamethrowers and light machine guns[33] that accompanied the German riflemen had little work to do in this phase of the battle. The Russians defending the trenches were poorly led, poorly equipped, and demoralized by continuous defeat, poor living conditions, and revolutionary propaganda. After being gassed and shelled all morning, most of the Russians at Riga required only the glint of a German bayonet to cause them to pull back or surrender.

Either the Russians had placed no machine guns in the forward trenches, or the crews had abandoned them during the bombardment, for no German skirmish line ran into the flanking fire that would have brought its advance to a standstill. Within a few minutes, the attacking Germans had passed through the first Russian position and were pushing on to the second. The secure beach was quickly filled with pioneers lashing together the pontoon bridges, which soon creaked under the jackboots of the follow-up regiments.

THE RUSSIAN EVACUATION

On the south bank, the German artillery had been unable to obtain fire superiority. The overwhelming majority of the guns available had been concentrated to support the river crossing. As a result, the three divisions conducting the supporting and diversionary attacks south of the Dvina had to make do with their organic field guns and light field howitzers. Because of this imbalance, the Russians were able to bombard many of the German jumping-off trenches. Directly south of Riga, the 3rd Reserve Infantry Regiment was unable to leave its trenches because of the heavy Russian artillery fire.[34]

The Russians on the south bank used this fire superiority not to counterattack against the Germans, but rather to mask their retreat. Soon after midday, German patrols sent out during a break in the German artillery fire discovered that the Russians had evacuated their positions. A similar phenomenon occurred along the Baltic Coast, where at dawn of the second day of the attack, the German 406th Infantry Regiment discovered that the Russian trenches were empty.[35]

On the peninsula, the Germans arriving at the second Russian position found that it, too, had been evacuated by the Russians. The few detachments that remained—a rear guard, perhaps—were quickly subdued and the Germans pushed further inland. Special detachments of German artillerymen took over the guns that the Russians had left behind. Other artillery support for the continuation of the attack was provided by light field guns that had come over in boats with the first wave. The mainstay of the German artillery effort, however, came from the heavy batteries on the south bank of the river, most of which had sufficient range to engage the Russians throughout the first day.

The only serious fighting that took place on the first day of the operation occurred on the Klein Jägel, a small river located behind the Russian second position. There the 14th Bavarian Division took part in what was perhaps the fiercest combat of the battle. On the second day, however, this pocket of resistance collapsed and the 14th Bavarian Division, which, along with the other two divisions that made up Group Berrer, was to march north to the river Aa and close the ring around the Russian 12th Army, continued its advance.[36]

Group Berrer again met resistance on the Grosse Jägel, a small river running east to west that provided the Russians with an opportunity to establish a remnant of a defensive line. Resistance was quickly overcome, however, by the tactical application of a favorite German operational maneuver—the double envelopment. German infantry got around both flanks of the Russian position on the Grosse Jägel and surrounded the defenders.[37]

EXPLOITATION

The buildup of German forces on the north bank was accomplished as quickly as the march north by Group Berrer. By the evening of the first day, six German divisions had crossed the Dvina. Three more infantry divisions, as well as cavalry, artillery, and supply wagons, followed the next day. This buildup permitted the expansion of the bridgehead to the west, east, and north—an expansion which, by the afternoon of the third day, resulted in German troops entering Riga on the heels of the retreating Russians.

A few hours later, the three German divisions on the south bank of the Dvina finished the task of clearing the southern suburbs of Riga. The Russians, seeing little virtue in fighting three divisions in front of them when nine divisions were about to cut off their line of retreat, had abandoned the strong fortifications that guarded the permanent bridges connecting these towns with the city across the river. Before they left, however, the Russians that had been defending the south bank succeeded in destroying the permanent bridges across the Dvina.

Before conceding defeat, the Russians launched a series of counterattacks to prevent the closing of the pincer. In trucks and on foot, Russian reinforcements had been streaming south since the beginning of the German operation. In hastily prepared counterattacks, the Russian reserves attempted to trade their lives for time. Attacking without artillery support, the Russians in their thick skirmish lines succeeded in giving up their lives but not in disrupting the German timetable.

Despite their rapid advance into Russian territory, the Germans were unable to finish their battle of encirclement at Riga. On September 3, only hours before the first German troops entered the city of Riga, the German High Command ordered General von Hutier to suspend operations. The British and Dominion troops fighting the Third Battle of Ypres had been more successful than the High Command had anticipated and some of von Hutier's troops were therefore needed to bolster the German position in Flanders.

Von Hutier continued the operation for two days in order to "bag" as many Russians as possible, for the latter were now in full retreat. An attempt by the 1st Cavalry Division and the 1st Guard Division to close the gap through which the Russians were escaping failed, in part because of the sacrificial assaults of all-female "Death's Battalions" that slowed their advance. Five days after it had begun, the battle of Riga was over.

RESULTS

While the Eighth Army failed to accomplish its mission of annihilating the Russian 12th Army, the Battle of Riga must nevertheless be considered a German victory. The 50,000 German inhabitants of Riga were liberated from the depredations of a Russian garrison whose discipline had collapsed. Twenty-five thousand Russian soldiers were rendered hors de combat and 262 guns—enough to equip five divisions—were captured. Most important, the Battle of Riga kept up the pressure on an enemy that was on the point of losing its will to continue the war.

By the standards of World War I, German losses at Riga were slight. Forty-two hundred Germans were killed or seriously wounded. A disproportionate share of these casualties, a full quarter, took place in the ranks of the infantry regiments of the 14th Bavarian Division. Other units got off relatively easily. The 2nd Guard Grenadier Regiment, for example, a unit that had suffered such great losses crossing a few hundred yards of open ground during the First Battle of Ypres, lost only one officer and 24 men at Riga.[38]

Von Hutier's victory at Riga made a deep impression on the High Command. Ludendorff's view that he could end the war on the western front with a series of tactical victories before the Americans arrived in force was strengthened. Both von Hutier and Bruchmüller were transferred west to take part in the preparations for this operation. It would be an exaggeration, however, to say that either von Hutier or Bruchmüller had practiced a new style of warfare at Riga. The Battle of Riga followed the pattern of earlier German operations on the eastern front—bombardment, breakthrough, and encirclement.

The techniques used by the various arms at Riga, moreover, were somewhat less than state of the art. The cavalry performed its traditional role—exploitation of the breakthrough and reconnaissance—in a traditional manner. The infantry likewise fought as they might have had the attack taken place in 1914. Although they crossed the Dvina as squads, the German infantrymen formed into company strength skirmish lines as soon as they reached the north bank of the river. Only the artillery was employed in a manner that came close to meeting the standards that had been established on the western front, the only major deficiency of the artillery being the employment of many unregistered guns which led, in some cases, to a degradation in accuracy.

The role played by elite assault units was small. One platoon of the 18th Assault Company took part in the crossing of the Dvina. Its mission was to help clear a single trench line on Borkowitz, one of the Russian-occupied islands in the middle of the river. The rest of the 18th Assault Company remained in Army reserve for most of the battle. Its only employment as a unit was a reconnaissance patrol over the Aa on September 3.[39]

It was thus at the operational, rather than the tactical level, that the Battle of Riga was to serve as a model for later German offensives. Riga proved the value of the attainment of surprise, the concentration of superior forces against the weak spots in the enemy disposition, and the deep penetration of that weak spot in order to encircle a portion of the enemy force. These aspects of the Battle of Riga, however, had been characteristic of German operational art for over half a century. It is therefore probable that the German offensives of 1918 would have had the same operational characteristics even if the Battle of Riga had not taken place.

NOTES

1.   Erich Ludendorff, *Ludendorff's Own Story* (New York: Harper and Brothers Publishers, 1919), p. 274.

2.   Balck, *Development of Tactics—World War*, p. 110.

3.   A good firsthand account of infantry combat on the eastern front is Adolf von Schell's *Battle Leadership* (Quantico, VA: The Marine Corps Association, 1982).

4.   Abteilung, German General Staff, "Die Entwickelung der Deutschen Infanterie im Weltkrieg 1914–1918," *Militärwissenschaftliche Rundschau* 3 (1938), p. 404.

5.   These towns, still known by the same name, are currently within the borders of Poland.

6.   The Eleventh Army had originally been formed on the western front for a planned operation to drive the mostly British and Belgian forces out of Flanders. For a description of this plan, see Fritz von Lossberg, *Meine Tätigkeit im Weltkrieg 1914–1918* (Berlin: E.S. Mittler & Sohn, 1939), pp. 136–44.

7.   *Der Weltkrieg* 7, pp. 369–70.

8.   Gordon Craig, *The Politics of the Prussian Army, 1640–1945* (New York: Oxford University Press, 1955), p. 383.

9.   For a description of the plans for this operation, see Fritz von Lossberg, *Meine Tätigkeit im Weltkreige 1914–1918* (Berlin: E.S. Mittler & Sohn, 1939), pp. 136–44.

10.   *Der Weltkrieg* 7, p. 368; and Edmund Glaise-Horstenau, ed., *Österreich-Ungarns letzter Krieg* II (Vienna: Verlag der Militärwissenschaftlichen Mittelungen, 1931–1936), p. 316.

11.   *Der Weltkrieg* 7, p. 370.

12.   Ibid., p. 372.

13.   Ibid., p. 375.

14.   Once located, the Russian machine guns were fired upon, over open sights, by pairs of German field guns that had been placed in the forwardmost German trenches for that express purpose.

15.   Richard von Berendt, *Das 1. Garde Fußartillerie Regiment im Weltkrieg* (Berlin: Druck und Verlag von Gerhard Stalling, 1928), pp. 140–42; Scheel, *Das Reserve Feldartillerie Regiment Nr. 70* (Berlin: Druck und Verlag von Gerhard Stalling, 1923), pp. 16–19; and Herrmann Köhn, *Erstes Garde Feldartillerie Regiment und seine reitende Abteilung* (Berlin: Druck und Verlag von Gerhard Stalling, 1928), pp. 148–51.

16.   Karl von Unger, "Gorlice-Tarnow" in Ernst von Eisenhart Rothe and Dr. Martin Lezius, *Das Ehrenbuch der Garde*, pp. 176–79.

17.   Babendieck, "Staszkowka und die Lipier Höhe," in ibid., pp. 187–93.

18.   Paderstein, "Erinnerungen an Staszkowka" in ibid., pp. 181–82.

19.   Glaise-Horstenau, *Osterreich-Ungarns letzter Krieg* II, p. 320.

20.   Glaise-Horstenau, ibid., p. 322.

21.   Georg Bruchmüller, *Die Deutsche Artillerie beim Angriff im Stellungskriegs* (Charlottenberg: Verlag "Offene Worte," 1926), pp. 15–19 and 41–42, hereafter referred to as Bruchmüller, *Angriff.*

22.   Max Hofmann, *The War of Lost Opportunities* (London: Kegan Paul, 1924), p. 135. The counterattack at Lake Narocz was a complete success for the Germans. Although they were outnumbered by the Russians by seven or eight to one, the Germans regained all of the territory that they had lost to an earlier Russian attack. See Norman Stone, *The Eastern Front 1914–1917* (New York: Charles Scribner's Sons, 1975), pp. 230–31.

23.   Hofmann, *The War of Lost Opportunities*, p. 135.

24.   Whether the "rolling barrage" was developed by Bruchmüller in the east or von Behrendt in the west was a subject of much acrimonious debate in the 1920s. Who "invented" the "rolling barrage," however, like the question of whether Leibnitz or Newton discovered the calculus, is a moot point. The German field artillery had entered the war with the idea that its principal task was to help the infantry gain fire superiority over an enemy who was most likely deployed in a line. In the attacks "with limited objectives" that began in the fall of 1914, artillery fire on the forward enemy trench was often used to facilitate the crossing of "no man's land." A few seconds before the attacking infantry were to enter the trench, the artillery barrage would shift to targets to the rear of the first line. The only changes needed to turn this sort of artillery fire into a "rolling bar-

rage" were a schedule and the placing of fire in the open ground *between* enemy positions. See Bruchmüller, *Durchbruchschlachten*, pp. 106–09.

25. Bruchmüller, *Durchbruchschlachten*, pp. 44–48.

26. Bruchmüller, *Angriff*, p. 29.

27. An officer who took part in the Riga operation in 2nd Guard Division wrote that there was a trench mortar for every 15 meters of front. Major A. D. Lichnock, "Dünaübergang 1. September, 1917," in Heinrici, *Das Ehrenbuch der Deutschen Pioniere*, p. 326.

28. Bruchmüller, *Angriff*, p. 66 and attached maps.

29. von Winterfeldt, *Das Kaiser Franz Garde-Grenadier*, p. 56.

30. Lichnock, "Dünaübergang," p. 326.

31. Bruchmüller, *Angriff*, p. 62.

32. U.S. Army War College, *Gas Warfare, Part II, Methods of Defense Against Gas Attacks* (Washington, DC: War Department, 1918), p. 19.

33. Most regiments had only one light machine gun per company.

34. Verein der Offiziere des ehem. Preuss. Res.-Inf.-Regts. 3., *Reserve Infanterie Regiment Nr. 3* (Berlin: Gerhard Stalling, 1926), p. 146.

35. Fritz Kaelich, *Das Infanterie Regiment Nr. 406* (Berlin: Gerhard Stalling, 1922), p. 21.

36. *Der Weltkrieg 1914–1918*, vol. 13, pp. 194–95.

37. Rolf Brandt, *Um Riga und Oesell* (Leipzig: Velhagen & Klasing, 1917), p. 8.

38. von Winterfeldt, *Das Kaiser Franz Garde-Grenadier*, p. 56.

39. Gruss, *Aufbau und Verwendung*, p. 90.

8

Mountain Warfare

The ruling principle for any offensive in the mountains is the con-
quest and holding of the crests, in order to get to the next objective by
these land bridges. . . . Every column on the heights must move forward without hesitation; by doing so opportunities will arise to help a
neighbor who cannot get on, by swinging round in rear of the enemy
opposing him.

Otto von Below,[1]
Order to the Fourteenth Army

Within days of the capture of Riga, four of the divisions that had fought
there had boarded trains and were rolling west to France and Belgium.
This was the beginning of a great transfer of forces from the east, where
victory had already been won, to the west, where defeat of the German
forces in the field was still a real possibility. In the ensuing three months,
the best divisions were pulled off the eastern front, leaving only second
line formations and that remnant of the German cavalry that still retained its horses to maintain order and guard against the unlikely eventu-
ality of a revival of Russian interest in the war.

Not all of the troops leaving the eastern front, however, found themselves heading for France and Belgium. A few selected formations—three
infantry divisions and the elite Alpine Corps—were sent south to the Italian Alps. There they joined three infantry divisions from the west and the
newly formed *Jäger* Division in preparation for what was to be the most
complete German victory of World War I.

TERRAIN AND SITUATION

Until the summer of 1917, the war between Italy and Austria-Hungary
had not been a major concern of the German High Command. For two
whole years the Italian and Austro-Hungarian armies had battered each
other along the mountainous border that separated the two nations. In
the course of these two years, little progress had been made on either side
toward winning a decisive victory. Thus, insofar as Germany was con-

cerned, Italy's main effect on the conduct of the war as a whole was to draw Austro-Hungarian troops away from the eastern front.

The German High Command became interested in Italy only when it appeared that the Austro-Hungarian forces in Italy were on the verge of collapse. The Italian strategy, hatched by the arch-attritionist General Luigi Cadorna, had been to bleed the Austro-Hungarians regardless of the cost to Italy. After two years of fighting, this strategy was beginning to bear fruit.

In the summer of 1917, General Konrad Krafft von Dellmensingen,[2] the former commander of the German Alpine Corps[3] and one of the few German generals with more than an academic knowledge of mountain warfare, made a tour of the Austro-Hungarian forces in Italy. At the end of this tour, General Krafft reported to the High Command that the Austro-Hungarians could not effectively resist the next Italian offensive. In order to forestall this debacle, the German High Command decided to launch an offensive of its own in Italy.

The place chosen by the High Command for the offensive was the valley of the Isonzo River (see Illustration 8). As the Isonzo runs from the Julian Alps south toward the Adriatic, along what is now the border between Italy and Yugoslavia, the river forms an "S". A few miles west of this great "S" the mountains give way to the great plain that reaches to Venice and beyond. Further south, where the Isonzo empties into the Adriatic, lay the city of Trieste, an Austrian possession long coveted by the Italians.

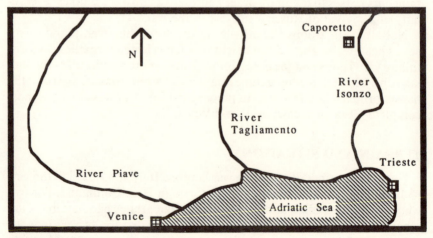

Illustration 8
The Venetian Plain

Throughout the war between Italy and Austria-Hungary, flat land had been at a premium. Every place where Italians and Austro-Hungarians faced each other was located high in the mountains that formed the borders between the two countries. The difficulty of moving troops and supplies through these mountains made it almost impossible for either side to exploit local successes.

It is not surprising, therefore, that the Italians chose the valley of the Isonzo as the scene of most of their offensives. The mountains on either side of the river were as formidable as any mountains along the front. They were, however, far fewer in number than those located in other sections of the front and soon gave way to flatter ground. As a further aid to movement, there were, to the north and south of the town of Caporetto,[4] a number of valleys that ran east to west into the valley of the Isonzo. These would provide useful highways to any attacker.

THE FOURTEENTH ARMY

The spearhead of the Austro-German offensive across the Isonzo was to be the German Fourteenth Army. Despite its name, only six out of the 14 divisions that made up the Fourteenth Army were from the German Army. The other eight were Austro-Hungarian formations that provided the Fourteenth Army with most of its trained mountain troopers—men whose expertise in high altitude warfare would be needed if the Italian positions that barred the way to open ground were to be cracked.[5]

The commanding general of the Fourteenth Army was Otto von Below. Von Below was a graduate of the German General Staff Academy, the institution in the German Army most concerned with the study of war at the operational level. As a corps commander on the eastern front, he had had ample opportunity to put this knowledge of operational art to practice. At Tannenberg and the Masurian Lakes, in Poland, and later in Macedonia, his corps took part in the kind of operational level maneuver that the General Staff had long considered the classical way to fight a campaign—a double envelopment of the enemy's field army. These campaigns had brought Germany victory against Russia, Serbia, and Romania, and provided von Below with a model for his campaign on the Isonzo.[6]

The Fourteenth Army's chief of staff, the same Krafft von Dellmensingen who had proposed the offensive to the High Command, did not share von Below's optimism. Despite a temperament that inclined him toward offensive action—the Austrian general Alfred Krauss called him "full of freshness and eagerness to attack"[7]—Krafft was aware of the inherent difficulties of movement in the mountains. He knew, from his own experience, how a small band of intrepid defenders could block a valley and thus keep an entire division from participating in a battle. As a result, the goal that he proposed for the operation was somewhat more modest than von Below's. He would be satisfied with a spoiling attack with the express aim of preventing the collapse of the Austro-Hungarian Army.

The relationship between Krafft and von Below was not typical of the traditional commanding general/chief of staff relationship that had been established in the early days of the German Empire by Hellmuth von Moltke the Elder. In part because the chiefs of staff were so well trained and had a direct line to the chief of the general staff, and in part because most German generals of Moltke's time gained their commands by virtue of their princely birth or their seniority, Moltke succeeded in raising the position of the chief of staff of an army to the point where commanders concentrated on the routine and the ceremonial while the chiefs of staff planned operations and made key decisions. Indeed, such was the power of the chief of staff of an army that, in a case where his commander gave an order against the chief of staff's advice, the latter was expected to record his dissension in writing. If the chief of staff did not do this and the order resulted in failure, it was the chief of staff, and not the commander, who was "relieved for cause."

Krafft, however, did not dissent from von Below's ambitious plan. Perhaps he recognized that von Below was a thoroughly professional practitioner of the art of war and linked his fate to the wishes of his commander out of respect and confidence. Krafft may also have realized that even if the Fourteenth Army failed to complete the destruction of the Italian forces on the Isonzo, his goal of relieving the pressure on Austria-Hungary would still have been attained.

The infantry and mountain infantry divisions of von Below's Fourteenth Army were organized into four "groups" (*Gruppen*), each of which was commanded by a corps commander and his staff. North of Caporetto, the Austrian General Alfred Krauss had four divisions—three Austrian and one German. Southeast of Group Krauss, the German General von Stein commanded three German divisions. South of Group Stein, the same General von Berrer who had commanded Group Berrer at Riga commanded a different formation with the same name. The new Group Berrer consisted of two German infantry divisions. Still farther south, the Austrian Fieldmarshall-Lieutenant Scotti commanded two Austro-Hungarian infantry divisions.[8]

Group Krauss and Group Stein were to cooperate in a double envelopment, the two wings of which were to attack along the west bank of the Isonzo until they met at Caporetto. If successfully carried out, this maneuver would permit the trapping of the Italian forces east of the Isonzo as well as provide a springboard for further penetration through the valleys that led west to the Venetian Plain. Group Berrer and Group Scotti, on the other hand, were to take possession of the mountains south of Tolmino and then move southwest along the valleys that ran parallel to that of the Isonzo.

PREPARATIONS

Throughout the months of September and October of 1917, the troops assigned to the Fourteenth Army arrived on the Italian Front and began their preparations for the offensive (see Illustration 9). A systematic training program was set in motion by each division. Training patrols and mock assaults gave the troops and their leaders a chance to become familiar with combat in the mountains. Acclimatization to the thin mountain air was also high on the list of training priorities. For the troops detailed for the offensive, each day brought a longer march with a heavier pack.[9]

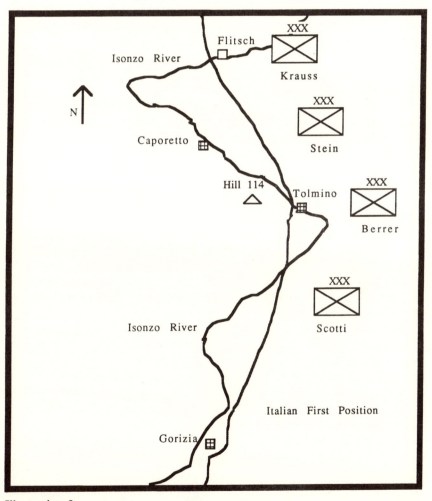

Illustration 9
Situation along the Isonzo, October 24, 1917

Enough time was left over after the route marches and battle exercises to conduct thorough training in the use of the 08/15 Maxim light machine gun. Many of the German infantry regiments had been issued their first light machine guns immediately before arriving on the Italian front and had yet to become familiar with them.[10] Other units, particularly those that had come from the western front, had had their allowance of light machine guns increased from one per company to six per company. Both developments required the training of a large number of new machine gunners.[11]

Insofar as their small unit tactics were concerned, the three divisions of the 14th Army that had come from the western front were state of the art. All three divisions had been in armies where the Assault Battalions had been conducting training courses and participating in operations for almost a full year. In addition, the soldiers who had joined these divisions in the course of the past year had, during their recruit training, been trained by instructors who had passed through teacher training courses held by the Assault Battalions.[12]

The formations specially trained and equipped for mountain warfare—the Alpine Corps, the *Jäger* Division, the 196th and 200th Infantry Divisions, and the Austrian mountain divisions—were also quite up to date in their tactics. The battalions that made up the German mountain divisions were, for the most part, *Jäger* battalions. The combination of prewar Boer tactics, early experience in the Vosges, attendance at training courses given by the Assault Battalions, and subsequent experience in the Carpathians, the Tyrol, and the Vosges, made the individual *Jäger* into a close copy of the stormtrooper. In August of 1916, moreover, each German *Jäger* battalion was given an additional machine gun company (for a total of two per battalion) and a trench mortar company of eight light trench mortars. This additional organic firepower, combined with the liberal attachment of mountain guns[13] and the training of the individual *Jäger* troops, made these *Jäger* battalions the functional equivalent of assault battalions.

The two infantry units assigned to the Fourteenth Army that were not formed from *Jäger* battalions were the Württemberg Mountain Battalion and the Bavarian Life Guard Regiment. The former was a special mountain unit that had been formed in October 1915 from volunteers drawn from all arms of service of Württemberg's semiautonomous little army.[14] Larger than an ordinary battalion, it consisted of six line companies (three light machine guns), three machine gun companies of 12 heavy machine guns each, and a trench mortar company of four light trench mortars and six grenade launchers. For combat, detachments (*Abteilungen*) that ranged in size from a reinforced company to the equivalent of a normal-sized infantry battalion were task organized.[15]

Since its formation, the Württemberg Mountain Battalion had fought primarily against the Rumanians and Russians in the Carpathians. These campaigns had been fluid even by the standards of the eastern front, with little opportunity for the enemy to establish himself in one position before his flanks were threatened and even less occasion to fortify properly a piece of ground. Nevertheless, the Württemberg mountaineers developed a style of warfare that was remarkably similar to that of the Assault Battalions. Like the *Jägers* of other German mountain units, many of the men of the Württemberg Mountain Battalion had fought in the Vosges or the Argonne in 1915. As evidenced by the use of *Stosstrupps* to lead the attack into enemy positions, a portion of the officers and NCOs of the Württemberg Mountain Battalion must have attended courses given by one or more of the Assault Battalions. Because of its inability to call upon artillery to provide indirect fire support, however, the Württemberg Mountain Battalion became even more adept than the Assault Battalions on supporting its maneuver with machine gun, mountain gun, and trench mortar fire.[16]

While the Württemberg Mountain Battalion was a new unit whose elite status derived from its special training and experience in mountain warfare, the Bavarian Life Guards were an old regiment with traditions dating back to the seventeenth century. With an officer corps drawn largely from the Bavarian higher nobility, the Life Guards served in peacetime as the ceremonial bodyguard for the King of Bavaria.[17] However, neither the regiment's high social status nor the fact that one of its battalions was commanded by the son of that monarch prevented it from being sent into some of the fiercest fighting in the war.

Despite these superficial differences between these two units, both of which were assigned to the Alpine Corps, their tactics and fighting qualities were remarkably similar. The formative tactical experience for the overwhelming majority of the officers and NCOs of these units was the trench warfare of the western front. Mountain fighting had reinforced the tendencies toward independent movement of squads and the attachment of supporting arms to platoons and companies that the Württembergers had picked up in the Argonne. The seminal experience for the Bavarian Life Guards, on the other hand, was the half-year-long battle for Verdun, where they took part in a large number of attacks "with limited objectives."

ARTILLERY

In addition to the mountain artillery attached to the infantry, the Fourteenth Army had at its disposal artillery that was much more powerful than that which had been available to General von Hutier's Eighth Army at Riga. General Richard von Behrendt, the artillery commander for the Fourteenth Army, mustered 1822 guns for the operation.[18] Colonel Bruchmüller, on the other hand, had had only about 680 guns at Riga.

The task facing von Behrendt's gunners, however, was far more daunting than the one dealt with by the German gunners at Riga. The Italians along the Isonzo were well equipped with modern artillery, much of which was heavy and some of which had been sheltered in caverns along the front. The German guns and howitzers at Caporetto, moreover, had to compensate for the small numbers of trench mortars available. Von Behrendt had less than one half of the trench mortars that Bruchmüller had had at Riga, although a somewhat larger proportion of von Behrendt's trench mortars were of the heavy and medium variety.

Despite this difference of scale, the German artillery bombardment at Caporetto followed the general pattern of the bombardment at Riga. At 2:00 on the morning of October 24, 1917, all available guns, howitzers, and trench mortars began firing Blue Cross and Green Cross shells at the Italian forward trenches and artillery positions. Additional Green Cross shells were fired by the over 1000 gas projectors of the 35th Pioneer Battalion, a unit that specialized in large-scale gas bombardments. The chief difference lay in the preparations for the bombardment. While Bruchmüller had kept registration of his guns to a minimum at Riga, von Behrendt had his artillery units register over the course of five days.[19]

Where the Italians were caught unaware by large concentrations of the German gas, whole platoons were killed.[20] The sentries often succumbed too quickly to wake those asleep and the sleeping died where they lay. Where the gas was weaker, the tactical effect was less dramatic. In some places, the Italian gun crews simply ran away.[21] In other locations, the gas merely irritated the artillerymen—who had been equipped with good quality gas masks—but killed the unprotected ammunition mules.

COUNTER-BOMBARDMENT

The immediate Italian response to the gassing was to launch a counter-bombardment against the German and Austrian positions. While this caused casualties among the troops moving up to the attack, it failed to impede the Fourteenth Army in the execution of its plan. The Italian batteries, especially the heavy batteries that were dependent upon mules to move ammunition up to the guns, were too hard hit by the gas to produce a respectable volume of fire.

What fire there was, moreover, was not very accurate. The positions of the German and Austrian batteries were largely unknown to the Italian artillery spotters. Even after the Austro-German bombardment began, the Italians were not able to locate the sources of it because the heavy fog in the valleys and the rain in the mountains made it difficult to identify the flash of individual guns.[22]

The gassing of the Italians lasted for two hours. Between 4:00 and 6:00 A.M., relative calm reigned along the Isonzo. With the exception of the artillery and the trench mortars firing in support of Group Krauss,[23] the

Germans and Austrians had stopped firing while the Italians were only capable of sending over the occasional round. A few minutes after 6:00 A.M., however, the bulk of the German and Austrian artillery and trench mortars resumed the bombardment, this time with high explosive. Although the rain and fog made observation difficult, the accuracy of the Fourteenth Army's artillery was quite good. Painstaking prebattle reconnaissance on the part of artillery and trench mortar officers paid off when the first or second round from each tube landed squarely on its target.[24]

THE INFANTRY ATTACKS

During this bombardment, which lasted a few minutes less than two hours, the infantry and mountain troops, as well as the pioneer detachments, machine gun companies, and mountain batteries that accompanied them, moved into their attack positions. At 8:00 A.M., the bombardment of the Italian forward position ceased. The howitzers and trench mortars concentrated their fire on the Italian second position and on the machine gun nests that lay between the first and second Italian positions. At the same time, the fire of the field guns formed the creeping barrage. Led by lower echelon stormtroops, the infantry followed the barrage in thin columns, as the terrain rarely permitted any other sort of formation.

The garrison of the Italian forward position did little to hinder the advance of the Fourteenth Army. German and Austrian battalions, concerned more with reaching the high ground than with maintaining contact with neighboring units, pushed across the Italian forward position as fast as they could. The effect of this disregard for any semblance of a linear advance was exacerbated by the irregularity of the terrain. It was therefore very difficult for some units to keep up with their creeping barrage, while others had to fire their signal rockets to request that the barrage be moved forward ahead of schedule. The advance was so rapid, moreover, that by midday many of the German and Austrian units had pushed so far that they were beyond the range of their field guns.

By the time that the first elements of the Fourteenth Army reached the second Italian position, the attack had broken up into a series of battalion- and company-sized engagements—seizing hilltops and racing through valleys. Machine gun nests and small groups of Italian mountain troops offered the bulk of resistance that was encountered. This resistance, however, was largely uncoordinated and was easily overcome. The most popular German technique for doing this was to pin down the defenders with machine gun fire so that a squad could get around an open flank and reduce the strong point with hand grenades.[25]

As would be the case until the end of the war, however, a vestigial fondness for frontal attacks was still present in the minds of some officers. Early on the first day of the attack, the 10th Company of the Bavarian Life

Guards attempted a frontal assault on an Italian strong point in the Valley of the Isonzo. Without having first deceived the enemy as to their intentions or first attaining fire superiority, the Bavarians formed a rough skirmish line and rushed forward. The regimental history of the Life Guards records that the assault was repulsed with "significant casualties."[26]

On a larger scale, flank attacks were used to reduce the larger (company- and battalion-sized) Italian strongpoints that were positioned so as to bar the path of entire divisions. One such strongpoint was the battalion position on Hill 1114, the easternmost peak of a ridge that overlooked a 13-kilometer-long stretch of the Isonzo between Tolmino and Caporetto. Two belts of trenches surrounded a central bastion with deep dugouts capable of protecting the garrison from all but direct hits from heavy howitzers. Thick barbed wire obstacles completed the fortification.

The battalion commander of the Third Battalion of the Bavarian Life Guards, the unit assigned the task of taking Hill 1114, first signalled, by means of a salvo of green signal rockets and a messenger pigeon, for the siege mortars that had been shelling the Italian strong point all day to cease their fire. This accomplished, he sent two companies forward to attack from opposite directions. Each of these companies, in turn, infiltrated patrols through gaps in the Italian wire and caught the defenders of the outermost belt in a crossfire.

As darkness fell, a third company, led by Second Lieutenant Ferdinand Schörner, infiltrated a platoon through yet another gap in the wire. This platoon then cleared that section of the Italian trench that commanded that part of the wire obstacle that barred the way of the second platoon of Schörner's company. Before the outermost belt was cleared, stormtroops from each platoon sprung forward and proceeded to roll up the second (inner) belt, forcing the surviving Italians to take shelter in the bastion.

After a short pause to allow the rest of the company to enter the position, the assault on the bastion began. Three squads were sent against suspected weak points. Two of these were repulsed. One succeeded in breaking in to the bastion. The breach was immediately exploited and Schörner's company was soon rolling up trenches and clearing out dugouts. The Italian resistance, at first fierce, collapsed soon after the exploitation of the breach. Three hundred of the defenders surrendered, handing over to Schörner a number of machine guns and large stores of food and ammunition.[27]

GROUP KRAUSS

North of Caporetto, Group Krauss pushed forward into the Italian lines at 9:00 A.M.. Attacking with one regiment on a narrow front, Group Krauss quickly broke through the Italian trenches and the ruined town of Flitsch—obstacles that had been rendered harmless by the early morning gas attack. After passing through Flitsch, General Krauss, who had made his reputation before the war as a writer of books on military theory, violated what was then a central tenet of mountain warfare. Sacrificing security for speed, Krauss declined to take the ridges along his route of march, preferring instead to send three of his four divisions one after the other through that part of the Valley of the Isonzo that led from the town of Flitsch, just north of Mount Krl, to the village of Saga.

Surprised by this unorthodox move, the Italians who might have been in a position to resist the advance of Group Krauss were unable to offer any significant resistance—the Germans and Austrians had gotten behind the bulk of the Italian defenders during the morning's advance and left them stranded and impotent on the mountaintops while they pushed on. The first day's advance of Group Krauss was halted only when the lead regiment of the long column marching along the banks of the Isonzo ran into a German artillery barrage. Messages sent to the artillery headquarters to lift the barrage didn't get through, so Group Krauss had to wait until the next day to make any further progress.[28]

In a maneuver similar to that of Group Krauss, the German 12th Division (Group Stein) marched northwest towards Caporetto along both banks of the Isonzo. As the march of the 12th Division was literally under the guns of the Italian third position, the bulk of Group Stein, including the elite Alpine Corps, was devoted to the capture of that position. Another division, the German 50th Division, supported the movement of the 12th Division by attacking westwards towards the Isonzo. This was aimed at preventing the Italians on the east bank of the Isonzo from taking advantage of their "interior lines" and concentrating against either Group Krauss or the 12th Division.

The advance of the 12th Division was swift. In a classic application of stormtroop tactics, the infantry of the 12th Division rolled up the first Italian position. They then formed into march columns and marched up the Isonzo at a rate of three to four kilometers an hour. Close behind the infantry followed the division artillery and services—the Valley of the Isonzo was one of the few places in the area where an entire division could march as a single formation. Around noon, the infantry of the 12th Division, aided by a creeping barrage provided by their own artillery, broke through that portion of the Italian second line that crossed the Isonzo just south of the town of Caporetto. At 3:30 the Germans stormed the town and, after a few minutes of street fighting, took it. They then turned east, marching through the valley that would eventually take them to the Venetian Plain.[29]

By nightfall of the first day, the Italians were in disarray. The Germans and Austrians seemed to be everywhere, penetrating three lines of resistance almost simultaneously and leaving behind them isolated groups of stragglers who, dispirited and leaderless, were often quite amenable to surrender. The poor morale of the Italian Army, encouraged by the seemingly senseless tactics of attrition that had been practiced for the past two years, was exacerbated by an officer corps notorious for its disregard for the welfare of the enlisted men. While the daring tactics of the Germans and Austrians led to many Italian units being surrounded, the sorry state of leadership in the Italian Army led to the rapid surrender of those surrounded units.

Even those Italian units whose members were willing to keep on fighting, however, often found themselves in untenable situations. Cut off from their higher headquarters and unable to coordinate their actions with other units, diehard battalions and companies were soon surrounded in their strong points and found themselves faced with a choice between surrender and the systematic reduction of their little fortresses by the German and Austrian troops that followed the first wave of the attack.

EXPLOITATION

Early on the second day of the attack, the men of the Fourteenth Army, refreshed by captured Italian rations, resumed the attack. The German *Jäger* Division (Group Krauss) completed the envelopment of the Italian troops on the east bank of the Isonzo. The rest of the Fourteenth Army pushed on towards the Venetian Plain, the forward elements marching through valleys whenever possible and leaving the reduction of isolated Italian units and strong points to those behind them. Ahead of the Fourteenth Army, the Italians retreated in confusion. A few uncoordinated counterattacks were a nuisance to the advancing Germans and Austrians, but did little to slow down their progress toward open ground. By October 27, the forward elements of the Fourteenth Army had left the mountains behind them.

Once on the Venetian Plain, the character of the battle changed. The three rivers that ran across the Plain into the Adriatic provided the Italians with barriers behind which they could attempt to establish defensive positions. The first two Italian attempts in this regard, on the Torre and on the Tagliamento, failed. The Germans and Austrians managed to cross each river in force before the Italians could consolidate their position. The third Italian attempt to form a defensive position, this time on the Piave, succeeded. After almost a month of advancing, the Fourteenth Army had been stopped.

By any standard, the attack of the Central Powers along the Isonzo was a success. Of the 2 million Italian soldiers arrayed against the Austro-Hungarian Empire at the beginning of the offensive, somewhere between 800,000 and 1,000,000 had been killed, wounded, or captured. Over 3000 guns, half of the Italian inventory, as well as 1700 trench mortars and 3000 machine guns were captured. At a time when they were already suffering from a shortage of military manpower, both France and Britain felt compelled to dispatch large expeditionary forces (a total of 11 divisions) to shore up their prostrate ally. At the very least, the victory at Caporetto meant that the German High Command needed no longer to worry about the imminent collapse of the Austro-Hungarian armed forces.

NOTES

1. From von Below's last order to the Fourteenth Army. Quoted and translated by John Keegan, "Blitzkrieg in the Mountains. The Battle of Caporetto," *Military Review*, January 1965.
2. Krafft von Dellmensingen, who started his career in the Bavarian Heavy Artillery, was selected for the Bavarian General Staff. He began the war as Chief of the General Staff of the Sixth Army, taking command of the Alpine Corps in May of 1915. Rudolf von Kramer et al., *Der königlich bayerische Militär-Max-Joseph-Orden: Kriegstaten und Ehrenbuch, 1914–1918* (Munich: Selbsverlag des königlich bayerische Militär-Max-Joseph-Orden, 1966), p. 340.
3. The Alpine Corps was not an army corps but rather a reinforced infantry division.
4. This town, which the Austrians called Karfreit, is currently located in the Yugoslav Republic of Slovenia and is known as Kobarid.
5. Only two of the German divisions, the 200th Infantry Division and the Alpine Corps, had any significant experience in mountain warfare. *Der Weltkrieg 1914–1918*, vol. 13, p. 231 and Konrad Krafft von Dellmensingen, *Der Durchbruch am Isonzo* (Berlin: Druck and Verlag von Gerhard Stalling, 1926), p. 19.
6. Francesco Fadini, *Caporetto dalla Parte del Vincitore: La Biografia del Generale Otto von Below e il suo Diario inedito sulla Campagna d'Italia del 1917* (Florence: Vallechi, 1974), passim.
7. Alfred Krauß, *Das Wunder von Karfreit: Der Durchbruch bei Flitsch* (Munich: I. F. Lehman's Verlag, 1926), p. 15.
8. Holding a military rank exclusive to the Hapsburg Empire, a fieldmarshall lieutenant was the equivalent of an American or British major general.
9. Krafft von Dellmensingen, *Der Durchbruch*, p. 24.
10. Rommel, *Attacks*, p. 201; and Ritter von Reiß et al., *Das Königlich Bayerische Infanterie Leib*, p. 298–300.
11. von Reiß et al., ibid., p. 300.
12. Week long training courses for officers and NCOs training recruits were first held in the summer of 1916 for instructors at the recruit depots of the Prussian XI Corps District. The idea caught on and, in December of 1916, all of the military districts that sent recruits to the western front sent their "drill instructors" to courses held by the various assault battalions. Gruss, *Aufbau und Verwendung*, pp. 85–86.
13. See Seeger, *Die Württembergische Gebirgs-Artillerie im Weltkrieg 1915–*

1918 (Stuttgart: C. Belser, 1920), passim, for a thorough discussion of the use of mountain guns during World War I.

14.   Rommel, *Attacks*, p. 91. The XIII Corps of the Prussian Army was composed entirely of units from the Grand Duchy of Württemberg.

15.   F. T. Schmidt, "Die Württembergischen Gebirgsschützen," *Der Feldgrau* 3, 1954, pp. 45–48.

16.   See Rommel, *Attacks*, passim.

17.   Nikolaus von Preradovich, *Die militärische und soziale Herkunft der Generalität des Deutschen Heeres, 1. Mai, 1944* (Osnabrück: Biblio-Verlag, 1978), p. 55.

18.   Hans Killian, *Wir Stürmten durchs Friaul* (Neckargemünd: Kurt Vowincker Verlag, 1978), p. 247.

19.   Georg Bruchmüller, *Die Artillerie beim Angriff in Stellungskrieg*, p. 116.

20.   Killian, *Totentanz*, p. 76 and Glaise-Horstenau, *Österreich-Ungarns letzter Krieg*, p. 525.

21.   Rommel, *Attack*, pp. 214–15.

22.   Fadini, *Caporetto*, pp. 262–64.

23.   Group Krauss, which was separated from the rest of the Fourteenth Army by Mount Krn, was on a separate timetable.

24.   Killian, *Totentanz*, p. 17.

25.   See Rommel, *Attack*, pp. 215–17, for examples of the squad and platoon tactics used by the Württemberg Mountain Battalion at Caporetto.

26.   von Reiß, et al., *Das Königlich Bayerische Infanterie Leib*, p. 311.

27.   Lieutenant Schörner was awarded the *Pour le Mérite* for his exploits on Hill 1114. von Reiß et al., *Das Königlich Bayerische Infanterie Leib*, pp. 314–15.

28.   Glaise-Horstenau, *Österreich-Ungarns letzter Krieg*, pp. 526–27.

29.   Killian, *Totentanz*, p. 86–91.

9

Cambrai

Each attack offers opportunities for self-designated activity and mission-oriented action, even down to the level of the individual soldier.

The Attack in Position Warfare

The successful exploitation of the breakthrough at Caporetto proved to Ludendorff that the German Army had developed a tactical system capable of breaking the deadlock of trench warfare and thus permitting the resumption of maneuver at the operational level. During the three years that it took the German Army to develop this system, however, Germany's enemies were not idle. While no contemporary army encouraged tactical innovation the way that the German Army did, all major belligerents made attempts to solve the problem of trench warfare by changing the way that their armies fought. The most significant of these innovations was the tank.[1]

As is well known, the first successful use of the tank in battle was at Cambrai. On November 20, 1917, 400 British tanks and six British infantry divisions attacked two understrength German infantry divisions along a front of 12 kilometers. Within 24 hours, the British had driven the Germans back five miles—a feat unprecedented on the western front. For the first time since the outbreak of the war, church bells rang in Britain.

The British accomplishment at Cambrai had cost the Germans two infantry divisions and 40 square miles of territory. It had, moreover, caused much worry at the High Command, where it was feared that the English would press their advantage and attack again. The salient driven into the German lines presented more than a threat. The exposed flanks of the British position provided the German Army with an opportunity to try its new tactics on a large scale on the western front. The army defeated at

Caporetto had been poorly led, poorly trained, and demoralized by years of apparently senseless slaughter exploited by socialist agitation. In 1917, however, the army fielded by the British Empire was still a formidable opponent.

Ten days after the British attack began, the Germans were ready to counterattack (see Illustration 10). Von der Marwitz, commanding general of the Second Army, had amassed 13 infantry divisions, nine of which were from the "pools" of divisions held by the Army Group Crown Prince Rupprecht and the High Command. These he organized into three oversized army corps. In the north, Group Arras, consisting of four divisions in the first line and two in corps reserve, was to attack towards the south. In the east, Groups Caudry and Busigny, each with three divisions in the first line and one in corps reserve, were to attack toward the west.

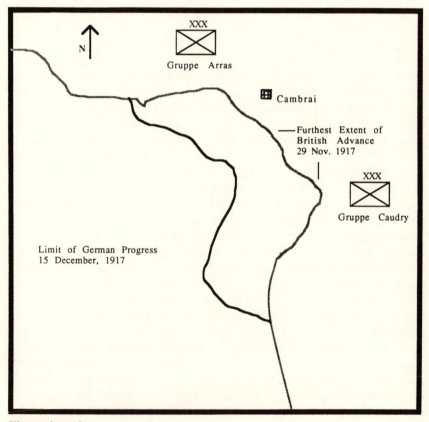

Illustration 10
The Cambrai Counteroffensive, November 30, 1917

In the instructions given by the High Command, the attack toward the west was designated the "main thrust" (*Hauptstoβ*) with the chief mission of Group Arras being to support that attack by drawing off as many British formations and as much British attention as possible.[2] The timing of the attack, while somewhat unusual, was in keeping with this conception. Rather than having the two groups attack simultaneously, von der Marwitz ordered Groups Caudry and Bussigny to attack at 8:50 A.M. and Group Arras three hours later at 11:50. This, he hoped, would convince the British that his attack was limited to the southeastern portion of the Cambrai salient and, in turn, lead them to denude the northern portion of the salient at the very moment when Group Arras was to attack.[3]

CREEPING BARRAGE

Each division's attack was prepared according to the model of Caporetto, Riga, and the attacks "with limited objectives" of the previous two and a half years. Gas and high explosive neutralized the British batteries while shrapnel and high explosive rained on the riflemen and machine gunners in the British trenches. At Caporetto, the chief work of the Austro-German artillery had been counter-battery fire. At Cambrai, on the other hand, where the British did not have quantities of well protected heavy artillery, the main business of the artillery was the creeping barrage. It was perhaps because of this that each division retained control over most of its organic artillery and organized its own creeping barrage with little direction from above.

One optimistic division commander planned for his barrage to move a hundred meters every minute. Some of his more cautious colleagues, on the other hand, set a schedule of a hundred meters every five minutes. In case the creeping barrage advanced too slowly, infantry battalion commanders were able to speed it up by firing signal rockets or jets from a flamethrower into the air. No provision, however, had been made to slow down the creeping barrage in case the infantry couldn't keep up with it.

ELITE ASSAULT UNITS

In most divisions, the first Germans to cross into the British trenches were members of elite assault units. The Second Army's assault battalion, the 3rd *Jäger*-Assault Battalion, was at less than half-strength. The majority of the battalion had been sent to Italy to take part in the offensive along the Isonzo and had not yet returned to the western front. The Second Army, therefore, could only provide stormtroopers for two of the ten attacking divisions.[4] Those divisions not receiving army-level stormtroopers, therefore, had to rely on their organic assault units— division and regimental assault detachments and companies to provide the dozen or so assault squads that each division needed to lead it into the British position.

Prior to the counterattack, the companies and platoons of the 3rd *Jäger*-Assault Battalion were broken down into their component squads which, in turn, were reassembled into "assault blocks" (*Sturmblocks*). Each assault block was an ad hoc unit commanded by a second lieutenant or staff sergeant whose size and composition depended on the mission that it was assigned. The 2nd Assault Company, for example, which had the mission of leading the 109th Infantry Regiment through two English trench systems of three trenches each, was task organized into two assault blocks and a "security block" (*Sicherungsblock*). Each of the assault blocks, consisting of assault squads, light machine gun squads, flame-thrower squads, and one or two grenade launchers, was given the task of breaking through one of the trench systems.[5]

THE BREAKTHROUGH

Despite the fact that neither the stormtroops nor the ordinary infantry that followed them had had the opportunity to rehearse the attack on the British first trench system at Cambrai, the first phase of the counter-offensive—the attack of Group Caudry out of the east—went well for the Germans. The lack of ostentatious preparations on the part of the Germans had given them strategic surprise. The short length and ferocity of the bombardment, as well as the speed with which the stormtroops broke into the first trench system, gave the Germans the advantage of tactical surprise as well. The first wave of stormtroops, reinforced by pioneers and supported by the suppressive fire of the creeping barrage, quickly overran the first trench system and pushed forward, leaving the reduction of the first line to the following waves of ordinary infantry.

Once they passed through the first trench system, the ordinary infantry moved forward in a formation that the Germans still insisted on calling skirmish lines, although it could be more accurately described as a line of squads, each of which advanced in a formation that conformed to its particular situation. Unlike that of the Italians at Caporetto, however, the British will to resist at Cambrai did not collapse with the loss of the first trench system. Each village or wood, and practically every old communications trench, provided a rallying point for groups of stragglers determined to make the Germans pay for every mile. To clear its path of such resistance, the German "skirmish line" broke up into component squads. These squads, supported by whatever heavy weapons were at hand, closed with the enemy using the same techniques that had served the German infantry so well during countless raids and attacks "with limited objectives."

As a further aid in this kind of fighting, the German infantry was equipped with artillery of its own, guns that supported the infantry by providing direct fire against such point targets as machine gun nests. These guns came from the field artillery regiments of the infantry divisions. A battery of four light (7.7cm) field guns was assigned to each attacking infantry regiment. These batteries, referred to as "infantry accompanying batteries," were often reinforced with pioneers—to remove obstacles in the path of the horse-drawn guns—and light machine gun teams.

Although the German infantry at Cambrai, both the designated stormtroopers and the ordinary follow-on troops, were organized and equipped for a trench raid or attack "with limited objectives," they did not have the advantage of being able to prepare for weeks or even months for an advance of a few hundred meters. Once the first trench system was breached, there was no time for a detailed reconnaissance that allowed a leader to pinpoint the location of every machine gun on a 1:10,000 scale map. The decision to attack, and the approach used was decided instantly, on the basis of a quick look at a large-scale map and a hasty analysis of the situation. Painstaking preparation and repeated rehearsal had been replaced by rapid improvisation and the almost instinctive execution of battle drills.

The hasty attacks, despite their improvised nature, bore enough of a semblance to a trench raid so that there was no doubt as to the paternity of the technique. Ernst Jünger, who led a company of the 73rd (Hannoverian) Infantry Regiment at Cambrai, wrote down his impressions of one of these little battles in his diary.

We went on, and a moment later a fresh stand was encountered. Bombs flew on both sides and burst with a resounding din. Now the technique of the storm troop came into play. A chain of bombs went from hand to hand along the trench. Snipers took up positions behind traverses ready to draw a bead on enemy bombers; the platoon commander kept an eye out over the top to see a counterattack in the nick of time; and the light machine gun section mounted their guns where there was a good field of fire.[6]

In one division, some of the infantry that followed the first waves of the attack were organized into company- and battalion-size task forces that were, like the much smaller task forces of the 3rd *Jäger*-Assault Battalion, called "assault blocks." Company-size assault blocks consisted of three to five platoons of infantry, four light trench mortars, and three or four heavy machine guns. The larger assault blocks contained a full infantry battalion (four companies of infantry, four to eight light trench mortars, and a full machine gun company of 12 heavy machine guns) reinforced by field guns from an infantry accompanying battery.[7] Like their antecedents at Verdun, the assault blocks at Cambrai were held in reserve until the forward waves ran into resistance that could not easily be overcome or safely bypassed. At that point, an assault block would be sent forward under the command of a particularly skilled officer. Strict orders were given that the assault blocks not be wasted on the "feeding" of the forward line, but only be used to maintain the momentum of the attack.[8]

Despite the fact that they were fighting in unfamiliar terrain, the stormtroopers and follow-on forces of Groups Caudry and Busigny made excellent progress the first day. By noon, they had pushed a distance of five miles into the British lines on a front ten miles long. Their success, however, was not repeated by Group Arras. Warned by the attack of Groups Caudry and Busigny, the British alerted and reinforced their troops facing north. Without the advantage of surprise and with their rolling barrage rolling on ahead of them, the stormtroopers of Group Arras had to fight a slow and difficult battle against intact British units.

AN UNEXPECTED ALLY

Although the fighting in the terrain in between and behind the British trench systems was more difficult than the taking of the trenches themselves, the German infantry continued to push forward for over 48 hours. After the first two days of the operation, however, the British recovered from the initial shock of the attack. They began their own counterattacks just as the effect of two days of fighting began to slow down the Germans. Nevertheless, the Germans continued to advance. By the seventh day of the operation, the Second Army had recovered all of the territory that had been lost to the British tanks as well as a considerable piece of ground that the Allies had held since the fall of 1914.

In stopping the Germans from advancing even further, the British found an unexpected ally in their own supply dumps. For over a year, the German nation had been subsisting on substandard food. The German soldier, who before the war had been the best fed in Europe, was reduced to a daily ration of adulterated rye bread and turnips. This diet contained insufficient vitamins to keep soldiers healthy, insufficient calories to maintain body weight, and was insufficiently enticing to keep the attacking infantry from spending a great deal of time looting the stores that the retreating British had left behind.

This looting, exacerbated in places by the discovery of stocks of rum, did much to slow the momentum of the German counteroffensive. Crown Prince Rupprecht, who as commanding general of Army Group Crown Prince Rupprecht was von der Marwitz's immediate superior, wrote soon after the battle that "the looting of enemy dugouts, depots, and baggage of food, etc., weakens the front quicker than enemy fire and attrition."[9] By nightfall on December 7, the exhausted German infantry

had stopped moving forward and the British took the opportunity to reform their line.

The breakdown in discipline notwithstanding, the Cambrai counteroffensive was a great success for the Germans. While the territory regained
had no particular value, the rapidity with which it had been recaptured
convinced many high-level decision makers, not the least of whom was
Ludendorff, that the new tactics of the German infantry were effective
against a first-class enemy. Had these tactics failed at Cambrai, on the
other hand, Ludendorff might have had second thoughts about his plan
for an offensive leading to a war-winning victory in the west. As these tactics did succeed, however, he went ahead with his plans.

TRAINING

The first prerequisite for an offensive in the west was a sufficient number of troops trained in the new tactics. Units that had been on the western front for a year or more could be counted on to be familiar with major
portions of the new tactical system. The recruits reporting to their depots,
the veterans of the first year of the war returned to active service by the
"combing" of the factories and the farms, and the men transferred from
the eastern front, however, had to undergo a thorough apprenticeship before they could be judged competent to practice the new tactics. The German High Command therefore dedicated the winter of 1917–1918 to
completing the transformation of the German Army in the west.

The training undergone by the troops who were to take part in the
spring offensive was a mixture of the old and the new. While stormtrooper tactics were a radical departure from even the most advanced tactics taught during peacetime, they nevertheless grew out of the way that
German soldiers had been taught to fight before the war. During the
course of the war, when recruits were regularly sent to the front with as little as eight weeks of training, the military fundamentals had been neglected. Thus, the task of retraining much of the German Army had to be
preceded by a bit of remedial basic training.

The first step was the establishment of a climate of discipline. Veteran
trench fighter and green recruit alike were so lacking in the military bearing that the old Regular Army had tried so hard to inculcate in its soldiers
that senior German officers regularly referred to the German Army of
1917–1918 as a "militia." Time in the training schedule was therefore set
aside for close order drill—including the "goosestep"—and classes on
military courtesy.[10]

Rifle marksmanship, a skill that had atrophied in the course of the war,
was emphasized throughout the training period. Ludendorff had come to
the conclusion that, because of the primacy of the hand grenade, the German infantryman had lost confidence in his rifle. This confidence,

Ludendorff believed, could only be regained through constant practice in firing under different conditions. Thus, although he did not issue detailed instructions—as usual, such matters were left to the discretion of company and battalion commanders—Ludendorff ordered that marksmanship training be given a high priority.

In the crowded villages behind the German lines, "every little slope was in use as a range, so that the bullets whistled about the country very much as in a battle." As many riflemen as possible were also trained in the use of the light machine gun. All of this live fire sometimes resulted in accidents. In one case, a machine gunner inadvertently shot the commanding officer of a neighboring unit off his horse while the latter was reviewing his troops.[11]

To ensure that the attacking infantry would be able to rapidly exploit any breakthrough, units were marched long distances to and from their training sites. Daily marches of 30 kilometers in each direction (for a total of 60 kilometers a day) were not uncommon. Strenuous as these marches were, however, they were more than mere physical training. Rather, they provided the infantry with practice in attacking on the move. At Riga and at Caporetto the Germans had maintained the momentum of their offensive by placing reserves a few kilometers behind the front and starting them towards the battlefield as soon as the movement of the first line troops gave them room. By the time that these reserves ran into the enemy, they would have marched 11 or more kilometers. The ability to deploy for the attack after such an exertion would be a prerequisite for the success of the offensive.

The chief formation into which the German infantry were trained to deploy for battle was the skirmish line. This was not, however, the solid bayonet walls of 1914. Within the skirmish line of 1918 squads advanced as individual units, the particular formation taken by each squad depending on the tactical situation. For rapid movement across uncontested territory, a variety of irregular columns were practiced. Within these columns, squads and platoons had the same flexibility of formation as they did in the skirmish line.

For advanced training in stormtroop tactics, a large number of dummy trench systems were built in the training areas. Like the ones built in preparation for trench raids, these were modeled after actual French and British positions that had been photographed from the air. Live fire exercises were held on these positions. Both defenders and attackers fired their rifles, machine guns, and even flamethrowers, over each others' heads. Half-charge hand grenades were thrown with intent to miss. Needless to say, the live fire exercises sometimes resulted in casualties.

The same decentralization of authority that had permitted the development of stormtroop tactics in the first place also played an important role in its dissemination. The actual execution of the training mandated by Ludendorff was left to regimental, battalion, and, in particular, company commanders. That most company commanders at this time were second lieutenants, many who had been commissioned from the ranks of the war volunteers after a six-week training course, seems not to have reduced the professional discretion enjoyed by officers holding that billet.

The freedom allowed to regimental, battalion, and company commanders resulted in the troops receiving training with a wide variety of emphases. A deserter from the 449th Infantry Regiment reported to the French that he had received no training at the company or platoon level, but that all of the exercises that he had participated in had dealt with squad tactics. At the same time, a deserter from a neighboring unit, the 448th Infantry Regiment, told his captors that he had undergone many company drills.

The training of infantry accompanying batteries was similar to that of the infantry. It began with the training of the cannoneers as infantrymen, so that they might defend their guns from counterattacks and, in case their guns were destroyed, so that they might serve as infantry. After this individual training, the batteries underwent maneuvers in the rapid movement of the guns and the conduct of direct fire.

GUIDELINES

The officers and NCOs retraining the German infantry were guided in their work by a number of field manuals, pamphlets, and memoranda issued under Ludendorff's signature during the winter of 1917–1918. The writers of these guidelines varied. Some were front line officers recording their battle experiences. Others were General Staff officers trying to reduce the combination of the new tactics and the old operational art to words. Still others were technical experts describing new ways of using old weapons (e.g. direct fire for trench mortars and indirect fire for heavy machine guns) as well as introducing relatively new weapons (e.g. the light machine gun).

For leaders at the company level and below, the chief reference was the second edition of the *Training Manual for Foot Troops in War* (*Ausbildungsvorschrift für die Fusstruppen im Kriege*). This edition, dated January 1, 1918, was a radical departure from the first edition.[12] It expressed, for the first time in an official document, Ludendorff's command that every German infantryman be trained as a stormtrooper and described exercises, similar to those already in use by the assault battalions, to help commanders attain this goal.[13] In keeping with this idea, no mention was made of assault units within the infantry platoon, company, or even battalion, even though almost all infantry companies and a fair proportion of platoons at this time maintained specialized stormtroops.

In addition to endorsing the methods of the assault battalions, the second edition of the *Training Manual for Foot Troops in War* put special emphasis on the idea that the squad was a tactical unit in its own right. This acknowledgement manifested itself in unambiguous statements— "The squad is the smallest unit in open order"[14]—and numerous diagrams wherein the neat pairs of lines that in previous manuals had designated platoons and companies were replaced by little map symbols that designated squads, machine guns, and light trench mortars— discrete elements capable of independent action.[15] What Captain Rohr had known for over two years was now official.

Although the *Training Manual for Foot Troops in War* described the light machine gun as the chief means by which the infantry could provide for its own movement and promulgated a table of organization for an infantry company in which six of its 18 squads were light machine gun squads, it also included a great deal of information on the offensive use of heavy machine guns. The use of heavy machine guns as an auxiliary weapon in attacks "with limited objectives" and raids was, of course, well established by the end of 1917. German machine gunners had gotten very good at locating and suppressing enemy machine gun nests, covering the flanks of an attack, and sweeping the parapets of enemy trenches. Some had even mastered the art of indirect machine gunfire—a technique introduced by the Canadians in 1917—that called for the machine gun to fire at high angles so as to form a barrage on the far side of a low hill.[16]

The chief limitation on the use of the heavy machine gun as an offensive weapon remained its great weight. When this was mitigated in 1917 by the introduction of a relatively light tripod to replace the heavy sledge formerly used to support the weapon, the possibility of adding heavy machine guns to a force penetrating deeply—that is to say, beyond 400 meters—into an enemy position was raised. The *Training Manual for Foot Troops in War* heartily recommended this practice and included descriptions of how a machine gun company should be deployed for battle beyond the enemy's front line trench—to do for the infantry battalion what the light machine gun did for the infantry platoon.

From the point of view of techniques, the second edition of the *Training Manual for Foot Troops in War* had little new information for those who had been fighting on the western front. It did serve, nevertheless, an important doctrinal function—it legitimized and systematized what had been going on at the front for almost two years. Perhaps more importantly, the 1918 edition of the *Training Manual for Foot Troops in War* finished the work that had been started with the first (December 1916) version: It gave those training recruits in Germany official permission to train them in a way that was more in line with the realities of modern warfare.

THE ATTACK IN POSITION WARFARE

The largest unit that the second edition of the *Training Manual for Foot Troops in War* dealt with in any detail was the battalion. It was the battalion commander who personally coordinated the fire of heavy machine guns, light trench mortars, accompanying artillery, and indirectly firing artillery with the maneuver of companies, platoons, and even squads by designating targets and issuing "commands" (*Befehle*).[17] Above the battalion level, however, commanders commanded by means of "battle missions" (*Gefechtsauftrage*),[18] assignments that told a subordinate commander what needed to be done but rarely went into the technical details of how it was to be accomplished. As a general rule, battle missions gave a subordinate a goal to accomplish, but usually left the coordination of fire support, particularly the coordination of machine gun and light trench mortar fire, to the battalion commander.[19]

This dichotomy between "commands" and "battle assignments," a difference that was crucial to the German style of fighting, was reflected in the fact that a separate manual was written for those commanding units larger than battalions. Dated January 26, 1918, the *Attack in Position Warfare* (*Der Angriff im Stellungskrieg*) was, like the *Training Manual for Foot Troops in War*, an important departure from previous manuals. Its author, Captain Hermann Geyer of the Operations Section of the German General Staff,[20] took the techniques that had been developed during three years of attacks "with limited objectives" and pressed them into the service of what he called the "attack battle" (*Angriffsschlacht*)—the breaking through of the enemy trench system with the hope of resuming operational maneuver.

To make the marriage between trench warfare and the prewar tradition of operational maneuver work, Geyer had to reconcile the need for detailed, systematic preparation with the requirement that the exploitation of the rupture of the enemy position be as rapid as possible. The offensive at Caporetto and the counteroffensive at Cambrai proved to Geyer that this union could work. Of these two operations, however, Geyer seems to have been most influenced by the success of the Cambrai operation. There is such a similarity between *The Attack in Position Warfare* and Crown Prince Rupprecht's after action report "Lessons of the Cambrai Counteroffensive" that it is likely that Geyer had a copy of the latter document on his desk as he wrote the former.[21]

The lessons learned in other operations, however, were also taken into account. In November of 1917, General Ludendorff had asked the commanding general of each army to provide him with ideas for the upcoming manual. These provided Geyer, an officer who had had no front line experience, with a varied picture of trench warfare. The Operations Section of the General Staff, headed by the same Lieutenant Colonel Max

Bauer who had fostered the early growth of the Assault Battalions, contributed to the sources available to Geyer with its monograph on operations on the eastern front. This study, entitled *Lessons from Offensive Enterprises 1917*, paid particular attention to the Battle of Riga.

One document that we can be sure that Geyer consulted at the time—he mentions it by name in *The Attack in Position Warfare*—was *Accounts of Minor Operations Carried Out by the Vailly Group (XI Corps) During May and June of 1917 (Anlage kleiner Angriffsunternehmungen bei Gruppe Vailly im Mai/Juni 1917)*. This document provided detailed descriptions of state of the art attacks "with limited objectives" that had been carried out by units of the Seventh Army in the spring and summer of 1917. Ludendorff considered this study so useful, in fact, that he had it distributed throughout the army.

The key to the synthesis of the attack "with limited objectives" and operational maneuver was knowing precisely what needed to be centrally controlled and what needed to be left to subordinate commanders. "The attack," wrote Geyer, "even more so than the defense, demands strict leadership, careful and thorough direction for the cooperation of all arms within the fighting units and between neighboring units, especially clear designation of the goals of an attack. On the other hand, each attack *offers opportunities for self-designated activity and mission-oriented action,*[22] even down to the level of the individual soldier."[23]

Because the tactics of German units had already been worked out and promulgated, the bulk of *The Attack in Trench Warfare* dealt with those things that were amenable to centralized control—logistic preparations, secrecy, and the preliminary bombardment. A great deal of attention was also paid to a reiteration of some of the traditional aspects of German operational art. Chief among these were the idea of the *Schwerpunkt*, the critical point on the battlefield where the commander should focus his attention and his efforts, and the practice of *Weisungsführung*, the belief that a subordinate commander should follow not so much the express orders of his superior but rather regulate his actions according to what his superior is trying to accomplish (i.e., the "battle mission" given to the superior by the commander at the next higher level).

Despite this concentration on issues of interest to officers at the regimental level and higher, Geyer managed to devote a few lines of his work to the combat of smaller units. After reaffirming the High Command's commitment to stormtroop tactics, he stressed that, whenever possible, enemy strong points should be taken in the flank or the rear. If any particular unit was not able to get around to the flank or the rear of a strong point in its path, it should not resort to a frontal attack but rather call in suppressive artillery or machine gun fire on the objective and wait for neighboring units to take it in the flank or the rear.[24]

This technique, which had broken the resistance on the Klein Jägel at

Riga, was one of the keys to the rapid advance through the enemy defensive system. As the elevation of the squad to the rank of independent tactical unit had freed the infantry platoon and company from the necessity to advance in a straight line, this technique freed entire regiments and divisions. The insight that brought about both of these changes was the same. Captain Rohr had realized that letting a single squad push deep into an enemy position made it quite possible that the enemy might take the attacking squad in its own flank. He also knew, however, that the attacker, if he moved quickly enough, could hit the defender in the flank or rear before the defender was able to gather his wits about him and react. The same dynamic was at work at the company or battalion level. Liberating attacking units from the line meant that the attacker had very vulnerable flanks. Captain Geyer knew, however, that the defender had neither the inclination nor the opportunity to exploit those flanks, especially if he were being bombarded by artillery or machine gun fire at the same time.

THE FORMATION OF ELITE DIVISIONS

Even Ludendorff, who was a major proponent of the idea that all German infantrymen should attain the standards reached by the Assault Battalions, realized that the German Army of 1918 was composed of many men who were simply not capable of becoming proper stormtroopers. The Assault Battalions had been composed of young bachelors who were at the peak of their physical and mental powers. The army as a whole, however, was full of married men in their thirties, forties, and, in the case of the Landsturm, fifties. These soldiers had neither the stamina nor the right frame of mind to throw themselves enthusiastically into battle. Attempting to train and equip them as stormtroopers would only waste scarce resources that could otherwise be concentrated upon more suitable candidates.

The solution to this problem was to designate about a quarter of the German infantry divisions as "attack divisions" (*Angriffsdivisionen*). These units, for the most part divisions that had gone to war with a high proportion of active duty soldiers, were given priority for high quality replacements, supplies, and new equipment such as light machine guns, the tripods for heavy machine guns, the new light carriages for the light trench mortars, and the newer model field guns and howitzers coming out of the Krupp factories. These formations spent most of the winter of 1917–1918 in training.

By the end of the training period, the infantry of these divisions were, from the point of view of their tactics, stormtroopers. In recognition of this, some attack divisions even went so far as to dissolve their elite assault units. This, in turn, resulted in a change in the meaning of the word

Stosstrupp. No longer did it distinguish the trench fighter from the prewar infantryman but rather referred only to those squads within the infantry platoon who had as their primary task the closing with the enemy as opposed to the protection of the light machine gun or other crew-served weapons.

The adoption of stormtrooper tactics by whole divisions, however, did not mean that each infantryman in those divisions was up to the standard of the assault battalions. To fill the ranks of the attack divisions, the War Ministry had to assign to them men who, by virtue of their age alone, would have been disqualified for service in an assault battalion. (The assault battalions rarely accepted a volunteer over 25 years of age. The attack divisions, on the other hand, were full of men between the ages of 25 and 35.) In addition to accepting older men, the attack divisions accepted a large number of men who were not only not volunteers, but who were already weary of the war.

While the attack divisions trained, the other three-quarters of the German Army were occupied with holding the trenches. These latter divisions, referred to as "trench divisions" (*Stellungsdivisionen*) had to make do with older equipment and older men. While their division, regimental, and battalion elite assault units might contain stormtroopers every bit as effective as the men of the attack divisions, the quality of the average soldier was poor. For these formations, stormtroop tactics remained a specialized skill.

By the end of the winter of 1917–1918, however, enough German soldiers had been trained in stormtrooper tactics to permit Ludendorff to believe that he could finish the war by virtue of the fact that his tactics were better than those of the enemy. It was time for the Peace Offensive.

NOTES

1.   While the French built quite a few tanks, the tactical system that they used during the last two years of World War I relied on the systematic destruction of every inch of an objective by heavy artillery. While this system was effective tactically—the French formations using it invariably succeeded in taking their objectives—it required so much time to carry out that it was incompatible with operational maneuver.

2.   *Der Weltkrieg* 9, pp. 135–36. Another interpretation of the concept of the operation was that the attacks from the north and east were intended to form the two arms of a pincer attack the aim of which was to cut off all British forces in the Cambrai salient. See Ludwig Lange, "Das Problem der Abschnürungsangriffe," *Wissen und Wehr*, March, 1931, pp. 125–27.

3.   Lange, "Das Problem," pp. 125–27.

4.   The other two assault companies, the other machine gun company and infantry gun battery, the trench mortar company, and the flamethrower platoon were still in Italy.

5.   F. Müller, *Brandenburgisches Jäger Batallion Nr. 3* (Berlin: Gerhard Stalling, 1922), pp. 87–88.

6.   Ernst Jünger (Basil Creighton, trans.), *Storm of Steel* (London: Chatto and Windus, 1929), pp. 227–28.

7.   In some cases, as many as two of the infantry companies from these reinforced battalions were removed for duty elsewhere, forming a unit in which the supporting arms predominated.

8.   After Action Report of Army Group Crown Prince Rupprecht, December 24, 1917 (*2. Fortsetzung zu den Erfahrungen aus den Angriffskämpfen bei Cambrai für die "Angriffsschlact," Heeres Gruppe Ia d Nr. 4812, 24 Dezember, 1917*), reprinted in Crown Prince Rupprecht of Bavaria, *In treue Fest: Mein Kriegstagebuch* 3 (München: Deutscher National Verlag, 1929), pp. 207–10.

9.   Ibid., p. 210. Ludendorff echoed this observation, "The success was not as complete as it might have been because a good division, instead of pressing on, stopped to go through an enemy supply depot." Ludendorff, *Ludendorff's Own Story*, p. 497.

10.   Letter of Emil Aman to Author, March 3, 1983.

11.   Jünger, *The Storm of Steel*, p. 240.

12.   The first edition, drafted by the headquarters of the Second Army and issued in December 1916 as a supplement to the Drill Regulations of 1906, called for the training of as many officers and NCOs as possible in stormtrooper tactics. One of its major assumptions, however, was that infantry tactics would revert, more or less, to those which had been taught in peacetime once the war of movement resumed. Ludendorff, *Ludendorff's Own Story*, p. 574 and Friedrich Bertkau, "Sturmtruppen," in Hermann Franke, ed., *Handbuch der neuzeitlichen Wehrwissenschaften* (Berlin: Verlag von Walter de Grouter & Co., 1937), p. 683.

13.   *Ausbildungsvorschrift für die Fusstruppen im Kriege, 2. Entwurf* (Berlin: Reichsdruckerei, 1918), pp. 97–99. Hereafter cited as *AVF II*.

14.   *AVF II*, p. 78.

15.   "The light trench mortar was part of the infantry battalion which became more and more the tactical unit of the division, just as the group was the tactical unit of the battalion." Ludendorff, *Ludendorff's Own Story*, p. 574.

16.   A separate manual dealing with the technique of indirect machine gunfire, *Vorschrift für das indirekte Schießen mit M. G. 08*, was issued in March of 1918.

17.   *AVF II*, p. 164.

18.   Ibid., p. 173.

19.   The German words *Befehl* and *Auftrag* have very different meanings, much more so than the difference in the meanings of their closest English counterparts, "command" and "assignment," would indicate. A *Befehl* is the direct descendent of the paradeground command, something to obey with little thought and no hesitation. On the battlefield, a *Befehl* triggers a battle drill. An *Auftrag*, on the other hand, not only permits but requires thought on the part of its recipient. It corresponds not with an automatic response but with a desired outcome of events.

20.   Captain Geyer worked for Lieutenant Colonel Max Bauer. It is interesting to note that the task of writing the *Attack in Position Warfare* went to Geyer,

whose other duties were concerned with artillery, rather than Captain von Gozler, the "duty expert" on gas, flamethrowers, trench mortars, rocket pistols, pioneer stores, infantry armor, and steel helmets. *Summary of Information*, No. 250, January 11, 1919.

21. Crown Prince Rupprecht of Bavaria, *In treue Fest* 3, pp. 206–10.

22. *"Gelegenheit zu freier Betätigung und zu entschlußfreudigem Handeln."* In the original German, the emphasis that is here made by italics was indicated by spaced type.

23. Prussia, Kriegsministerium, "Der Angriff im Stellungskrieg," reprinted in Erich Ludendorff, *Urkunden der Obersten Heeresleitung über ihre Tätigkeit 1916/ 1918 II* (Berlin: Ernst Siegfried Mittler und Sohn, 1920), p. 641.

24. Prussia, Kriegsministerium, "Der Angriff im Stellungskrieg," pp. 641–75.

10

The Peace Offensive

> Our wars should be short and lively, for it is not in our interest to pro-
> tract matters; for a long struggle little by little wears down our admi-
> rable discipline, and only results in the depopulation of our country
> and the exhaustion of our resources.
>
> *Frederick the Great*

While Ludendorff's new army was being trained, he and his staff were busy determining the location and targets for the Spring Offensive. An operation in a secondary front—Italy, Russia, or Macedonia—was ruled out at an early stage. Earlier victories had rendered the enemy forces on these fronts incapable of threatening Germany. Even a brilliant victory, moreover, against the Russians, Italians, or the Allied expeditionary forces in Macedonia would do nothing to prevent the build-up of U.S. forces in France. By the first week of November, 1917, Ludendorff had decided, with the concurrence of most members of the General Staff, that, for these strategic reasons, the offensive would have to take place in the west.[1]

Once this was decided, the next question before Ludendorff was "Against whom should the offensive be directed?" In answering this question, Ludendorff and his staff took into account both strategic and tactical reasons. From the point of view of tactical skill, the British Army was considered to be significantly weaker than the French. From the point of view of strategy, on the other hand, the destruction of the ability of the French Army to continue the war would necessarily result in the capitulation of France while the defeat of the British Expeditionary Force did not mean the defeat of Great Britain, which would still be shielded by the Royal Navy.

The scales were tipped in favor of an attack on the British by a consideration of concerns at the operational level. On November 20, 1917, in a discussion with the chiefs of staff of Army Group "Crown Prince

Rupprecht" and Army Group "German Crown Prince,"[2] Ludendorff confessed that he could only spare, from his strategic reserves, 35 divisions and 1000 pieces of heavy artillery for the coming offensive.[3] An attack on this scale could not deliver, in his estimation, a crushing attack on the French, who, at this time, fielded seven armies in the west. The areas that the French Army occupied, moreover, were either unsuitable for an offensive because of rough terrain (e.g. the Vosges Mountains) or provided the French Army with room in which to pull back and reform their line.

The British, on the other hand, with four armies in northern France and Belgium, were a much better target from the point of view of scale. Furthermore, the British Expeditionary Force occupied territory that provided the Germans with the possibility of getting around their flank and cutting off their retreat, thereby turning a tactical victory (the breaking through of the British position) into an operational one (the destruction of a significant portion of the British expeditionary force).[4] As the plans were refined in the course of the winter, however, this operational consideration was pushed further and further into the background. It still remained an implicit part of the plan; in fact, it remained the key justification for the offensive. Nevertheless, the difficulty of breaking through the British trench system, not what was to be done after that had been accomplished, occupied almost all of the attention of Ludendorff and his staff.[5]

THE BRITISH DEFENSIVE SYSTEM

During the winter of 1917–1918, while the Germans were organizing their forces for the great offensive, the armies of the British Empire were preparing for a series of defensive battles. The experience of 1917, that is to say the costly attacks at Passchendaele and Messines Ridge, had given the British an abiding respect for the new German defensive tactics and they resolved to copy them. Armed with captured German regulations and aerial photographs, they laid out their defenses according to the method developed by the Germans in 1916. The three parallel trench systems were replaced by three successive "zones"—the "forward," "battle," and "rearward"—each with a particular mission.

The forward zone consisted largely of concealed machine guns the fire of which covered barbed wire obstacles. Its purpose, according to the British General Headquarters memorandum that promulgated the new defensive scheme, was to "guard against surprise, to break up the enemy's attacks and compel him to expend large quantities of ammunition, and employ strong forces for its capture." In other words, it was a combination alarm system and economy of force measure—the trench warfare equivalent to a cavalry screen.

Behind the forward zone, the battle zone consisted of a series of larger strongpoints. Laid out for defense against flank as well as frontal attacks, these strongpoints were expected, in the event that the Germans succeeded in penetrating other portions of the battle zone, to hold out until counterattacking British forces restored the line. To give the counterattacking reserves a place to make a stand, diagonal trenches were dug in the ground between the strong points.

Farthest to the rear, the rearward zone extended some four to eight miles behind the battle zone. Its principle purpose was to provide a location for supply dumps, headquarters, and the longer-range artillery units. So as to provide a fall back position in a "worst case scenario," additional strong points were planned for the rearward zone, although their construction was not to begin until after the forward and battle zones had been completed.[6]

While the British were successful in copying the outward appearance of the German defensive system, they were unable to adopt its substance. The key to the German elastic defense was its reliance upon the initiative and good judgement of the man on the spot, whether he were a sergeant in command of a squad or a captain in charge of all of the units counterattacking within his battalion's sector. While this system was not incompatible with British society as a whole—Britain being the foremost decentralized society in Europe and the Dominions being even more decentralized than the Mother Country—such reliance on junior commanders was anathema to a system of command that valued, above all else, adherence to established procedure.[7]

COMMAND

By March 10, these plans had become sufficiently well developed for Ludendorff to issue the definitive order for the operation. Three armies, the Seventeenth, the Second, and the Eighteenth, were detailed for the attack. The first two of these armies, directly subordinate to the Army Group of Crown Prince Rupprecht of Bavaria, were to attack between Arras and Perronne, along a path roughly parallel to the course of the River Somme. Their first task was a lopsided pincer movement, with the Seventeenth Army doing most of the work, to cut off the British forces in what remained of the Cambrai salient. The Eighteenth Army, part of the Army Group of the German Crown Prince, was to support this attack with a less ambitious thrust along the south bank of the Somme.

Of the three armies, two, the Seventeenth and the Eighteenth, had been formed expressly for the operation. The third, the Second Army, had been thoroughly reconstituted after the Cambrai counteroffensive. About half of its 16 divisions had taken part in that operation; the rest had been transferred in during the winter. The overwhelming majority of divisions in these three armies were "attack divisions," with a handful of "trench divisions" remaining to hold sectors that were not suitable to offensive action.[8]

In addition to receiving the best divisions, the three armies were well equipped with the nondivisional combat and combat support units needed for the breaking through of the British position—army-level assault battalions, *Jäger* battalions, trench mortar battalions, mountain gun batteries, flamethrower companies, machine gun sharpshooter detachments, special gas projector battalions, infantry gun batteries, and heavy artillery batteries (see Illustration 11). For the exploitation that was to follow, the three armies were provided with reserves of horses, fodder, supplies, labor units, and road-building materials.

The commanding generals of the three armies—Otto von Below (Seventeenth), Oskar von Hutier (Eighteenth) and George von der Marwitz (Second)—were proven practitioners of offensive warfare at the operational level. Von Below, the victor of Caporetto, and von Hutier, the victor of Riga, both retained the services of the chiefs of staff (Generals Krafft von Dellmensingen and von Sauberzweig, respectively) who had served them during 1917. Von der Marwitz, on the other hand, lost Lieutenant Colonel Stapff, the chief of staff who had worked with him at Cambrai. Less than a month before the offensive was to begin, Stapff was transferred to the eastern front to serve as chief of staff to the Tenth Army.[9] His replacement was Colonel von Tschischwitz, the scion of an old Prussian military family who had most recently been the chief of staff of the XXIII Reserve Corps, a formation that had taken part in the successful breakthrough in Eastern Galicia in the summer of 1917.[10]

Despite the demonstrated competence in operational art of all three army commanders and two out of three of the army chiefs of staff, the Spring Offensive was to be on such a scale that Ludendorff himself would conduct the battle at the operational level. He would maneuver his armies in the same way that the victors of Riga, Caporetto, and Cambrai had maneuvered corps. This decision, to seek one large operational victory rather than a series of smaller ones, relegated the army commanders to the role of tactical, rather than operational leaders. Although his direct means of influencing the battle consisted only of the five infantry divisions of his operational reserve, Ludendorff became the linchpin of the offensive, the one who would give the orders to push on or stand fast and, ultimately, the one who would receive the credit for victory or the blame for defeat.

Ludendorff's centralization of operational control in his own person did not extend to the artillery preparation. There was no artillery commander for the whole operation—the artillery virtuosos von Behrendt and Bruchmüller served as artillery commanders at the army level. In the cases of the Second and Eighteenth Armies, Ludendorff merely

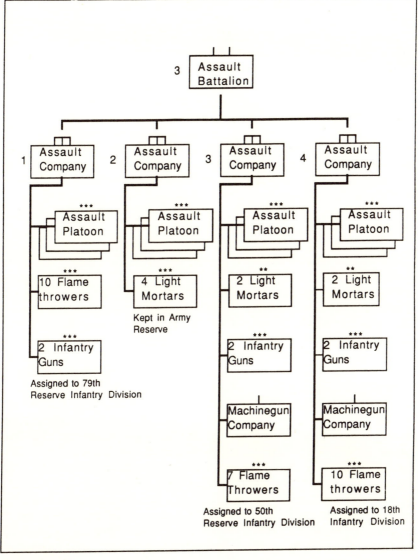

Illustration 11
Task Organization of the Third Jäger–Assault Battalion (Second Army),
March 21, 1918

stipulated the length of the preparatory bombardment. In the case of the
Seventeenth Army, that decision was delegated to the headquarters of
Crown Prince Rupprecht.[11] Apart from these coordination measures,
which were agreed to at a conference shortly before the attack, each army-

level artillery commander was able to custom tailor his fire support to his particular situation.

General von Hutier, for example, amassed a far greater number of guns, howitzers, and light mortars for the attack of the Eighteenth Army than did General von Below and his Seventeenth Army. The artillery park of the Eighteenth Army consisted of 1568 light field pieces; 1028 heavy guns and howitzers; 27 super-heavy guns, howitzers, and mortars[12]; and 1257 trench mortars. The Seventeenth Army's artillery, on the other hand, mustered 1408 light field pieces, 801 heavy guns and howitzers, 25 super-heavy weapons, and 1197 trench mortars.[13] The density of artillery in the Eighteenth Army, however, was somewhat less than that of the Seventeenth Army, for von Hutier had to stretch his guns over 20 divisions while von Below had only 16 divisions to provide for.

SUPPORTING OPERATIONS

The artillery pieces massed for the attack under the control of the Second, Seventeenth, and Eighteenth Armies were not the only ones participating in the operation. Thousands of additional guns, howitzers, and trench mortars fired in support of the great offensive even though they were never moved to the actual battlefield. Their first task was to support the many raids carried out in January, February, and March of 1918. The second was to participate in the dumping of mustard gas on those French and British positions that were not scheduled to be overrun by the three attacking armies.

The increase in the number of trench raids carried out by the German forces in the west served three purposes. First, it tended to reduce French, British, and Belgian raiding activity, thus making even the routine gathering of order of battle intelligence by the enemy much less effective. Second, it masked the intensive (and telltale) logistical preparations for the offensive. Third, because the troops that took part in these raids were told that they were preparing for an offensive in their own sectors, those raiders who were captured by the enemy aided in the disinformation effort.[14]

The gassing, with Yellow Cross shells, of British, French, and Belgian positions all along the western front began on March 9 and lasted until the nineteenth. This operation not only resulted in tens of thousands of enemy casualties—the British Third Army alone was deprived of the services of 4800 men—but also aided in the effort to keep Germany's enemies from discovering the exact time and place of the long-awaited offensive. Mustard gas, after all, while accounting for very few deaths, was very effective in occupying every available minute of the troops who were unfortunate enough to be in its vicinity. Those who did not become casualties were so preoccupied with the business of decontamination of themselves, their equipment, and their surroundings that any thought of a trench raid or even of a patrol into "no man's land" was out of the question.

On March 19, the general bombardment with Yellow Cross shells was replaced with a more selective treatment. Those areas of the front that the Germans were sure that they would not pass over in the course of the offensive—sections to the north and the south of the three armies and strong points within the planned battlefield that could safely be bypassed—were bombarded with still more mustard gas. Other areas, the broad highways through which the three armies would march, were shelled with a mixture of Blue Cross and Green Cross.[15]

This change in the pattern of gas bombardment, of course, would have disclosed the exact locations where the Germans planned to attack, had a British observer been thinking like the Germans. For the British, however, gas warfare was, at best, a specialized branch of the art of war, a paramilitary ghetto where civilian chemists with temporary commissions were given permission to harass the enemy. The idea of making gas warfare an integral part of a battle plan was alien to British decision makers. As a result, the exact location of the attack remained a surprise until the moment that the preparatory bombardment began.

THE PULKOWSKI METHOD

One aspect of the German preparations that might have caught the attention of the British, however, was the registration of artillery pieces. By 1918, much of the German artillery inventory was suffering from excessive barrel wear. This significantly reduced the accuracy of these weapons, and made the prebattle registration of guns and howitzers all the more important. The registration of guns for a raid or attack "with limited objectives" could be disguised as routine harassing fire. This technique, however, could not be used to register the over 6000 tubes that were scheduled to take place during the offensive.

The solution was found in mathematics. Many of the artillery pieces scheduled for the offensive were transported to firing ranges behind the lines. There they were test fired to determine the "peculiarities" of each gun and each was provided with a set of firing tables customized by a professional mathematician. These firing tables, moreover, were designed to allow the fire direction officer to take into account such factors as wind speed, barometric pressure, moisture content of the air, and, in the case of some of the largest pieces, the rotation of the earth.

This method, usually credited to an artilleryman named Captain Pulkowsky, required many changes in the way that the German artillery conducted routine business—it was certainly a far cry from the pre-1914 vision of a horse-drawn battery galloping on to the field to deliver a few volleys into the ranks of a visible enemy. The winter of 1917–1918, however, had provided Captain Pulkowsky with the opportunity to teach this method to over 6000 artillery officers and NCOs.

A critical element in the success of the German plan to fire without registration was the quality of the maps in the hands of the artillery officers. This problem was solved by a stroke of luck—the battlefield over which the German infantry would attack had been the rear of the German position in France from late 1914 until the middle of 1917. This area had been made the subject of many precise surveys and from this raw material, first-class maps were made and issued to the artillery.

THE FIRST DAY

The Peace Offensive officially began at 4:40 A.M. on March 21, the moment when the preparatory bombardment began in earnest (see Illustration 12). As had been the case at Riga and at Caporetto, the first phase of the bombardment consisted largely of Blue and Green Cross shells, although some of the heavier guns (10cm and 15cm) used high explosive against targets in the British rear areas. In the sector of the Second Army, two gas projector battalions of the kind that had served at Caporetto dropped an extra ration of phosgene on the British positions in the "nose" of the Cambrai salient.[16]

Five hours, to the second, after the preparatory bombardment began, the light field batteries and trench mortars fired the first salvo, a mixture of high explosive and Blue Cross, on the creeping barrage. The first troops to follow this barrage were stormtroopers from elite assault units. As had been the case at Cambrai with Second Army's 3rd *Jäger*-Assault Battalion, army level assault battalions were divided into *Sturmblocks*, task forces composed of an assault company reinforced with machine guns, light trench mortars, flamethrowers, and infantry guns.[17] These *Sturmblocks* were attached to divisions, and, in the case of the 50th Infantry Division, regiments in the first line of attack.[18] Even though some of the armies not involved in the offensive lent their assault battalions to the armies that were engaged, there were not enough army level stormtroopers to go around. As a result, some divisions had to make do with their organic assault troops.[19]

The stormtroopers of the *Sturmblocks* were to push as far into the enemy position as possible. While the heavy machine guns that were available to all *Sturmblocks*, and the infantry guns, trench mortars, and flamethrowers that were available to most *Sturmblocks*, gave these units the means of reducing obstacles that blocked their path, *Sturmblocks* were to avoid strong points the reduction of which might slow them down.[20] The goal set for most divisions, after all, was to penetrate the 8000 or so meters that stood between "no man's land" and the British

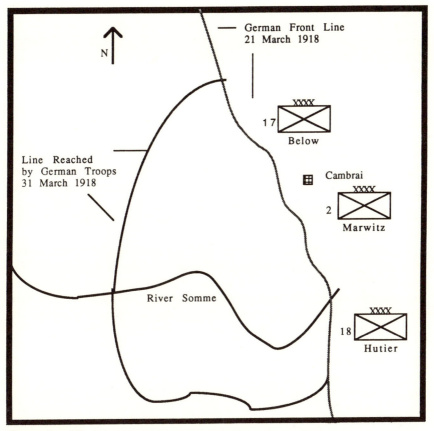

Illustration 12
The German Spring Offensive, March 21–31, 1918

field artillery emplacements, and the stormtroops had only 12 hours of daylight in which to accomplish this.

Those strongpoints that did not surrender when it was discovered that they were surrounded could be dealt with by the infantry regiments that followed the *Sturmblocks* by as little as a hundred meters. The regiments were well equipped with additional heavy machine guns, light trench mortars, infantry guns, and light field guns[21] and were considered quite capable of reducing machine gun nests and other strong points. Insofar as possible, this task was to be accomplished from the flanks or the rear. The troops and commanders that were to take part in the Peace Offensive had been inculcated with the technique that, at the regimental level, had succeeded in breaking Russian resistance at the Klein Jägel during the battle of Riga and at the battalion level had proved so useful at Caporetto.

As a general rule, the latter [reserves] are not engaged at the points where the attack has been stopped by strong points and supporting points which would exact useless sacrifices, but at points where the attack is still progressing and its advance may be facilitated. This is done with a view to breaking down the enemy's resistance in the neighboring sectors by turning the flanks and getting around in the rear.[22]

Crossing "no man's land" posed little difficulty for the stormtroopers leading the infantry regiments of the Seventeenth and Eighteenth Armies. "No man's land," after all, was the part of the battlefield in which the stormtroops had the most experience, where the creeping barrage was most thorough in its suppression of the British positions, and where the thick fog that laid over most of the battlefield for most of the morning prevented those few British machine gun teams which were not directly effected by the barrage from seeing the grey-clad attackers until a few seconds before they were overrun.

The stormtroopers of the Second Army, on the other hand, were not so successful. Their progress was slowed considerably by indirect artillery and machine gun fire. The preliminary bombardment and the continuous counterbattery fire that continued through the day was not completely successful in suppressing the British artillery opposite the Second Army. To make matters worse, the wind had shifted, blowing much of the German gas into the German positions. By noon, British artillery was able to lay harassing fire, not only on "no man's land," where the burning off of the morning's fog left the attackers exposed to British observation, but also on the German positions through which the follow-on echelons were marching.[23]

Bullet storms produced by batteries of heavy machine guns sited on reverse slopes were even more damaging. At Villers-Guislan, on the far right of the Second Army's sector, the indirect fire of the 9th Battalion of the British Machine Gun Corps prevented the German 107th Infantry Division from reaching the first British line for the entire first day of the attack.[24] Other formations on the right wing of the Second Army fared little better, with only one division managing to take its assigned portion of the British forward zone. On the left wing, the stormtroops made some progress, advancing as far as four and a half kilometers into the British position in some places, but nowhere managing to reach the battle zone where the bulk of the British combat power was located.[25]

The Seventeenth and Eighteenth Armies did not run into serious difficulties until they passed the British first line of resistance. It was during the fighting for the British forward zone that most German units lost control of their creeping barrage. At first, each army's creeping barrage had moved forward as a single wall of explosions, flying shell splinters, gas, and smoke. Each barrage maintained its constant rate of march as long as the stormtroops were able to overrun or bypass the obstacles in their way. Where the stormtroopers were slowed down, however, and the artillery observers failed to see the green signal rockets fired by the front line commanders, the creeping barrage continued to creep forward according to its ambitious timetable.

Without the aid of the creeping barrage, the infantry and stormtroopers of the Seventeenth and Eighteenth Armies had to fight the "Battle of the Intermediate Zone" with their organic weapons. While, as a general rule, they were up to this task, the need to coordinate infantry gun, trench mortar, and heavy machine gun fire for each hasty attack against a machine gun nest or diehard platoon cost the Germans precious time. By nightfall, neither the Seventeenth nor the Eighteenth Army had completely broken through the British battle zone. Only in the sector of the Eighteenth Army did significant numbers of Germans succeed in reaching the British artillery positions, a fact demonstrated by the capture of 88 artillery pieces.[26]

The failure of almost all units to reach their first day's objective, however, did not mean that the attack did not succeed in throwing the defenders completely off balance. The Eighteenth Army captured 7000 prisoners on the first day. The Seventeenth Army captured 2300 and the Second Army 4000.[27] This haul of prisoners gives some indication of the effect that the German tactics had on the British and Portuguese defenders. Completely untrained for independent action, small units were isolated psychologically by the bombardment and physically by the "infiltration" of the stormtroopers between strong points. Once cut off, many of the men of these small units could imagine no other course but surrender.

THE SECOND DAY

For most of March 22, the German infantry were in the unenviable position of having pushed too far for their own artillery to support them but not far enough to deny the British the use of their own guns. The difficulties of moving the German artillery forward across the mud, shell holes, and barbed wire of "no man's land" meant that the German infantry would, once again, have to rely largely on organic resources to provide the firepower that was so necessary to their successful maneuver. Against the disorganized remnants of the British trench garrison, these resources sufficed, and progress was made throughout the second day. The Second Army succeeded in breaking through the entire British forward zone in its sector while the Seventeenth and Eighteenth Armies completed the breakthrough of the British battle zone.

As had been the case on the first day of the offensive, the ability of the British to defend themselves against the German attack in a coordinated fashion was severely hindered by the slow reflexes of the British command system. As a British captain of engineers who observed the entire battle later commented that "The day closed with Divisional Headquarters bowing under a welter of orders and counter orders from Corps, most of which took two hours to deliver and were too late for action when received."[28] Orders to hold certain lines or "switches" were received long after the terrain in question had fallen to the Germans, and some units retreated while others remained in action.

This confusion notwithstanding, the British managed, in keeping with their new defensive doctrine, to launch a number of small counterattacks, many of which were supported by tanks, against units of the Second and Seventeenth Armies. Although the Germans succeeded in stopping all of these counterattacks, the fact that they had so little artillery, and what they had often had to be used in a direct fire role against tanks, meant that the casualties that they suffered in recently conquered ground were high.[29] The casualties suffered by the units of the Eighteenth Army, on the other hand, resulted from attacks through the British battle zone and, in some cases, the rearward zone. As had been the case on the first day of the attack, the greatest killers of Germans were artillery pieces and machine guns firing in the indirect mode, weapons that were most effective when they could shelter behind an "infiltration resistant" obstacle such as the Crozat Canal.[30]

By the evening of the second day, the British had begun to make use of their motor transport fleet and were counterattacking with whole divisions brought up from army reserves. By this time, however, most of the German field artillery batteries had rejoined their parent divisions. The British counterattacks, moreover, were still local affairs, reactions to the growing momentum of the German attack rather than coordinated parts of a plan to strike a decisive blow against the attackers, and where the British were not attacking, the Germans were.

OPEN WARFARE

The third day brought even more progress for the Germans. The Eighteenth Army kept up its furious march through those remnants of the British Fifth Army that were not in full retreat, while the Second and Seventeenth Armies pushed into the British rearward zone. By the evening of the twenty-third, Ludendorff was satisfied that he had broken through the British defensive system and that the 80-kilometer-wide gap that his three armies had driven into the British position meant that he was free to resume the war of movement. This realization forced him to make a decision.

For the first three days of the offensive, Ludendorff had pursued the rather modest goal of cutting off the Cambrai salient by providing the

Second and Seventeenth Armies with fresh divisions from his own, rather small, operational reserve. While these reinforcements failed to trap the British garrison in the salient, the Second and Seventeenth Armies had succeeded in driving all British forces before them back towards the Channel Coast. This limited success gave Ludendorff cause to hope that the British Expeditionary Force could be pushed even farther in that direction and perhaps even knocked out of the war altogether. To that end, he ordered the Second and Seventeenth Armies to swing north, while the Fourth and Sixth Armies, which had hitherto limited their role in the battle to holding their positions in northern France and Flanders, were to attack towards the west.[31]

Von Hutier's Eighteenth Army retained its mission of protecting the operation as a whole from a French counteroffensive. The only difference between the mission that von Hutier received on March 10 (when the orders for the first day of the offensive were given) and March 23 was the depth to which he was to penetrate. In fact, it might be argued that it was the phenomenal success of the Eighteenth Army that permitted Ludendorff to expand the scope of the offensive—much of what was to have become the southern flank of the Second Army was already protected by von Hutier's advancing divisions.[32]

The exploitation of the 80-kilometer-wide gap in the British position, unlike either the exploitation phase of the successful German offensives on the eastern front or the even more dramatic pursuit, the battle of Caporetto, was not a rapid one. The "green fields beyond" were not the empty plains of Russia. Rather they were full of towns, canals, forests, and rivers that provided opportunities for the fresh British forces continually arriving on the battlefield to establish new lines of resistance and, in places, to counterattack in force. Breaking through the hasty defenses often required deliberate attacks. These, in turn, often required that the infantry wait until the artillery, which was suffering from a shortage of horses, caught up with them. The counterattacks also served to reduce the momentum of the attack, even, by March 25, in the sector of the hitherto unstoppable Eighteenth Army.

Exhaustion was also reducing the ability of the German infantrymen to act independently on the battlefield. Fatigue dulled the will to fight that was such an essential part of stormtrooper tactics. A tired man could be put in a dense formation and pushed into battle—that was one of the virtues of close order tactics. The stormtrooper, on the other hand, had to provide his own motive force. By the third or fourth day of the attack, that motive force was wearing thin and troops were observed not only stopping to loot the British supply depots that were falling into German hands by this time, but also getting drunk on captured rum.

For a while, there were enough reasonably fresh German soldiers to keep the armies moving forward. Stormtroop tactics, after all, did not require that all units move forward at the same pace. By the ninth day of the attack, however, the will of individual German soldiers to push forward collapsed. For all practical purposes the armies stopped moving forward, and the British were finally able to reconstitute a line and start building a new defensive system. For six more days the Germans tried, without success, to break through this new line. On April 5, 1918, Ludendorff officially ended the operation.

Although the gains that the Germans made during the Peace Offensive were impressive by the standards of the Western Front—90,000 prisoners and 1300 guns were taken, 212,000 enemy soldiers were killed or seriously wounded, and an entire British army (the Fifth) was rendered worthless as a military formation—the cost of the Peace Offensive had been high. The casualties—dead and seriously wounded—were officially estimated at 239,800 officers and men. Some divisions were reduced to half strength, many companies could muster only 40 or 50 men.

The Peace Offensive succeeded in attaining its immediate goal of breaking through the British defensive system, although the fact that this took three days rather than one made it possible for the British to bring up their reserves and thus confound any significant exploitation. This failure of stormtrooper tactics to live up to Ludendorff's expectations, however, did not reduce his faith in the new methods. The Peace Offensive was soon followed by three more offensives on the same pattern, each of which began with stunning tactical victories and ended with exhausted stormtroopers unable to push forward against a shattered enemy. The last of these offensives, launched on August 4, lasted only four days. When it ended, not only had German troops stopped moving forward, but they were beginning to retreat. This long, slow retreat lasted until November 11, when an armistice precipitated by revolution in Germany ended the fighting in the west.

NOTES

1.   Hermann von Kuhl (Henry Hossfeld, trans.), *The Execution and Failure of the Offensive* II, pp. 1–4. This source is an unpublished translation of *Entstehung, Durchführung und Zusammenbruch der Offensive von 1918* (Berlin: Deutsche Verlagsgesellschaft für Politik und Geschichte, 1927) and is hereafter cited as von Kuhl, *Execution and Failure of the Offensive of 1918*.

2.   Crown Prince Wilhelm was known as the "German Crown Prince" because, unlike the other crown princes who were heirs only to their kingdoms (i.e., Bavaria and Saxony), he was also heir to the German imperial throne.

3.   To these divisions and guns would be added the divisions and guns already committed to the front in question.

4.   Von Kuhl, *The Execution and Failure of the Offensive* II, pp. 7–11.

5.   At this point in time, Ludendorff was not only the de facto chief of the general staff for the whole German Army, but also the de facto head of govern-

ment, the de facto minister of munitions, the theater commander for the western front, and the head of a team that was trying to codify the new tactics. Despite his prodigious capacity for work, Ludendorff could not keep on top of all these duties. While he focused on tactical and industrial problems, he seems to have placed operational considerations in the background sometime during the winter of 1917–1918 and kept them there until the end of the war.

6.   Great Britain, War Office, British Expeditionary Force, "G.H.Q. Memorandum on Defensive Measures, 14 December, 1917," reprinted in Historical Section, Committee of Imperial Defense, *Military Operations France and Belgium, 1918, The German March Offensive and Its Preliminaries, Appendices* (London: Macmillan and Co., 1935), pp. 22–28.

7.   For an excellent and accessible discussion of the British command and control system of World War I, see Martin van Creveld, *Command in War* (Cambridge, MA: Harvard University Press, 1985), pp. 148–88.

8.   The Seventeenth Army had 11 "attack divisions" and five "trench divisions," the Eighteenth Army 17 "attack divisions" and three "trench divisions," and the Second Army 14 "attack divisions" and two "trench divisions."

9.   *Der Weltkrieg 1914–1918*, 14, p. 116.

10.   Bruchmüller, *Die Artillerie beim Angriff im Stellungskrieg*, p. 47.

11.   Ibid., p. 97.

12.   This category consisted of pieces of 17cm caliber or greater.

13.   *Der Weltkrieg 1914–1918*, 14, p. 108 and 124.

14.   Ibid., p. 100.

15.   Rudolf Hanslian, *Der chemische Krieg* (Berlin: Verlag von E.S. Mittler und Sohn, 1937), pp. 142–43.

16.   *Der Weltkrieg 1914–1918* 14, p. 116.

17.   F. Müller, *Brandenburgisches Jäger Battalion Nr. 3*, pp. 92–93.

18.   The two front-line regiments of the 50th Infantry Division were perhaps the most heavily reinforced of the infantry regiments taking part in the offensive. Each had a company from Assault Battalion "Rohr," a divisional assault detachment, one or two companies of machine guns (one from Assault Battalion "Rohr"), one or two companies of trench mortars, a battery of light field guns, two batteries of infantry guns (one from Assault Battalion "Rohr"), and a flamethrower platoon. In addition to this, one of the regiments received a detachment of five tanks. Gruss, *Aufbau und Verwendung*, p. 103 and Great Britain, General Staff, *Summary of Information*, No. 7, April, 1918.

19.   There was even one case where three *Jäger* Battalions were used to lead the attack of a two division task force (Group Gayl) that had the mission of establishing a bridgehead over the Crozat Canal on the first day of the offensive. These battalions, however, although they were composed of first-class troops who were well trained in stormtroop tactics, were neither organized as *Sturmblocks* nor equipped with infantry guns or flamethrowers. A. Fehrtman, *Reserve Jäger Bn. Nr. 19* (Berlin: Gerhard Stalling, 1929), pp. 152–60.

20.   Gruss, *Aufbau und Verwendung*, p. 100.

21.   As a rule, each regiment attacking in the first line received a battery of four light field guns from one of the division's two field artillery regiments. In most cases, this was supplemented by an additional infantry gun, mountain, or

horse artillery battery. This provided each of two front line battalions with a full "accompanying battery." Bruchmüller, *Die Deutsche Artillerie in den Durchbruch-Schlachten,* p. 108.

22.   Prussia. Heer. Oberste Heersleitung. "Memorandum on Offensive Combat" (Ia/II Nr. 6220 dated 1/25/18), translated and reprinted in Commander in Chief of the Allied Armies, *Supplement to Memorandum No. 1672 of June 27, 1918. Translation of German Documents.*

23.   *Der Weltkrieg 1914–1918* 14, p. 118.

24.   G.S. Hutchinson, *Machine Guns, Their History and Tactical Employment* (London: Macmillan and Co., 1938), pp. 286–87; and *Der Weltkrieg 1914–1918* 14, p. 119.

25.   Ibid., pp. 121–22.

26.   Ibid., p. 130.

27.   Ibid., pp. 114, 121, and 130.

28.   G. MacLeod Ross, "The Death of a Division: The 39th Division in March, 1918," *The Fighting Forces,* April 1930, p. 29.

29.   *Der Weltkrieg 1914–1918* does not give details of the casualties suffered in these counterattacks, but simply refers to them as "considerable" (*erheblich*).

30.   *Der Weltkrieg 1914–1918* p. 146. The Crozat Canal ran perpendicular to the axis of advance of the Eighteenth Army.

31.   Ibid., Vol. 15, pp. 165–69.

32.   For an alternate interpretation of the change in Ludendorff's operational conception, which has become the "orthodox" one among English-speaking historians, see Martin van Creveld's *Command in War* (Cambridge, MA: Harvard University Press, 1985), pp. 180–81.

Conclusion

German infantry tactics did not stop developing after the end of the Peace Offensive. The casualties of the offensives, as well as the losses from the influenza epidemic that had begun to spread through the ill-fed German population, resulted in a German Army that was rich in supporting arms but poor in riflemen. Companies of less than 50 men had six or more light machine guns and battalions of less than 200 men retained their full complement of 12 heavy machine guns. The introduction of the Bergmann submachine gun gave the German stormtrooper an additional edge in close combat, and further reduced the number of men who were armed primarily with the rifle. The radical change in German tactics, however, had already taken place.

The infantryman was no longer armed exclusively with the rifle and bayonet. His tactical repertoire was expanded to include hand grenades, pistols, daggers, and sharpened spades. If he were a specialist, he also mastered a machine gun (light or heavy), a grenade launcher, a trench mortar, a flamethrower, or an infantry gun. Infantry units, moreover, from the battalion down to the squad, ceased being uniformly armed masses of riflemen and became combined arms units in their own right, possessing a greater variety as well as a greater quantity of firepower than ever before.

The revolution in armament coincided with a revolution in movement on the battlefield. The squad, aided by its own firepower and that of its neighbors, became capable of maneuvering by itself by the end of 1915. By the end of the war, those squads which contained both a light machine gun *Trupp* and a *Strosstrupp* had gone a step further. They were capable of maneuvering *within* themselves, forshadowing the fire team concept which was not universally accepted until well after World War II.

The twin decentralization of firepower and maneuver was related to yet a third, that of command. It was no longer sufficient for the small unit leader to be the bravest member of the battle line. Lieutenants and NCOs became key decision makers upon whose shoulders rested complete responsibility for the outcome of the one of the thousands of little combats into which battle had disintegrated. A battalion commander, on the other hand, though exposed to a great deal of "stray" fire, was involved in very little combat at all. On the contrary, his business became a miniature version of the operational art. He pushed resources toward the squad or platoon whose success would most contribute to the accomplishment of his mission.

CAUSES OF CHANGE

Demonstrating that German infantry tactics changed during World War I is far easier than explaining why they changed. However, unless one believes in the inherent superiority of the German soldier over both his allies and his enemies, one is forced to ask the question "Why didn't other armies that fought in the First World War innovate to the same degree that the Germans did?" The facile answer, often repeated in general works on World War I, is that the Western Allies sought a technological solution (i.e., the tank) to the problem of trench warfare while the Germans sought a tactical solution (i.e., infiltration tactics).

This answer, however, is unsatisfactory for two reasons. First, the German tactical solution involved a number of new weapons—the flamethrower, the infantry gun, the trench mortar, the light machine gun, the grenade thrower, the stick grenade, the bangalore torpedo, gas shells, and, at the very end of the war, the submachine gun. Second, both the French and the British tried tactical solutions of their own. Week-long bombardments, indirect machine gun fire, and "artillery conquers, infantry occupies" had not been taught at prewar general staff academies any more than stormtroop tactics. In short, all belligerents were innovative in the use of both new technology and new tactics.

Perhaps a better question to ask would be, "Why did the Germans innovate in the particular way that they did?" One part of the answer lies in the fact that the German Army was a highly decentralized, mission-oriented organization that placed a great deal of trust in its officers. Thus, front line commanders were permitted to tailor their tactics to the situation, Colonel Bauer could set up the first assault battalion without having to clear his proposal with a score or more bureaucrats, and Captain Rohr was able to train his troops with no other instructions than "make the best use of your experience at the front." Decentralization and trust, however, like the habit of self-education that characterized the German officer corps, only provided a framework in which innovation took place. The actual spur to change fighting methods came from other phenomena —the preexisting methods of the pioneers, the tactical debates of the prewar years, the weapons that were available, the peculiar situation in which the German Army found itself, the personalities of key individuals such as Ludendorff, Crown Prince Wilhelm, Captain Rohr, and Colonel Bruchmüller, and the centuries-old *Jäger* tradition.

DECENTRALIZATION

With the exception of the assignment of operational missions, which was a prerogative tightly controlled by the General Staff, tactical and administrative decisions in the German Army were made at comparatively low echelons of command. A British company or battalion returning from a period of trench duty would be sent to a camp such as the infamous "Bull Ring" at Étaples, where specialist instructors following a curriculum approved at the highest level would relieve the unit's officers and NCOs of the burden of conducting training. A French unit would similarly be deprived of its officers and run through a period of training designed, to the last detail, by an officer of the General Staff. A German company that had been pulled out of line, on the other hand, remained under the direct control of its commander, even if he was a 20-year-old second lieutenant with a reserve commission.

Centralization prevented the British and French Armies from adapting quickly to new situations because it required that proposals for change be written up, passed up the chain of command, turned into policy, and then promulgated down the chain of command. The French, in particular, had a number of bright young officers[1] who proposed tactical reforms similar to those being adopted by the Germans. While these proposals were warmly received by high-ranking officers, they got lost in the bureaucracy and had little effect on the way the French infantry actually fought.

Decentralization alone, however, cannot explain the entire phenomenon of German success with tactical innovation. The Italian Army of World War I, being, like the German Army, a relatively recent amalgamation of the armies of subnational states, was also quite decentralized. While this decentralization permitted the Italians to develop their *Arditi* units to such a high degree, it did not cause ordinary infantry units to change the way that they fought. The Italians thus had the means of developing new infantry tactics, but not disseminating them.

SELF-EDUCATION

The element that made German decentralization work was a self-educating officer corps. Although the General Staff siphoned off some of the best brains in the army to practice operational art and foolish school masters talked of the inherent bellicosity of the German soldier, the vast majority of German officers believed that Germany's fate depended directly upon their tactical competence. With first-class NCOs to train recruits and perform the myriad "management" functions necessary to a well run garrison, German officers had plenty of time for map problems, staff rides, war games, maneuvers, and, last but not least, following the frequent and heated debates in the military press about the tactical meaning of the latest technological innovation.

This is not to say that German officers were intellectually inclined. On the contrary, German regimental officers were far less well educated in the general sense than their colleagues in other armies and prided themselves in being "practical" men. This was particularly true of those officers, like Captain Rohr, who had passed through the cadet schools. Nevertheless, however disinclined he may have been to read philosophy or visit museums, the German officer possessed the habit of regularly and systematically studying the more pedestrian aspects of the art of war. A great spur to such study was the sure knowledge that, for those German officers not fortunate to have been born the son of the emperor, a king, or a royal duke, the only path to promotion beyond the command of a regiment was admission to the General Staff Academy. This, in turn, required attention to tactics. For, while the ultimate goal of the General Staff was excellence in operational art, the entrance exam consisted almost entirely of tactical problems.

Other factors which contributed to the ability of the German officer to pay attention to the phenomenon of tactics were the slowness with which he was promoted and the small number of nonregimental billets to which he could be assigned. Captain Rohr's career was typical in its emphasis on the handling of units smaller than a regiment. Even if his years at cadet schools are discounted, he had four full years as a platoon commander in the 66th Infantry Regiment before being posted to the NCO school at Potsdam. The five years of staff duty following the four years at the NCO school found him working first as a battalion and then as a regimental adjutant in his old regiment. (If the frequent mentions in German regimental histories of adjutants being killed and wounded is any indication, a German adjutant of the first two decades of this century was not a deskbound bureaucrat. In fact, in most German infantry battalions, he was the only commissioned officer who was not in command of a fighting unit.) This staff duty was topped off by four years of company command.[2] Thus, in his 19 years of commissioned service,

Rohr commanded infantry units for eight of them, taught soldiers or aspirant NCOs for five, and never served on a staff above the regimental level.

The infantry officers of most other armies did not share the German enthusiasm for serious study of the art of war. Despite the establishment of a General Staff and a substantial increase in the educational attainments of the average officer during the last three decades of the nineteenth century, most British officers worked hard to maintain an air of detached amateurism and snubbed the "mug" who neglected hunting and polo in favor of maps and military history. This became even more true as the war progressed and those few regular officers who took their profession seriously found themselves concentrated on staffs, leaving small unit leadership to enthusiastic but tactically incompetent schoolboys.

Almost all U.S. officers were commissioned directly from civilian life after the outbreak of the war and got what little military training they did from French or British instructors. The tiny band of regular officers, rapidly promoted to ranks that they could not even dream of in peacetime, were, like their British counterparts, assigned primarily to staff work. Regular and volunteer alike were even then burdened with a military culture that valued "efficient management" over tactical skill and, with the exception of the occasional officer who had taken the time to educate himself in the art of war, believed victory in battle to be axiomatic, a function of the inherent virtue of the New World, the righteousness of the cause, and the unfailing aim of natural-born riflemen. The net result was an American Expeditionary Force whose leaders focused their eyes on routine and politics rather than operations or tactics.

The French officers, on the other hand, were as industrious as the Germans. French infantry officers, perhaps the best educated in Europe in terms of their knowledge of mathematics, history, science, and literature, suffered from a crippling tendency to substitute intricate systems developed at the highest level for informed judgement by trusted subordinates. This tendency was reinforced by the fact that there was a great gulf between educated officers, particularly those on the General Staff who were selected for that honor by virtue of their command of civilian as well as military subjects, and those whom they led. Neither the French NCO nor those company officers who had been commissioned after long service as NCOs were considered capable of the kind of independent action that, by the end of the war, was universally expected of German NCOs.

Russian and Italian infantry units had the same defects as their French counterparts without their countervailing virtues. Infantry officers in both countries had a reputation for intellectual sloth, high living, and indifference to the needs of their men. Moreover, neither Russia nor Italy, the bulk of whose people considered military service a calamity rather than an honor, succeeded in developing a strong NCO corps. Not only were the largely peasant conscripts whose families had only been released from peonage within living memory reluctant to show the minimal initiative required of an NCO in any army, but the lower middle classes whose members provided the raw material from which Germany built her NCO corps were far smaller (in proportion to the population) in Russia and Italy and were totally devoid of any interest in a military career.

In short, the French were provided with the answers to tactical questions before they were asked and the British, Americans, Russians, and Italians, at least at the regimental level, rarely even bothered to ask what the questions were. Only the Germans were in the habit of being asked, in the course of their training as officer candidates and lieutenants as well as on the entrance examination to the General Staff Academy, questions like "How would you storm that hill?," "How would you employ a machine gun in support of your attack?," "How would you move across that ravine in the face of enemy fire?"

The answers that the Germans derived from this process and carried with them into battle in 1914 were often no better than the copybook maxims of the French. The habit of questioning, however, gave the German Army a definite advantage when it came to adapting to unforeseen conditions. Their peacetime training had given them an equation that was a fairly good approximation of infantry combat; all they needed to do was plug in the new numbers to match the facts that they discovered on the battlefield. In short, a self-educating officer corps with the freedom to train their units as they saw fit gave the German Army a capacity for self-reform that no other military organization of the time could approach.

A HEAD START

The final reason for the success of the German infantry in adapting its tactics to the conditions at hand, ironically, has little to do with the infantry itself. Some of the most dramatic instances of innovation in recent military history have occurred outside of the organization that one would expect would most feel the need to innovate. Thus, early in the American Civil War, the U.S. Navy bought the Spencer repeating rifle years before the army got interested in self-loading firearms. During World War I, it was the Royal Naval Air Service, not the British cavalry, that first acquired armored cars. The Germans benefitted from this phenomenon of "innovation at the margin" when their pioneers (albeit with the help of the *Jäger* Captain Rohr) established a "fast track" for tactical evolution in the form of the first Assault Battalion. While German tactics would most likely have evolved in the direction that they did without the help of the Assault Battalions, the work of the German pioneers gave the German infantry an initial impetus that should not be discounted.

The reasons that the German pioneers, rather than line infantry, were able to innovate so quickly are many. In 1914, the pioneers were already used to working, with very little supervision, in squad-sized teams. Pioneers were trained for fortress warfare before the outbreak of hostilities. This gave them a head start in thinking about the problem of crossing "no man's land," which, after all, is an easier proposition than crossing the glacis of the masonry fortress, as well as providing them with the tools, particularly hand grenades, of trench warfare. Pioneers were, moreover, free of romantic notions about battle. War to them was a dangerous job, like the digging of a mine or the building of a bridge over a fast moving river. Martial virtue consisted in finding the most efficient way of doing the job, not in the *beau geste* of a bayonet charge. Finally, pioneers, whose training in prewar infantry tactical forms was not as thorough as that of the infantry, had fewer bad habits to break.

OPERATIONAL ART

That the excellence that was achieved in the realm of tactics did not win the war for Germany does not make the revolution that occurred between 1914 and 1918 any less significant. Good tactics, after all, are worthless unless the battles that are won with them are combined to make a successful campaign and the campaigns are fought in a way that supports strategic goals. The failure of the German Army in 1918 was not a failure then of German tactics at the squad, platoon, company, battalion, regimental, division, or even army level, but a failure of German operational art, German strategy, and German national policy.

The German Army had entered World War I with the expectation that the conflict would be won at the operational level, that the fighting of battles was of secondary importance to the winning of campaigns. As a result, the German Army's brain power was concentrated in the General Staff in order to produce excellence in operational art; the "best and the brightest" focused on railroads rather than fire fights. This attitude directly contributed to decisive operational victories against four of Germany's enemies—Russia, Rumania, Serbia, and Italy.

The failure of German operational art to defeat the Western Allies, however, led to two related concepts that had succeeded, by the end of the war, in destroying the faith of many influential German officers in the wisdom of concentrating their attention on the operational level. The first was the belief, the greatest expositor of which was von Falkenhayn, that tactical action alone—the mere destruction of enemy soldiers—was an efficient means of bringing about a strategic end. The second was the

idea, one that grew out of the experience of countless attacks "with limited objectives" and trench raids, that combat had become so difficult an
enterprise that operational considerations had to be subordinated to tactical ones.

Both of these concepts made major contributions to the defeat of Germany. Verdun, the tactical solution to a strategic problem, deprived
Germany of about 300,000 soldiers, a disproportionate number of whom
were irreplaceable officers and NCOs of the regular army. The Peace Offensive, launched on a scale so great that operational level decisions were
made not by army commanders but by Ludendorff himself, the de facto
warlord of the German Empire playing the role of army group commander, also resulted in Germany losing another 300,000 of its best soldiers without gaining a victory at the operational level. In the first case,
operational art was dispensed with. In the second, its requirements were
improperly calculated.

If we focus on the operational level, we can see that the weapon that
kept the German Army from winning a war of maneuver on the western
front was not the machine gun but the railroad. As thousands of trench
raids and attacks "with limited objectives," as well as the successful
breaking through of heavily fortified positions at Caporetto and during
the great offensives of 1918, proved, stormtroop tactics were an
efficient way of releasing the German Army from the "grip of Hiram
Maxim." No tactical system, however, could solve the fundamental operational problem that the German Army faced in the west—the fact
that the enemy's railroads and motor transport columns could always
bring up more fresh troops.

The means of dealing with this problem would have to wait until the
next war. Beginning in 1939, the fully motorized and partially armored
Panzer division gave the German Army the means to move troops toward, across, and around the battlefield faster than Germany's enemies
could move troops behind it. The innovation wasn't the tank—at
Cambrai the German-controlled railroads could move troops in the path
of the British tanks before the tanks could consolidate their tactical
victory—rather, it was the mobility of complete formations that could
quickly exploit gaps in the enemy disposition.

In 1918, the German infantry could use stormtroop tactics to tear
gaps. Given a sufficient number of battalions, those gaps could be
turned into gaping holes scores of kilometers wide. As long as the following formations depended on muscle power for mobility, however,
those holes could never be turned into war-winning victories. In the absence of suitable transport, the stormtrooper and his tactics remained
Germany's forlorn hope.

NOTES

1.   I am thinking in particular of Captains Baux and Laffargue, both of whom wrote essays that were well received by military authorities at the national level but were largely ignored by fighting units. See Charles Baux, *Études sur combat* (Paris: Payot & Co., 1921); and André Laffargue, *Fantassin de Gascogne. De mon jardin à la Marne et au Danube* (Paris: Flammarion, 1963). See also Appendix 3.

2.   Gruss, *Aufbau and Verwendung,* p. 20.

Appendix A:
The Wilhelm Raid

In July of 1916, the 229th Reserve Infantry Regiment occupied part of the German defensive system southwest of the French city of Lille. It was a quiet sector at this time, far from the battles raging at Verdun and on the Somme. Neither the Germans nor the British Empire troops opposite them let the sector remain totally calm. Once a week or so, a raiding party from one side or the other would slip over "no man's land" and attempt to take a few prisoners.

On July 12, 1916, the commanding officer of the 229th Reserve Infantry Regiment received a one-page letter from his immediate superior, the commanding general of the 50th Reserve Division, ordering him to plan a trench raid for the night of July 20. The plan, including an annex detailing the use of trench mortar and artillery fire, was to be ready in two days. Apart from an admonition to maintain secrecy, no additional instructions were given.

As his orders certainly did not require him to attack all of the enemy troops in his sector, the first task before the regimental commander was the choice of an exact objective. He and his staff looked for a piece of ground that could easily be cut off from the rest of the enemy position by a German box barrage and yet was not well covered by enemy machine gun or artillery fire. If possible, moreover, the ground to be attacked should be suitable for annexation to the German trench system. Only one section fulfilled all of these requirements, a protrusion in the British lines known as the "Bastion."

The water table in this part of French Flanders was high enough to prevent the digging of proper trenches. The Bastion was thus less of a trench than an old-fashioned earthwork, with walls of earth and sandbags that made it clearly visible to the Germans. Behind the Bastion, however, there was much that could only be seen from the air. Aerial photographs revealed to the German regimental commander that to the immediate rear of his chosen objective the British had built shallow communications trenches, a second defensive line, and what looked like an ammunition line. Also of note was the low ground immediately in front of the Bastion. In wet weather it became a quagmire that would do more to hinder an attacker than the barbed wire that the British were starting to put up.

The weight of artillery fire that the British could bring to bear on an attacker was also a consideration for those planning the raid. If the preparations for the raid were discovered, the most likely British response would be to lay a heavy barrage on the German front lines, thereby making it impossible for the raid even to begin. If the raiders succeeded in breaking in to the Bastion and holding on to it for any length of time, that position, too, would come under intense fire. The British, with their almost limitless supply of Chilean nitrates, could afford to spend the shells to pulverize the location of any suspected threat. In order to minimize this vulnerability, the regimental commander decided that the raiders should penetrate no deeper than 30 meters beyond the walls of the Bastion. The width of the objective was likewise to be limited by the 130-meter width of the Bastion itself.

TASK ORGANIZATION

The regimental commander and his staff then determined the composition of the raiding force. They decided that four officers, 12 NCOs, and 48 men of the regimental Assault Detachment would take part in the operation. For the purpose of moving across "no man's land," this force would be divided into two raiding parties. A third party was to serve as a rear guard for the raiding force, preventing an overeager enemy from following the withdrawing raiding party into the German lines.

Pioneer support for the raid came in the form of one officer, three NCOs, and 15 men from the Field Pioneer Battalion of the 50th Reserve Division. Three teams, each consisting of four pioneers, were to use satchel charges and bundles of stick grenades to blow up dugouts, trench mortar emplacements, and any tunnels that might be found in the Bastion. The other pioneers were assigned the task of cutting paths through the enemy wire with wire cutters and "Bangalore torpedos."

The raiding force would be provided with field telephones and wire by the artillery liaison team that was to be sent from the Field Artillery Regiment of the 50th Reserve Division. In the past year and a half of trench raiding, however, field telephones had shown themselves to be less than reliable means of communication. The regimental commander therefore decided that the chief means of communication between the raiding force and the regimental commander as well as between the regimental commander and the Field Artillery Regiment would be pyrotechnic signals. The secondary means of communication was a chain of runners established between the jumping-off point for the raid and the regimental command post.

FIRE SUPPORT

In addition to the machine guns and grenade launchers that were organic to the regiment, the available fire support consisted of five batteries of light field guns (20 guns), five heavy artillery batteries (20 heavy guns and howitzers), and divisions Trench Mortar Company (ten trench mortars). All of these assets were placed under the direct tactical control of the commander of the 229th.

The fire support annex to the raid plan called for three phases of artillery fire. First, artillery, trench mortars, and grenade launchers would fire on the Bastion for 45 minutes—cutting wire, causing casualties, and keeping heads down. After the first ten minutes of this preparation fire there would be a pause. The Germans hoped this would not only confuse the British but that the defending troops would react to this pause by sticking their heads out of their holes long enough to provide the shells of the second half of the preparation with something more than sandbags to hit.

To further confuse the enemy, the 231st Reserve Infantry Regiment, the neighbor to the north of the 229th, was to carry out a demonstration. During the preparation fire, it was to pepper the British position north of the Bastion with small arms fire and grenades. Some of the divisional artillery was also allotted to this demonstration. Near the end of the preparation fire, some light field guns were to shift their fire on the positions in "no man's land" to the left and the right of the path the raiders were to take. The time-fused high explosive and shrapnel shells fired by these guns would clear the area of any British patrols.

A few seconds before the last volley of the preparation was to be fired, the two raiding parties would leave the German trenches, cross "no man's land," and, as the last volley of shells fell on the enemy, burst into the Bastion. Simultaneously, the artillery, trench mortars, and grenade launchers would shift their fire and form a "box barrage"—a wall of low air bursts on the left, right, and rear of the Bastion to prevent the enemy from counterattacking during the raid.

The third phase of the fire support plan was an "on call" series of fires on the Bastion itself and the surrounding enemy positions. After the two raiding parties had left the Bastion, this series was to be fired to suppress any attempt to interfere with the safe return of the raiding parties.

During all three phases of this planned bombardment, some guns were held in reserve to deal with any enemy machine gun, field piece, or trench mortar that might open fire. Others were set aside to suppress known machine gun, artillery, or trench mortar batteries. Registration of all 50 tubes that were to take part in the raid was planned for July 18 and 19. Great care was to be taken to ensure that the registration would appear as normal harassment fire.

At the time of the raid, the regimental Assault Detachment of the 229th was not a permanently organized unit. A few months previously, selected officers, NCOs, and men had been brought together for a period of training and then returned to their companies, there to serve in their former capacities. A few days before each raid, the Assault Detachment would be brought together for further training and rehearsals. Immediately after each raid, the part-time stormtroopers would again be dispersed.

On the morning of July 14, the regimental order containing the details of the raid was sent to the division commander. From this point onward, the raid was to be known by the code name "Wilhelm." At the same time, the men of the Assault Detachment assembled in a training area far away from the battlefield and set about building a full-scale replica of the Bastion. In addition to studying aerial photos, large-scale maps, and reports from patrols, the stormtroopers tested a number of plans on the model trench system that they had built.

While the stormtroopers trained, the regimental commander worked out the problem of choosing the date for the raid. The twentieth, it turned out, would be a bad day for the raid. The regiment would be conducting reliefs that day, moving one battalion into the trenches and the other battalion out. This was a tricky operation requiring a great deal of coordination. Conducting a raid on the same day would only lead to confusion. The retaliatory bombardment that was sure to follow the raid, moreover, would fall on twice the number of Germans if it occurred during the relief. It was therefore decided to carry out the raid on the evening of the nineteenth.

Once these decisions were made, the regimental commander sat down with Lieutenant von Werner, the officer in charge of the Assault Detachment. Together they worked out the exact time that the raiding parties would leave the German lines, the routes that they would take through the German wire, and their formation. Questions of ammunition supply, what weapons were to be carried by the stormtroopers, and how many stretcher bearers to take along remained the province of Lieutenant von Werner. The regimental commander discussed these issues with him only to ensure that they had been thoroughly considered.

The questions of how deep to attack and how long to stay in the enemy position, however, were reserved for the regimental commander. It was he who coordinated the fire support for the raid, giving orders to the artillery for the "box barrage" that was to isolate the objective and the machine guns that were to protect the withdrawal of the raiding party. In these days before the introduction of portable radios, strict adherence to the schedule would be needed to prevent the raiding party from being hit by this "friendly fire."

EXECUTION

At 9:00 P.M. on the evening of July 19, the men of the raiding force formed up in the large concrete shelters that served as their assembly areas. Ten minutes later, the enemy, who were later identified as New Zealanders, began firing artillery, trench mortars, and small arms at the German position. No casualties were suffered by the raiding party as they were protected by shelters that were proof to all but a direct hit from a heavy howitzer.

At first, the Germans believed that the enemy had discovered their plans for the Wilhelm raid and were trying to interfere with it. The clouds of smoke that had been seen rising from the British position were believed to be clouds of poison gas, released into the atmosphere in the hopes that the wind would carry them into the German position. At 9:18 some of the men of the 229th reported that they felt nauseous, a fact that tended to support the "gas attack theory." The gas alarm was sounded and the Germans donned their gas masks.

Seven minutes later, however, the Germans discovered the real reason for the shelling and the gas attack. Five hundred meters to the north of the Bastion, in a sector occupied by the 231st Reserve Infantry Regiment,[1] the New Zealanders were conducting a raid of their own. In support of the New Zealanders' raid, the fire on the sector of the 229th was resumed.

The ensuing commotion almost caused the regimental commander of the 229th to call off the "Wilhelm" raid. Two considerations, however, caused him to order the continuation of the German operation. First, he believed that the German fire into "no man's land" would be sufficient to disperse the New Zealanders. Second, he believed that the shells from the New Zealanders' harassing fire falling on the German jump-off position would not seriously hinder the departure of the German raiding force.

At 10:15 P.M. the German artillery and trench mortars began to execute the first phase of the fire support plan for "Wilhelm." Low hanging smoke in "no man's land," however, made it impossible for the German artillery observers to see the strike of their own rounds or to pinpoint the origin of the New Zealand trench mortar fire that was striking the German jump-off position.

A few seconds before 11:25 P.M. the two German raiding parties left the shelter of their concrete bunkers and started moving towards the Bastion. The New Zealanders' trench mortar fire had made this movement easier by destroying not only a good proportion of the German barbed wire obstacles but much of their own wire that had been strung to protect the Bastion. Aided by this and the general confusion, the raiding party on the right crossed "no man's land" without incident. As the German artillery and trench mortars began the second phase of their fire plan, the rightward raiding party leapt into the Bastion.

Protected from enemy counterattacks by the "box barrage" planned by their regimental commander, the raiders inside the Bastion began the task of clearing out the enemy. In the darkness and smoke, they bombed along the trenches and tossed grenades into dugouts. Against less resolute defenders, the shock of the stormtroopers' attack would have led to the quick cessation of resistance. The New Zealanders, however, continued to fight as individuals long after they lost the ability to put up any concerted defense. The systematic clearing of the Bastion was thus frequently interrupted by the need to dispatch with pistol, club, or dagger a die-hard New Zealander suddenly popping up in the midst of the German raiding party.

The raiding party on the left did not make as good progress as its counterpart on the right. After crossing "no man's land," they found themselves caught in a wire obstacle swept by New Zealander machine gun fire. Smoke that lay between the source of the machine gun fire and the artillery liaison officer prevented the use of the artillery to suppress the machine guns. Directly in front of the Bastion, moreover, there were small groups of New Zealanders hiding in shell holes. They attacked the pinned German raiders with hand grenades. Although the Germans reacted in kind, the New Zealanders had the advantage of fighting from cover against an enemy trapped in the open. The Germans took heavy casualties, including the officer in charge. Convinced that further progress was futile, the NCO that took command of the raiding party decided to return to the German lines.

At 11:47 Lieutenant Werner gave the order to withdraw. His mission had been completed and he did not wish to allow the enemy time to prepare a barrage or counterattack against the Bastion. The raiding party on the right pulled back across "no man's land" carrying its wounded and leading two prisoners. As had been feared, the New Zealanders attempted to follow the raiding party back to the German lines. The rear guard of the raiding force, however, succeeded in preventing this.

Once they reached their lines, the men of the Assault Detachment moved to the rear of the German trench system and a well deserved rest. They were out of harm's way at 12:30 when the New Zealanders' retaliatory bombardment began. Even without their artillery, however, the New

Zealanders had inflicted severe losses on the men of the Assault Detachment. The German losses for the engagement were two officers and two men killed, two men missing and presumed dead, and 14 men wounded. Three New Zealanders were wounded, three were missing (two of whom were captured by the Germans), and one was killed.

For the Germans, the "Wilhelm" raid must be considered a partial success. The mission of discovering who occupied the Bastion and of destroying the dugouts there was accomplished, although the losses were far higher than had been anticipated. There were many small reasons for the large number of casualties. The smoke in "no man's land" hindered the calling in of artillery fire to suppress the machine guns that pinned the left raiding party. The left raiding party was further handicapped by the fact that many of its members had lost their grenades while crawling through barbed wire obstacles.[2]

Lieutenant Werner, in an article written after the war, expressed his belief that the size of the raiding party was too large, exposing too many men to enemy fire. Had it not been for the redundancy of two raiding parties, however, the mission may not have been accomplished. While only one party was needed to clear the Bastion, two parties may have been needed to ensure that one party reached the objective. The main cause of the heavy German casualties, however, seems to have been the spirited defense of the Bastion by an unexpectedly large number of New Zealanders.

NOTES

1. The 231st was also part of the 50th Reserve Division.
2. The raiders did not use grenade sacks, the technique favored by Captain Rohr. Instead, they clipped the grenades to their belts.

Appendix B:
The Jacobsbrunnen Raid

The art of trench raiding in the German Army reached its zenith in the year that passed between the end of the Battle of Verdun in the fall of 1916 and the beginning of the Battle of Cambrai in the fall of 1917. It was during the first three months of this year that most of the army-level Assault Battalions, as well as the majority of lower echelon elite assault units, were created. The lack of large-scale offensive activity in the west during the last nine months of this year made it possible for these units to perfect their technique without much distraction.

The raid, code-named *Jacobsbrunnen* ("Jacob's Well") and conducted under the auspices of the 7th Bavarian Landwehr Infantry Regiment in the early morning hours of November 3, 1917, is a good example of a "mature" German trench raid conducted using techniques developed by the Assault Battalions. Detailed records pertaining to it have survived because it was the first raid of the war in which Americans were taken prisoner,[1] and, immediately after the war, the Historical Section of the American Expeditionary Force took the trouble to search out, translate, and publish the various orders and maps associated with the raid.[2]

At the time of the raid, the 7th Bavarian *Landwehr* Infantry Regiment, part of the 1st Bavarian *Landwehr* Division , had occupied a quiet sector in Lorraine, east of Nancy and north of Lunéville, for almost a year. This allowed Major Bedall, the regimental commander, to make contingency plans for raids against various objectives in the French position. When, on October 29, 1917, the commanding general of the 1st Bavarian *Landwehr* Division ordered the regimental commander to organize a raid against three French dugouts on a hill known as the *Kapplerbuckel,* the latter simply dusted off the latest version of a plan that had first been written in April 1917.

The commanding general of the 1st Bavarian *Landwehr* Division had ordered the raid because he had received word that there were Americans occupying the French dugouts. The United States had been in the war since April, but half a year had passed without U.S. soldiers showing up on the front lines. German intelligence was eager not only to identify the units of the Americans rumored to be on the *Kapplerbuckel,* but was also interested in discovering something about their fighting qualities. The order that Major Bedall received therefore stressed the importance of capturing as many prisoners as possible.

Artillery support for the raid was provided by the light field (7.7cm) guns and light field (10.5cm) howitzers of the 1st *Landwehr* Field Artillery Regiment, the artillery regiment organic to the 1st Bavarian *Landwehr* Infantry Division. Additional artillery support came from the 10cm guns of the 24th Foot Artillery Regiment, the 12cm Belgian guns of the 26th Foot Artillery Regiment, and the heavy field (15cm) howitzers of the 2nd *Landwehr* Foot Artillery Regiment. In all, 17 batteries of guns and howitzers were set aside for the raid. These were registered on October 30.

The bulk of the raiding force—seven officers, four senior NCOs, 24 NCOs, and 112 infantrymen—came from the 7th Bavarian *Landwehr* Infantry Regiment. These were reinforced by detachments from the division's elite assault unit (one senior NCO, five NCOs, 43 stormtroopers, and one stretcher bearer), the 24th Pioneer Battalion (one officer, three NCOs, and 18 enlisted pioneers), and the 8th *Cheveaulegers,*[3] the cavalry regiment that provided the 1st Bavarian *Landwehr* Infantry Division with its organic squadron (two NCOs and four troopers). The *Weilheim Landsturm* Battalion provided one officer, one NCO, and 12 men. These, together with a handful of men from the 7th Bavarian *Landwehr,* were assigned the job of protecting the flanks of the raiding force during the operation. The assault troops were divided into three raiding parties, each led by a lieutenant and a senior NCO, and a wire-cutting party.

To confuse the enemy about the exact location of the raid, two separate diversions were to take place immediately before the actual operation. One lieutenant, one senior NCO, two squads of infantry, and three pioneers were to take part in a feigned raid against Hill 269, a French-held position a few hundred meters away from the *Kapplerbuckel.* They were to be supported by the indirect fire of six artillery pieces. A more sizable artillery operation—16 artillery pieces in all—was to be mounted against another nearby position known as the "Canal Narrows." This latter undertaking was to involve no German infantry at all.

The troops for the raid were relieved of trench duty on November 1, gathered together behind the lines, and intensively rehearsed. In the course of two days, repeated practice on dummy trenches took men from different companies and battalions and welded them into a unit capable of concerted action. This task was facilitated by the very age of the plan—a number of times before the raid had been ordered, rehearsed, and then cancelled at the last minute. The players were thus working on a familiar stage from a familiar script.

Forty-five minutes after midnight[4] on the morning of November 3, two officers of the raiding party crept forward from the German jumping-off position towards the U.S. position, unrolling behind them a thin strip of white cloth. By 2:30 A.M., the left and right flank guards were in position. These squad-sized detachments would stay in "no man's land" to prevent counterattacks against the raiding force when it withdrew from the objective. At 3:00 A.M. the artillery batteries involved in the operation reported their readiness to the commander of the raiding force, Second Lieutenant Wolf. At the same time, the assault troops reached their assembly positions.

At 3:25 A.M., the diversionary artillery fire was begun. At 3:29, the German artillery ceased fire in order to allow the gun crews to reorient their weapons for the next phase of fire. At 3:30 the Germans resumed fire, this time hitting both Hill 259—the site of the feigned raid—and the *Kapplerbuckel*. About this time, the French artillery began to reply to the German fire.

The German barrage on the *Kapplerbuckel* had been laid so precisely that the assault column was able to move right up to the wire that separated the three dugouts from "no man's land." At the front of the German column, a squad of pioneers placed a bangalore torpedo under the wire entanglement. As the artillery fire shifted toward the rear of the *Kapplerbuckel*, the pioneers detonated the torpedo and the stormtroopers rushed forward, each of the three parties going off in its predetermined direction.

The Americans were taken completely by surprise. Although they were regular soldiers who had seen combat along the Mexican border, they had been prepared for neither the ferocity of the bombardment nor the speed with which the Germans penetrated their position. With no plan for resisting such an attack and no leaders taking charge, the Americans were unable to resist as a unit. Individual Americans engaging in close combat were able to kill and wound individual Germans, but were unable to interfere with the execution of the raid.

Immediately after the explosion of the bangalore torpedo, the signal troops who had followed Lieutenant Wolf in the attack set about establishing an intact telephone line to Major Bedall at the regimental command post in the German position. At 3:38 A.M., Wolf used this line to report the capture of the first U.S. prisoners. A few minutes after that, he used the telephone to call in artillery fire on a U.S. machine gun that was firing into "no man's land" along the route that the raiding force would have to take if it was going to regain German lines. The artillery fire, from a battery that had been set aside for just this sort of contingency, immediately silenced the machine gun.

The three raiding parties continued to push deeper into the U.S. position, clearing trenches by the then venerable method of "rolling up" with hand grenades and destroying dugouts with bundles of "potato mashers." At 3:50, Lieutenant Wolf gave the signal to withdraw, and the Germans started to pull back. With them, they took 11 U.S. soldiers, two of whom were NCOs, and nine of their own number who had been wounded.[5] Behind them, they left the bodies of two stormtroopers who had died in the assault.

The withdrawal was carried out with no interference from either the Americans or their French neighbors. The majority of the raiders returned with the main body, though stragglers continued to return until 5:00 A.M. When, shortly after dawn, the raiders were counted, it was found that only one German soldier was unaccounted for. It was later learned that he had been captured by some resolute Americans during the raid.

Despite the fierce resistance of individual U.S. soldiers, the raiders had fulfilled their mission to the letter. Although their casualties had been higher than expected, they had caused comparable casualties among the Americans—11 of whom were paraded in front of the German propaganda cameras the next morning, three of whom were dead, and five of whom were seriously wounded. The raiders could return to their rest areas confident in the fact that they had earned the cash bonus that the paymaster had waiting for each of them at the regimental headquarters.

NOTES

1. Major Leslie J. McNair, *Raids* (Fort Leavenworth, KS: The General Service Schools, 1920), p. 1.

2. The documents from which this narrative was reconstructed are from the unpublished volume *World War Records, First Division, AEF, Regular: German Documents, Aisne, Marne, Soissons.*

3. *Cheveaulégers* were a type of light cavalry peculiar to Bavaria.

4. The times used here are German time. The Allies used French time which was one hour behind German time.

5. This narrative is an adaption of an article by the author entitled "The Jacobsbrunnen Raid" which appeared originally in *Der Angriff: A Journal of World War I Military History*, No. 23, March 1983. The information about the Americans involved comes from Richard A. Baumgartner's "Postscript" to the article on page 15 of the same issue.

Appendix C: André Laffargue

In the English language literature of World War I, the invention of the tactics that the German infantry used so successfully in 1917 and 1918 is often credited to a Frenchman, Captain André Laffargue. The history of this belief can be traced back to a brief passage in a book[1] written by Arnold Vieth von Golsenau, a left-wing soldier of fortune who had been a regular officer in the German Army both before and during World War I. From Golsenau's book, the story was picked up by Captain G.C. Wynne, whose mistitled book on German defensive tactics of World War I, *If Germany Attacks*, was the first book in English to deal with doctrinal change in the German Army during that period. From Wynne, the story has spread to the point that no book on the German tactics of World War I would be complete without a discussion of Captain Laffargue's role.

On May 9, 1915, Laffargue, then a second lieutenant only one year out of Saint Cyr, was commanding a company of the 153rd Infantry Regiment in an attack on Vimy ridge in Flanders. The attack on the first German trench had been successful but costly. Laffargue's company had only 80 men when it entered the cemetery at Neuville Saint Vaast and ran into two German machine guns. These prevented the company from moving forward for four hours, during which time the Germans had brought up reinforcements. During the next two days, two French regiments attempted to clear out the cemetery. The first failed. The second succeeded. Both suffered heavy casualties.

Although he was wounded during the attack, Laffargue could not help but notice the fact that if his company had been able to deal with the two

German machine guns, the French attack would have been able to push deep into the German position. The two regiments that were decimated trying to clear the cemetery would have been exploiting Laffargue's breakthrough rather than dealing with the German reserve brought forward under the cover of the machine guns.

THE ATTACK IN TRENCH WARFARE

During his convalescence, Laffargue described the problems he had faced in Flanders in a pamphlet called *The Attack in Trench Warfare* (*Étude sur l'Attaque dans la Période actuelle de la Guerre*).[2] This pamphlet also proposed a technique for breaking through a German trench system. To deal with the problem of machine guns, Laffargue advocated that mountain howitzers and 37mm guns be attached to the attacking infantry. He also advocated a swift advance into the enemy position with each company disregarding the progress of its neighbors. In these two recommendations, Laffargue's system resembled that of the first Assault Detachment.

There was, however, more of the old than the new in Laffargue's system. The smallest unit with an independent objective was the company, not the squad, as was the case with German stormtroopers. There was no mention of taking a trench in the flank or clearing it by "bombing along." The chief assault weapon of the infantry remained the bayonet. Finally, there was no provision for bypassing centers of resistance.

An attack conducted according to *The Attack in Trench Warfare* was to begin with the destruction of the first German trench by the fire of heavy trench mortars. Additional preparation fire would be provided by the ubiquitous 75mm field guns. The first wave of the attacking infantry would then form a skirmish line and move forward. Strict attention was to be paid to the maintenance of alignment "as on parade," in order to carry along those who would fall back and restrain the "enthusiasts."

Those wire obstacles that had not been destroyed by the fire of the "75s" would force the skirmish line to lie down. Individual soldiers would then cross the obstacle and commence firing once they reached the other side. When all had crossed, the line would reform and continue its march toward the enemy trench, which would be taken in a single rush. The primary weapon here would be the bayonet.

The first trench taken, the skirmish line would reform and proceed to march toward the second and third lines of trenches. A second and a third wave of infantry, also in neatly aligned skirmish lines, would follow the first wave. Further reserves would also move forward so as to be able to exploit the breakthrough.

It is clear that Captain Laffargue was on the verge of developing a system of infantry tactics that might be very similar to that of the Assault

Battalions. He was held back, however, by a desire, common to many military men, to maintain control over the attack by maintaining control over the attackers. He recognized, for example, that the enemy could be thrown off balance by rapid movement deep into his position. He advocated training troops on obstacle courses in order to develop their "agility and suppleness." He insisted, however, on the need to maintain the skirmish line formation until the point where, 50 meters from the enemy trench, bayonets were lowered and close combat began.

DISSEMINATION

Soon after Laffargue finished *The Attack in Trench Warfare*, he showed it to one of his former history teachers. This teacher, it turned out, was a friend of Marshall Foch, and recommended to Laffargue that he show his work to the Marshall. Foch liked the work and had it distributed to some of his generals. Early in 1916, the pamphlet was published commercially.

After publication of *The Attack in Trench Warfare*, Laffargue stopped working on tactics. The same wound that had provided Laffargue the leisure to write the pamphlet prevented his return to frontline service. He spent the rest of the war in staff jobs, first in the personnel department of the General Headquarters at Chantilly and then on the staff of a division.[3]

In the summer of 1916, a copy of *The Attack in Trench Warfare* was captured by German troops in the course of a trench raid and brought to the attention of their superiors. The pamphlet was translated into German and distributed to units.[4] Whether this was merely to inform the German units about possible French methods or to encourage them to imitate Laffargue's system, however, is not clear. According to Vieth von Golsenau, the pamphlet was used by some units as a training manual. No other German sources, however, make mention of the pamphlet or its use as a training manual.

Whether or not *The Attack in Trench Warfare* was used by any or all German units as a training manual, however, has little bearing on the question of how and why the German infantry changed its way of fighting during World War I. Those aspects of Laffargue's system that were also present in the German tactical system of 1918—the emphasis on rapid movement, the use of automatic rifles and trench mortars to gain fire superiority, the cultivation of the spirit of the offensive—were already present in the tactics of the Assault Battalions.

NOTES

1. Ludwig Renn, *Warfare*, p. 110. Ludwig Renn was the pseudonym of Vieth von Golsenau.

2.   André Laffargue, *The Attack in Trench Warfare: Impressions and Reflections of a Company Commander* (Washington, DC: The United States Infantry Association, 1916). The French edition was published in 1915 in Paris by the Army Geographic Service Press (*Imprimerie du Service Géographique de l'Armée*).

3.   André Laffargue. *Fantassin de Gascogne. De mon jardin à la Marne et au Danube* (Paris: Flammarion, 1962), pp. 79–117.

4.   General (ret.) André Laffargue, *Letter to Author*, 15 October, 1987.

Bibliography

Wherever possible, I have given the most recent English edition of a published work. In those cases where I have referred to both an English translation and a German original, both versions are listed.

Atteridge, A. Hillard. *The German Army in War.* New York: McBride, Nast, and Company, 1915.

Azan, Paul. *The Warfare of Today.* Boston: Houghton Mifflin, 1918.

Baehrecke, Fritz. "Tage vor Ypern." In Ernst von Eisenhart-Rothe and Martin Lezius. *Das Ehrenbuch der Garde. Die Preußische Garde im Weltkriege 1914–1919.* Berlin: Wilhelm Kolk and Verlag Oskar Hinderer, 1931.

Baentsch. "Die Infanterie in Durchbruchsschlacht." *Militärwissenshaftliche Rundschau* 3 (1938). Many German authors before World War II published books and articles without giving their first names.

Balck, Hermann. "Translation of a Taped Conversation with General Hermann Balck, 13 April, 1979." Columbus, OH: Battelle, Columbus Laboratories, Tactical Technology Center, 1979.

Balck, Wilhelm. *Development of Tactics—World War.* Fort Leavenworth, KS: The General Service Schools Press, 1922.

———. *Entwickelung der Taktik im Weltkriege.* Berlin: R. Eisenschmidt, 1922.

———. *Tactics.* Translated by Walter Krueger. Fort Leavenworth, KS: U.S. Cavalry Association, 1915.

"The Battle of the Intermediate Zone." *The Infantry Journal,* 15.

Baux, Charles. *Études sur Combat.* Paris: Payot & Cie., 1921.

Benary, Albert, ed. *Das Ehrenbuch der Deutschen Feldartillerie.* Berlin: Verlag Tradition Wilhelm Kolk, 1930.

Berendt, Richard von. *Das 1. Garde Fußartillerie Regiment im Weltkrieg.* Berlin: Druck und Verlag von Gerhard Stalling, 1928.

Bernhardi, Friedrich von. *On War Today.* London: Hugh Rees, Ltd., 1913.

_____. *Germany and the Next War.* London: E. Arnold, 1914.

Bertkau, Friedrich. "Sturmtruppen." In Franke, Hermann, ed., *Handbuch der Neuzeitlichen Wehrwissenschaften.* Berlin: Verlag von Walter de Grouter & Co., 1937.

Beumelburg, Werner. *Ypren, 1914.* Berlin: Druck und Verlag von Gerhard Stalling, 1925.

Bjornstad, A.W. *The German Army.* Fort Leavenworth, KS: Press of the Army Service Schools, 1916.

Brandis, Cordt von. *Der Sturmangriff. Kriegserfahrungen eines Frontoffiziers.* No publisher given, 1917.

Brandt, Rolf. *Um Riga und Oesell.* Leipzig: Velhagen & Klasing, 1917.

Brauns, Hans. *Maschinen-Gewehr-Scharffschützen-Abteilung Nr. 22.* Berlin: Gerhard Stalling, 1923.

Bruchmüller, Georg. "Die Artillerieführung bei den großen Deutschen Angriffen im Jahre 1918." *Wissen und Wehr,* No. 4, 1931.

_____. *Die Artillerie beim Angriff im Stellungskrieg.* Charlottenburg: Verlag "Offene Worte," 1926.

_____. *Die Deutsche Artillerie in den Durchbruchschlachten des Weltkrieges.* Berlin: E.S. Mittler und Sohn, 1922.

Brückner, E. "Der Durchbruchsangriff vor dem Weltkrieg in Anwendung und Theorie." *Militärwissenshaftliche Rundschau.* 3 (1938).

Carrias. "L'Armée allemande, son histoire, son organization, sa tactique." *Revue Militaire Française.* Oct. 1936, pp. 67–112.

Cochenhausen, "Artillery Preparation Fire in Trench and Open Warfare." In Schwarte, Max, *War Lessons in Examples Taken from the World War.* Unpublished manuscript, translation of *Kriegslehren, in Beispielen aus dem Weltkrieg,* located at U.S. Army Military History Institute, Carlisle Barracks, Carlisle, PA.

Comena D'Alameda, P. *L'Armée allemande avant et pendant la Guerre de 1914–1918.* Paris: Berger-Levrault, 1919.

"Conduct of the Infantry Attack." *The Infantry Journal* 15.

Craster, J.M., ed. *Fifteen Rounds a Minute. The Grenadiers at War: August to December 1914.* London: Macmillan, 1976.

Cron, Hermann. *Die Organization des Deutschen Heeres im Weltkrieg.* Berlin: Ernst Siegfried Mittler und Sohn, 1923.

Cuninghame, Sir T. "German Theories in the Attack and Defense." *The Infantry Journal* 16.

Demeter, Karl. *The German Officer Corps in Society and State 1650–1945.* New York: Frederick A. Praeger, 1965.

Ehrgott, H.W. "The Battle of Picardy and the Double Penetration." *The Infantry Journal* 33.

Ellison, G.F. "The Training of Recruits in the German Infantry." *Journal of the Royal United Services Institution* 33 (1889–1890).

Fadini, Francesco. *Caporetto dalla Parte del Vincitore: La βiografia del Generale Otto von Below e il suo Diario Inedito sulla Campagna d'Italia del 1917.* Florence: Vallechi, 1974.

Fehrenbach, T. "Meine Eindruck in der 2. württ. Sturmkp., Sturmbat. 16." *Allgemeine Schweizerische Militärzeitung.* 1932.

France. Ministère de la Guerre. État-Major de l'Armée. 2iéme Bureau. "Reports of Interrogations of German Prisoners of War by American and French Military Personnel 1918. U.S. National Archives Record Group 120, Boxes 5894, 5893, 5892, 5891 and 5910.

_____.*Notes on the German Army in the War, 1917.* Washington, DC: Government Printing Office, 1917.

"German Methods of Trench Warfare." *Professional Memoirs, Corps of Engineers, U.S.A.* 9 (1917).

"German Principles of Command in the Defensive Battle in Position Warfare." *The Infantry Journal* 14.

"German Tactics." *The Infantry Journal* 15.

Germany. Heer. *Vom westlichsten Teil der Westfront.* Herborn: Orania-Verlag, 1917. (History of the 52nd Infantry Division.)

_____. Generalstab. 7. (Kriegswissenschaftliche) Abteilung. "Die Entwickelung der Deutschen Infantrie im Weltkrieg 1914–1918." *Militärwissenschaftliche Rundschau* 3 (1938).

_____. Generalstab. 7. (Kriegswissenschaftliche) Abteilung. *Der Handstreich gegen Lüttich von 3. bis 7. August 1914.* Berlin: Ernst Siegfried Mittler und Sohn, 1939.

_____. Kriegsministerium. *Drill Regulations for the Infantry, German Army, 1906.* Washington, DC: Government Printing Office, 1907.

_____. Reichsministerium. *Cantigny Operations: Documents Pertaining to German Raids (May 27, 1918) and the American Attack and Capture of Cantigny.* U.S. Army, First Division, Historical Section, 1928.

_____. Various Agencies. *Der Weltrieg 1914–1918.* Berlin: E. S. Mittler und Sohn. (German official history of World War I, the last volume of which is currently being completed.)

Gies, Joseph. *Crisis, 1918.* New York: W.W. Norton and Company, Inc., 1974.

Glaise-Horstenau, Edmund, ed. *Österreich-Ungarns letzter Krieg.* Vienna: Verlag der Militärwissenschaftlichen Mittelungen, 1936.

Gold, Ludwig. *Die Tragödie von Verdun.* Berlin: Gerhard Stalling, 1926.

Goodspeed, D.J. *Ludendorff, Genius of World War I.* Boston: Houghton, Mifflin Company, 1966.

Gottberg, von. *Geschichte des Hannoverschen Jäger Battalions Nr. 10.* Berlin: E.S. Mittler, 1903.

Great Britain, War Office, General Staff. *The Austro-Hungarian Forces in the Field. March. 1918.* London: War Office, 1918.

_____. *Field Service Regulations of the German Army.* London: Harrison and Sons, 1908.

_____. *German Army Handbook,* April, 1918. New York: Hippocrene Books, 1977.

_____. *German Raid on the British Trenches near la Boisselle,* April 11, 1916.

_____. *Notes on Recent Fighting.* Army Printing and Stationary Service in France, 1918.

_____. *Summary of Recent Information Regarding the German Army and Its Methods.* London: War Office, 1917.

_____. *The Training and Employment of Bombers.* London: Harrison and Sons, 1916.

Groener, Wilhelm. *Lebenserinnerungen—Jugend, Generalstab, Weltkrieg.* Göttingen: Vandenhoeck & Ruprecht, 1957.

Gruss, Hellmuth. *Aufbau und Verwendung der Deutschen Sturmbataillone im Weltkrieg.* Berlin: Junker und Dunnhaupt Verlag, 1938.

Haber, L.F. *The Poisonous Cloud, Chemical Warfare in the First World War.* Oxford: Clarendon Press, 1986.

Hagen, von. *Geschichte des König l. Sächsichen l. Jäger Battalions Nr. 12.* Freiburg in Sachsen: Verlag von Craz und Gerlach, 1909.

Hanslian, Rudolf. *Der chemische Krieg.* Berlin: E.S. Mitter & Sohn, 1937.

Heinrici, Paul, ed. *Das Ehrenbuch der Deutschen Pioniere.* Berlin: Verlag Tradition Wilhelm Kolk, 1932.

Hoeppner Flatow, W. *Stosstrupp Markman greift ein. Der Kampf eines Frontsoldaten.* Berlin: Steiniger Verlag, 1939.

Hofmann, Max. *The War of Lost Opportunities.* London: Keegan, Paul, 1924.

"Instructions for the Employment of Flame Projectors." *The Infantry Journal* 14.

Jünger, Ernst. *Copse 125, A Chronicle of the Trench Warfare of 1918.* London: Chatto and Windus, 1930.

_____. *The Storm of Steel. From the Diary of a German Stormtroop Officer on the Western Front.* London: Chatto and Windus, 1929.

Kaelich, Fritz. *Das Infanterie Regiment Nr. 406.* Berlin: Gerhard Stalling, 1922.

Kaiser, Alexander. *Paderborner Infanterie-Regiment (7. Lothr.) Nr. 158.* Berlin: Gerhard Stalling, 1924.

Keegan, John D. "Blitzkrieg in the Mountains: The Battle of Caporetto." *Military Review.* (January 1965).

Killian, Hans. *Totentanz auf den Hartmansweilerkopf 1914–1917.* Neckargemünd: Kurt Vowincker Verlag, 1972.

_____. *Wir Stürmten durchs Friaul.* Neckargemünd: Kurt Vowincker Verlag, 1978.

Klietmann. "Beiträge zur Geschichte der Deutschen Handgranate." *Der Feldgrau,* 1971.

Köhn, Herrmann. *Erstes Garde Feldartillerie Regiment und seine reitende abteilung.* Berlin: Druck und Verlag von Gerhard Stalling, 1928.

Krafft von Dellmensingen, Konrad. *Der Durchbruch.* Munich: Bernhard Graefe Verlag, 1937.

_____. *Der Durchbruch am Isonzo.* Berlin: Druck und Verlag von Gerhard Stalling, 1926.

Kramer, Rudolf von, et al. *Der königlich bayerische Militär-Max-Joseph-Orden: Kriegstaten und Ehrenbuch, 1914–1918.* Munich: Selbsverlag des königlich bayerische Militär-Max-Joseph-Ordens, 1966.

Krauss, Alfred. *Das Wunder von Karfreit. Der Durchbruch bei Flitsch.* Munich:

T.F. Lehmanns Verlag, 1926.

———. *Theorie und Praxis in der Kriegskunst*. Munich: T.F. Lehmanns Verlag, 1926.

Kuhl, Hermann von. *The Execution and Failure of the Offensive*. Translated by Henry Hossfeld. This source is an unpublished translation of *Entstehung, Durchführung und Zusammenbruch der Offensive von 1918*. Berlin: Deutsche Verlagsgesellschaft für Politik und Geschichte, 1927.

———. *Der Weltkrieg*. Berlin: W. Kolk, 1929.

Laffargue, André. *The Attack in Trench Warfare: Impressions and Reflections of a Company Commander*. Washington: The United States Infantry Association, 1916.

———. *Fantassin de Gascogne. De mon jardin à la Marne et au Danube*. Paris: Flammarion, 1962.

Lange, Ludwig. "Das Problem der Abschnürungsangriffe." *Wissen und Wehr*, March, 1931.

Ledebur, Ferdinand Freiherr von. *Die Geschichte des Deutschen Unteroffiziers*. Berlin: Junker und Dunnhaupt Verlag, 1939.

Leed, Eric J. *No Man's Land: Combat and Identity in WWI*. London: Cambridge University Press, 1979.

Lossberg, Fritz von. *Meine Tätigkeit im Weltkreige 1914–1918*. Berlin: E.S. Mittler & Sohn, 1939.

Lucas, Pascal Marie Henri. *L'Évolution des idées tactiques en France et en Allemagne 1914–1918*. Paris: Berger-Levrault, eds., 1923.

Ludendorff, Erich. *Ludendorff's Own Story*. New York: Harper and Brothers Publishers, 1939.

Lundström, Richard J. "Cross Against Crescent: The 'Unknown' War between Germany and Turkey in the Caucasus, 1918." *Der Angriff. A Journal of World War I Military History*, No. 22, January, 1983.

Marshall, S.L.A. *Men Against Fire: The Problem of Battle Command in Future War*. Gloucester, MA: Peter Smith, 1978.

Matuschka, Edgar Graf von. "Organizationsgeshichte des Heeres, 1890–1918." *Handbuch zur Deutschen Militärgeschichte 1648–1939*. Frankfurt am Main: Bernhard and Graefe Verlag für Wehrwessen, 1968.

McNair, Lesley J. *Raids*. Fort Leavenworth, KS: The General Service Schools, 1920.

Meier-Welcker, Hans. *Seeckt*. Frankfurt am Main: Bernard & Graefe, 1967.

Middlebrook, Martin. *The Kaiser's Battle, 21 March, 1918: The First Day of the German Offensive*. London: Allen Lane, 1978.

"Moderne Handgranaten." *Militär-Wochenblatt*, Nr. 163 (1915).

Müller, F. *Brandenburgisches Jäger Bataillon Nr. 3*. Oldenburg i. O.: Gerhard Stalling, 1922.

Müller, Rudolf. *Das 3. Lotharingisches Infanterie-Regiment Nr. 135*. Berlin: Gerhard Stalling, 1922.

Paine, George H. "Accurate Shooting in Trench Warfare." *The Field Artillery Journal* VII, No. 4 (Oct–Dec. 1917): 440–48.

de Pardieu. *A Critical Study of German Tactics and of the New German Regula-*

tions. Translated by Charles F. Martin. Fort Leavenworth, KS: U.S. Cavalry Association, 1912.

Pfeifer, Waldemar. *Entwurf eines Exerzierreglements für die Infanterie: Eine Privatarbeit*. Berlin: Verlag R. Eisenschmidt, 1921.

Platt, Grover Cleveland. *The Place of the Army in German Life*. Unpublished Ph.D. dissertation, State University of Iowa, 1941.

Preradovich, Nikolaus von. *Die militärische und soziale Herkunft der Generalität des Deutschen Heeres, 1. Mai, 1944*. Osnabrück: Biblio-Verlag, 1978.

Prussia. Kriegsministerium. *Drill Regulations for the Infantry, German Army, 1906*. Washington, DC: Government Printing Office, 1907.

Ramcke, Bernhard. *Vom Schiffsjüngen zum Fallschirmjäger-General*. Berlin: Verlag der Wehrmacht, 1943.

Reddemann, "Die Totenkopf Pioniere." In Paul Heinrici, ed., *Das Ehrenbuch der Deutschen Pioniere*. Berlin: Verlag Tradition Wilhelm Kolk, 1932.

Reiß, Ritter von, et al. *Das Königlich Bayerische Infanterie Leib Regiment im Weltkrieg, 1914–1918*. Munich: Max Schick, 1931.

Reichmann, Carl. *Observations on the German Imperial Maneuvers in 1893*. Fort Leavenworth, KS: The General Service Schools, 1894.

Reymann, Martin. *Das Infanterie Regiment von Alvensleben (6. Brandenbg.) Nr. 52 im Weltkriege 1914/1918*. Berlin: Gerhard Stalling, 1923.

Rieben, von. "Ypern." In Ernst von Eisenhart-Rothe and Martin Lezius. *Das Ehrenbuch der Garde, Die Preußische Garde im Weltkriege 1914–1919*. Berlin: Wilhelm Kolk and Verlag Oskar Hinderer, 1931.

Rohkohl, W. *Reserve Infanterie Regiment Nr. 226*. Berlin: Gerhard Stalling, 1923.

Rommel, Erwin. *Attacks*. Vienna, Virginia: Athena Press, 1979.

Rupprecht, Crown Prince of Bavaria. *In Treue Fest: Mein Kriegstagebuch*. Munich: Deutscher National Verlag, 1929.

Schäfer, George. "Deutschland 1916/1918. Divisions Sturm-Kompagnie." In *Zeitschrift für Heeres und Uniformkunde*, 1958.

———. "Jäger-Sturm Battalion 3." *Zeitschrift für Heeres und Uniformkunde*, 1957.

Schatz, Josef. *Geschichte des badischen (rheinischen) Reserve-Infanterie-Regiments 239*. Stuttgart: Chr. Belser A.G., 1927.

Schäwen. "Der erste Flammenangriff." In Paul Heinrici, ed., *Das Ehrenbuch der Deutschen Pioniere*. Berlin: Verlag Tradition Wilhelm Kolk, 1932.

Scheel. *Das Reserve Feldartillerie Regiment Nr. 70*. Berlin: Druck und Verlag von Gerhard Stalling, 1923.

Schell, Adolf von. *Battle Leadership*. Quantico, VA: The Marine Corps Association, 1982.

Schmeelke, Michael. "In the Vosges." *Der Angriff, A Journal of World War I History*, Nr. 20, September, 1982.

Schmidt, Ernst. *Argonnen*. Berlin: Gerhard Stalling, 1927.

Schmidt, F. T. "Die Württembergischen Gebirgsschützen." *Der Feldgrau* 3, 1954.

Schmidt-Richberg, Wiegand. "Die Regierungszeit Wilhelms II." In *Handbuch zur Deutschen Militärgeschichte 1648–1939*. Frankfurt am Main: Bernard & Grafe Verlag für Wehrwessen, 1968.

Schönfeldt, Ernst von. *Das Grenadier Regiment Prinz Karl von Preussen (2. Brandenburgisches. Nr. 12 im Weltkriege.* Berlin: Gerhard Stalling, 1924.

Schöning, H. *Leib-Grenadier Regiment König Friedrich Wilhelm III (1. Brandenbergisches) Nr. 8.* Berlin: Gerhard Stalling, 1924.

Schulte, Bernd F. *Die Deutsche Armee, 1900–1914, Zwischen Beharren und Verändern.* Dusseldorf: Droste Verlag, 1977.

Schwarte, Max. *War Lessons in Examples Taken from the World War.* Unpublished manuscript, translation of *Kriegslehren, in Beispielen aus dem Weltkrieg,* located at U.S. Army Military History Institute, Carlisle Barracks, Carlisle, PA.

Schwink, Otto. *Die Schlacht an der Yser und bei Ypren im Herbst 1914.* Oldenburg: Verlag von Gerhard Stalling, 1918.

Seeger. *Die Württembergische Gebirgs-Artillerie im Weltkrieg 1915–1918.* Stuttgart: C. Belser, 1920.

Seekt, Hans von. *Aus Meinem Leben.* Leipzig: v. Hase & Koehler, 1938.

Showalter, Dennis E. *Railroads and Rifles: Soldiers, Technology, and the Unification of Germany.* Hamden, CT: Archon Books, 1975.

Simon. *Instruktion für dem Einjärig Freiwilligen der Infanterie.* Berlin: Verlag von A. Bath, 1887.

Stein, Hans Rudolf von. "Die k.u.k. Infanterie und Jägertruppe im Weltkriege 1914–1918." *Zeitschrift für Heeres und Uniformkunde,* 1962.

———. "Die Minenwerfer Formationen 1914–1918." *Zeitschrift für Heeres und Uniformkunde,* 1959, 1960.

Stephanus. "Kriegserfahrungen und Infantriebewaffnung." *Militärwochenblatt,* Nrs. 104 and 105.

Sulzbach, Herbert. *With the German Guns.* London: Leo Cooper, Ltd., 1973.

Szczepanski, Max von. *Füsilier-Regiments Generalfeldmarschall Prinz Albrecht von Preßen (Hann.) Nr. 73 während des Weltkrieges 1914–1918.* Berlin: Gerhard Stalling, 1923.

Unger, F. von. "Der Angriff des Regiments Augusta am 11. November 1914 bei Ypern." In Ernst von Eisenhart-Rothe and Martin Lezius. *Das Ehrenbuch der Garde, Die Preußische Garde im Weltkriege 1914–1919.* Berlin: Wilhelm Kolk and Verlag Oskar Hinderer, 1931.

U.S. Adjutant General's Office. *Notes on Recent Operations. July, 1917.* Washington, DC: Government Printing Office, 1917.

U.S. Army Coast Artillery School, Fort Monroe, VA. *German Documents.* Fort Monroe, VA: Coast Artillery School, 1923.

U.S. Army Service Schools, Fort Leavenworth, Kansas. *Studies in Minor Tactics.* Washington, DC: Government Printing Office, 1917.

U.S. Army War College. *German and Austrian Tactical Studies.* Washington, DC: Government Printing Office, 1918.

———. *German Notes on Minor Tactics.* Washington, DC: Government Printing Office, 1918.

———. *Notes on Recent Operations No. 2.* Washington, DC: Government Printing Office, 1917.

———. *Notes on the Methods of Attack and Defense to Meet the Conditions of Modern Warfare.* Washington, DC: Government Printing Office, 1917.

U.S. War Department. Historical Sub-Section. General Staff. A.E.F. *A Survey of German Tactics, 1918.* Washington, DC: Government Printing Office, 1918.

_____. General Staff. A.E.F. *World War Records. First Division, A.E.F., Regular I-IV.* (Unpublished translations of German documents.)

Verein der Offiziere des ehem. Preuss. Res.-Inf.-Regts. 3. *Reserve Infanterie Regiment Nr. 3.* Berlin: Gerhard Stalling, 1926.

"Verwendung der Infanterie mit ihren Hilfswaffen im Angriff im Bewegungskrieg." *Militärwochenblatt,* Nrs. 104 and 105.

"A Visit to the German Front in Belgium: The Assault Battalions." *The Infantry Journal* 15.

Vogt, Adolf. *Oberst Max Bauer: Generalstabsoffizier im Zwielicht 1869–1929.* Osnabrück: Biblio-Verlag, 1974.

Willers, Hans. *Königlich Preussisches Reserve Infanterie Regiment Nr. 215.* Berlin: Verlag Gerhard Stalling, 1926.

von Winterfeldt. *Das Kaiser Franz Garde-Grenadier Regiment Nr. 2: 1914–1918.* Berlin: Gerhard Stalling, 1922.

Units Index

General Index

ABOUT THE AUTHOR

BRUCE GUDMUNDSSON is a military historian on the faculty of the Marine Corps Command and Staff College, Quantico, VA. Although his main interest is modern European military history, his management case studies in present day defense procurement have been taught at Harvard University, the Defense Systems Management College, and the Air War College. An officer in the Marine Corps Reserve, Mr. Gudmundsson is a frequent contributor to the *Marine Corps Gazette*. He currently lives in Fredericksburg, VA, with his wife and two children.